The
REVELATION
of
SAINT JOHN

The
REVELATION
of
SAINT JOHN

The Path to Soul Initiation

ZACHARY F. LANSDOWNE

WEISERBOOKS
San Francisco, CA / Newburyport, MA

First published in 2006 by
Red Wheel/Weiser, LLC
York Beach, ME
With offices at:
500 Third Street, Suite 230
San Francisco, CA 94107
www.redwheelweiser.com

Copyright © 2006 Zachary F. Lansdowne.

ISBN 1-57863-342-7

Typeset in Adobe Garamond by Dutton & Sherman Design

CONTENTS

ACKNOWLEDGMENTS

*I am grateful to Perry Havranek, George Karthas,
and Barbara Olson for their perceptive and helpful
comments on an early draft of this book.*

INTRODUCTION

The Revelation of Jesus Christ, which God gave unto him,
to shew unto his servants things which must shortly come to pass;
and he sent and signified it by his angel unto his servant
John. (Rev. 1:1)

The *Revelation of St. John*, the last book of the Bible, has been a mystery ever since it appeared about 2000 years ago. Sometimes called the *Apocalypse* or *Book of Revelation*, this enigmatic work is written entirely in symbols. Its vivid dramatic images have engendered praise from its admirers and scorn from its critics. No other part of the Bible has caused more controversy. Many think that it provides a key that unlocks the mysteries of life; others think it should be dropped from the Bible.

The *Revelation* is actually a veiled statement of an esoteric, or hidden, doctrine of early Christianity. When interpreted psychologically, it provides detailed and practical instructions for the spiritual journey—a roadmap to the awakening of higher consciousness. That spiritual journey can be characterized as the path of liberation or enlightenment, because it leads to complete freedom from sorrow and to a purely intuitive life. Although the *Revelation* appears in the holy book of the Judeo-Christian tradition, its instructions can be appreciated and applied by aspirants in all religious traditions.

TRADITIONAL INTERPRETATIONS

The *Revelation* has had a significant impact on Western civilization throughout the past two thousand years. Human fears and hopes are often expressed through words and images taken from it—apocalypse, millennium, four horsemen, hallelujah, Armageddon, and New Jerusalem. Many theologians, poets, scholars, painters, musicians, filmmakers, and politicians have been influenced by the rich imagery of the book.

The vast majority of published commentaries on the *Revelation* fall into three categories:[1]

- The *preterist* view holds that the *Revelation* describes issues and events in the first century. In particular, the major prophesies of the book are believed to have been fulfilled with the destruction of the city of Jerusalem in 70 A.D. The principal difficulty with this position is that the decisive victory of good over evil and the inauguration of the eternal reign of God portrayed in the latter part of the book seems not to have occurred.

- The *historical* view argues that the *Revelation* predicts the whole course of human history, from the founding of Christianity to the end of the world. Historical events and prominent leaders are identified as symbols in the visions. Proponents of this view find references to Roman emperors, various popes, Charlemagne, the Protestant Reformation, the French Revolution, and Mussolini in the symbolic narrative. A major difficulty with this approach is its subjectivity, as shown by widely diverse interpretations of the symbolism.

- The *futurist,* or eschatological, view contends that the *Revelation* predicts the events that will occur at the end of the world. It is characteristic of futurists to believe that the end of the world will occur very soon after they write. This view encompasses the difficulties of both the preterist and

---

1. A. W. Wainwright, *Mysterious Apocalypse: Interpreting the Book of Revelation* (Nashville, TN: Abingdon Press, 1993) provides a survey of the interpretive approaches to the *Revelation* that have been made from the second century to the present day.

historical views, since the time line is subjective and many of the events predicted did not, in fact, occur. Moreover, this view fails to identify any real significance the book may have had for the people to whom it was initially addressed—namely, the persecuted Christians of the first century.

These three traditional approaches can all be characterized as "external-temporal," because they all assume that the characters and episodes in the *Revelation* denote events that occur in the external world at definite past or future times.

Yet none of these approaches seems consistent with what the *Revelation* says about itself. According to Rev. 1.1, its purpose is to show "things which must shortly come to pass." Likewise, Rev. 1:3 states: "Blessed *is* he that readeth, and they that hear the words of this prophecy, and keep those things which are written therein: for the time *is* at hand." Thus, according to its own verses, the *Revelation of St. John* deals with the present—that is, with the present of whoever may be reading it. It thus contains information that any reader—including you or I—can apply to become blessed.

PSYCHOLOGICAL INTERPRETATION

This commentary embodies a psychological interpretation of the *Revelation* that differs radically from the foregoing external-temporal approaches. This interpretation is based on the following four principles:

- *Each of John's visions is similar to a dream.* John's visions contain symbols, just as dreams do. In fact, ancient Jewish scriptures often used the terms vision and dream interchangeably.[2] It is important to distinguish here between the John who is a writer and disciple of Jesus, and the John of the visions. An analogous distinction can be made between a person who is dreaming and the character that the person plays in the dream itself. For example, you may be a physician in your professional life and yet

---

2. In 1 Enoch 85:1, the visions of 83:1–3 are called dreams. In the Testament of Levi 8:18, the vision of 8:1 is a called a dream. In 4 Ezra 12:10. 13:21 and 25, the dreams of 11:1 and 13:1 are called visions. The texts for these ancient scriptures are given by J. H. Charlesworth, *The Old Testament Pseudepigrapha*, vol. I (New York: Doubleday, 1983).

appear in the role of a teacher, clown, or carpenter in your own dreams. Making this distinction helps resolve one of the major puzzles of the *Revelation*—an incident in which John appears to be rebuked twice for the same thing, namely, worshiping an angel. The first rebuke applies to the character that John plays in one of his visions (Rev. 19:10). The second applies to John himself in his normal consciousness (Rev. 22:9).

- *Each episode in a vision describes a stage on the spiritual journey.* Travelers on this journey include anyone who aspires to a higher way of life, no matter what religious tradition they follow. The name and connotations of any given symbol may lie in John's religious background (the Judaism of the Old Testament), but the specific meaning or denotation of the symbol may be part of other religious or philosophical traditions. Thus, in this commentary, analysis of the symbols refers to the Old Testament and to related concepts found in other traditions.

- *Each symbol represents some aspect of the consciousness of an aspirant who is at a corresponding stage on the spiritual journey.* Just as any part of a dream can represent a fragment of the dreamer's personality, the various beasts, seals, books, places, and angels that appear in John's visions depict fragments of an aspirant's inner life. For example, wars may refer to the internal struggles you face when trying to gain self-mastery. Even though some symbols may refer directly to external persons, places, and things, they do not represent anything that occurs outside of an aspirant's own consciousness.

- *John's role in the visions represents the aspirant's conscious attitude; the other symbols represent aspects of the aspirant's subconscious and super-conscious natures.* Here, "conscious attitude" refers to what aspirants know about themselves—their qualities, characteristics, and powers. "Subconscious nature" refers to the instinctual life of the physical body, as well as to suppressed or unrecognized desires and guilt. "Super-conscious nature" refers to powers and capacities that aspirants hold in potentia that are as yet unactivated or unrecognized.

The psychological interpretation of John's visions reveals the esoteric meaning of the *Revelation*. It provides detailed and practical instructions for a spiritual journey whose goal is what Christian mystics call "conscious union with God." Buddhists call it "enlightenment"; Hindus call it "self-realization"; transpersonal psychologists call it "self-actualization."

This spiritual map follows a logical plan. Chapter 1 gives introductory material. Chapters 2 and 3 present the intuitive instruction that aspirants will receive at seven different stages along the spiritual journey. Chapters 4 through 11 present the seven stages of the journey, along with experiences aspirants can expect to undergo if they follow the earlier instruction. Chapters 12 through 21 provide yet another description of the entire spiritual journey, but with a different emphasis, while chapter 22 summarizes the benefits of the spiritual journey and encourages aspirants to embark on it. The *Revelation* thus describes the same seven stages three times. (Analysis of any one of these sections, therefore, provides support for and insight into an analysis of the other two. Topics treated briefly and obscurely in one section are often given extensive treatment in another.)

From the third century to the present, commentators have noted that various episodes in the *Revelation* are repeated or occur in parallel, rather than follow a linear path. Most modern commentators agree with this view, called the "theory of recapitulation," even though they do not agree with the psychological method of analysis used in this commentary.[3]

Each numbered chapter in this commentary corresponds to a like-numbered chapter in the *Revelation*. The commentary provides text from the King James Version, also known as the "Authorized Version." Although about four

---

3. The basic structural question is whether the events depicted in the *Revelation* are meant to occur in a strict chronological order or whether some form of recapitulation is involved. R. H. Charles, *The Revelation of St. John*, vol. I (1920; reprint; Edinburgh: T. and T. Clark, 1985), p. xxiii, says, "the theory of Recapitulation . . . from the time of Victorinus of Pettau (circa 270 A.D.) has dominated practically every school of interpretation from that date to the present." R. H. Mounce, *The Book of Revelation* (revised; Grand Rapids, MI: William B. Eerdmans Publishing Company, 1998), p. 31, says, "The continuous chronological approach is not accepted by the majority of contemporary writers."

centuries old, this is still the most widely used biblical text in the English language, because it combines beauty in language with literal accuracy.[4] This original text is presented with verse-by-verse interpretations based on the psychological model discussed above. These interpretations are supported by footnotes
that contain citations of related material from earlier Jewish scriptures, as well
as quotations that are similar in meaning from various religious and philosophical traditions. Unless noted otherwise, all biblical quotations are taken from the
King James Version (KJV). Two appendices explore earlier interpretative efforts
and questions of authorship.

The *Revelation of St. John*, when seen through a psychological lens, contains
ideas associated with many diverse traditions—the redemptive power of love,
the efficacy of chakras and kundalini, the way of mindfulness, and the absolute
idealism of Platonic philosophy. Thus the *Revelation* reveals more than the hidden wisdom of esoteric Christianity. It reveals the essential harmony and unity
that binds the great world religions and philosophies together as one spiritual
truth.

---

4. The King James Version (KJV) provides a word-for-word translation of the original Greek
text. When the KJV includes additional words that are not found in the Greek text, those
additional words are italicized.

CHAPTER 1

THE SOUL

In John's initial vision, the aspirant becomes aware of the soul, which is the inner divine voice, and receives guidance concerning the seven chakras.

KING JAMES VERSION

1. The Revelation of Jesus Christ, which God gave unto him, to shew unto his servants things which must shortly come to pass; and he sent and signified *it* by his angel unto his servant John:

PSYCHOLOGICAL INTERPRETATION

1. The revelation given by God to Jesus Christ shows God's servants what must soon take place.[1] Jesus transmitted and certified this revelation by conveying his inspiration to his disciple John.[2]

---

1. The *Revelation* in verse 1 and elsewhere (1:3; 2:16; 3:11; 22:6, 7, 10, 12, 20) states that it is concerned with events that will or can happen immediately. This emphasis on immediacy is not consistent with the traditional methods of interpretation that treat the work as a chronicle of events in the distant past or future.
2. Angel is a translation of the Greek word (*aggelos*) that means "messenger," "envoy," or "one who is sent." In verse 1, the angel of Jesus is interpreted as inspiration that imparts instruction from Jesus. R. Steiner, *The Book of Revelation and the Work of the Priest* (London: Rudolf Steiner Press, 1998), p. 61, has a similar perspective when he refers to "the apocalyptist, writing through Inspiration." More generally, Paul, in 2 Tim. 3:16, says, "All scripture *is* given by inspiration of God." Unless stated otherwise, all biblical quotations come from the KJV.

2. Who bare record of the word of God, and of the testimony of Jesus Christ, and of all things that he saw.

3. Blessed *is* he that readeth, and they that hear the words of this prophecy, and keep those things which are written therein: for the time *is* at hand.

4. John to the seven churches which are in Asia: Grace *be* unto you, and peace, from him which is, and which was, and which is to come; and from the seven Spirits which are before his throne;

2. John recorded this revelation in three ways: intuition (immediate apprehension of truth), clairaudience (hearing the actual words dictated by Jesus), and clairvoyance (seeing images and visions).[3]

3. Happy is the person who reads or hears the words of this revelation, and who carefully studies these words, for they can be applied immediately.[4]

4. From John to the seven churches in Asia: "Grace and peace be unto you from God, who is eternal; and from the seven archangels,[5] who are in the presence of the heart of God;[6]

---

3. The phrase "word of God" is taken to be an intuition, which is the immediate knowing of something without the conscious use of reasoning. Heb. 4:12 appears to use this phrase in the same way: "For the word of God *is* quick, and powerful, and sharper than any twoedged sword, piercing even to the dividing asunder of soul and spirit, and of the joints and marrow, and *is* a discerner of the thoughts and intents of the heart."

4. The *Revelation* contains seven beatitudes, that is, phrases that begin with the word "blessed" in the KJV. Some other versions (e.g., the New English Bible (NEB)) translate this word as "happy." Verse 3 contains the first of these seven beatitudes.

5. C. W. Leadbeater, *The Masters and the Path* (1925; reprint; Adyar, Madras: Theosophical Publishing House, 1965), pp. 260–262, says that "the Seven Spirits of God" in the *Revelation* are the seven archangels. In the Jewish tradition, the archangels are "the seven holy angels who present the prayers of the saints and enter into the presence of the glory of the Holy One" (Tobit 12:15, Revised Standard Version (RSV)). See also 1 Enoch 20:1–7. H. P. Blavatsky, *The Secret Doctrine*, vol. I (1888; reprint; Pasadena, CA: Theosophical University Press, 1977), pp. 38, 339, 429, sometimes refers to the seven archangels as the "Dhyan Chohans," which literally means "Lords of Light," or as the "Elohim."

6. A throne is a point of contact with a king. In verse 4, the throne of God is taken to be what is sometimes called the "heart of God." For example, *A Course in Miracles* (*ACIM*) (second edition; Glen Ellen, CA: Foundation for Inner Peace, 1992) uses the expression "Heart of God" several times; e.g., vol. I, p. 340. A. A. Bailey uses this expression many times, such as in *Discipleship in the New Age*, vol. II (1955; reprint New York: Lucis Publishing Company, 1972), p. 437, "The 'light of love' which flows from the Heart of God." The role and functions of the heart of God are provided later, especially in chapters 4 and 7.

5. And from Jesus Christ, *who is* the faithful witness, *and* the first begotten of the dead, and the prince of the kings of the earth. Unto him that loved us, and washed us from our sins in his own blood,

6. And hath made us kings and priests unto God and his Father; to him *be* glory and dominion for ever and ever. Amen.

5. and from Jesus Christ, who is a faithful witness of truth—the first among us to fulfill the pattern of human evolution, and more powerful than any ruler on earth.[7] Jesus loved us, purified us with his love,[8]

6. and made us into a kingdom of priests who worship God,[9] the source of his own illumination.[10] Consequently, Jesus truly merits honor and authority forever. So it shall be."

---

7. The three-part title in verse 5 is based on earlier scriptures: John 18:37, Col. 1:18, and Psal. 89:27. *A Commentary on the Book of the Revelation Based on a Study of Twenty-Four Psychic Discourses by Edgar Cayce* (1945; reprint; Virginia Beach, VA: A.R.E. Press, 1969), p. 127, says that it was "Jesus . . . who first fulfilled the pattern of man's evolution." This quotation is not from Cayce himself, but is an interpretation that a study group made based on Cayce's messages.

8. The "blood" in verse 5 is interpreted as love for the following reason: it is able to remove sin, which is separation from God. But 1 John 4:7 states that "every one that loveth is born of God, and knoweth God," indicating that love can remove sin. O. M. Aivanhov, *The Book of Revelations: A Commentary* (second edition, Los Angeles: Prosveta, 1997), p. 36, and A. A. Bailey, *A Treatise on White Magic* (1934; reprint; New York: Lucis Publishing Company, 1979), p. 351, also consider blood to be a symbol of love.

9. In Exod. 19:6, God promised the Israelites that he would make them "a kingdom of priests, and an holy nation," if they obeyed his voice and kept his commandments. The Revised Standard Version (RSV) provides a translation of verse 6 that is closer to the promise in Exodus: "and made us a kingdom, priests to his God and Father." The early church understood itself to be the inheritors of the blessings promised Israel (1 Pet. 2:9).

10. James 1:17 speaks of God as "the Father of lights," meaning the source of both physical and spiritual illumination.

7. Behold, he cometh with clouds; and every eye shall see him, and they *also* which pierced him: and all kindreds of the earth shall wail because of him. Even so, Amen.

7. Through this revelation, Jesus comes to convey inspiration to human beings. Humanity as a whole will someday recognize Jesus as the source of various inspired writings[11]—even those who have been hostile toward him.[12] People throughout the world will mourn and repent because of his message. So it shall be.[13]

8. I am Alpha and Omega, the beginning and the ending, saith the Lord, which is, and which was, and which is to come, the Almighty.

8. God, speaking through Jesus (who in turn inspires John), says: "I am eternal and everlasting," which is true, because God is the same yesterday, today, and tomorrow, and is all-powerful.[14]

---

11. The first part of verse 7 is based on Dan. 7:13: "*one* like the Son of man came with the clouds of heaven." Several scriptural passages (Exod. 19:9, 34:5; Num. 11:25; Matt. 17:5) describe a divine voice that comes out of a cloud to provide revelation, and so a cloud symbolizes the conveyance of inspired revelation. A. A. Bailey, *Glamour: A World Problem* (1950; reprint; New York: Lucis Publishing Company, 1973), p. 189, says, "This is the significance of the words in the New Testament, 'every eye shall see Him'; humanity as a whole will recognise the revealing *One*."

12. Verse 7 is partly based on Zech. 12:10: "they shall look upon me whom they have pierced, and they shall mourn for him, as one mourneth for *his* only *son*." The piercing in verse 7 is taken as hostility, because a sharp arrow is sometimes used as a metaphor for false witness, wickedness, anger, or bitter words (Prov. 25:18; Psal. 11:2, 38:2, 64:3).

13. The mourning is taken as a sign of repentance, as in James 4:9–10: "Be afflicted, and mourn, and weep: let your laughter be turned to mourning, and *your* joy to heaviness. Humble yourselves in the sight of the Lord, and he shall lift you up." See also Matt. 5:4.

14. Verse 8 is similar to Isa. 44:6: "I *am* the first, and I *am* the last; and beside me *there is* no God." See also Isa. 41:4 and 48:12. Most modern translations of verse 8 (e.g., RSV, New Revised Standard Version (NRSV), New International Version (NIV)) use the phrase "Lord God" instead of just "Lord." Alpha and Omega are the first and last letters of the Greek alphabet. D. Fideler, *Jesus Christ, Sun of God* (Wheaton, IL: Theosophical Publishing House, 1993), p. 272, says, "In Hellenistic times, Alpha and Omega were symbols of Aeon, Eternity personified as a mythological being."

9. I John, who also am your brother, and companion in tribulation, and in the kingdom and patience of Jesus Christ, was in the isle that is called Patmos, for the word of God, and for the testimony of Jesus Christ.

9. John, who is a brother and companion in suffering to everyone studying this revelation, and who shares with them the fellowship and patient strength of Jesus, was banished to Patmos, a small rocky island in the Aegean, for promoting the teachings of God and Jesus.

10. I was in the Spirit on the Lord's day, and heard behind me a great voice, as of a trumpet,

10. John received a vision based on the spiritual journey.[15] The aspirant, who is John himself within the vision,[16] starts the spiritual journey when he intuitively hears an authoritative voice coming from beyond his mind.[17]

---

15. Verse 10 is the only place in the Bible in which the phrase "the Lord's Day" appears. Charles, *The Revelation of St. John*, vol. I, p. 23, says that this phrase refers to Sunday, and he cites evidence indicating that "the Lord's Day" was widely used in this way by Christians during the second century. Sunday was the day of Jesus' physical resurrection; it is taken as symbolizing the spiritual journey, which is a process of psychological resurrection.

16. To distinguish between the John who is having the vision (or who is dreaming) and the John who is within the vision (or who is within the dream), the latter is referred to as the aspirant. John was a man and so would appear in his own visions as a man. This commentary uses the pronoun "he" to denote the aspirant, because the latter is the role that John plays in his vision.

17. The word "great" is a translation of the Greek word (*megas*) that is sometimes used to denote people holding positions of authority (Mark 10:42). The trumpet was an instrument through which God spoke during Moses' experience in the Sinai; see Exod. 19:16, 19 and Heb. 12:19. The trumpet is interpreted as the intuition, because the latter is a faculty through which God speaks to a human being. For example, in 1 Kings 19:12, God spoke to Elijah through the intuition, described as "a still small voice." Paramahansa Yogananda, *The Science of Religion* (1953; reprint; Los Angeles: Self-Realization Fellowship, 1969), pp. 96–97, explains: "Every man has the power of intuition, as he has the power of thought. As thought can be cultivated, so intuition can be developed. In intuition we are in tune with Reality— with the world of Bliss, with the 'unity in diversity,' with the inner laws governing the spiritual world, with God."

11. Saying, I am Alpha and Omega, the first and the last: and, What thou seest, write in a book, and send *it* unto the seven churches which are in Asia; unto Ephesus, and unto Smyrna, and unto Pergamos, and unto Thyatira, and unto Sardis, and unto Philadelphia, and unto Laodicea.

11. This voice says, "I am eternal and everlasting; whatever teachings you understand,[18] apply[19] them to your personality,[20] so that those teachings can affect the seven major centers of energy[21] that lie within your inner nature:[22] the sacral, solar-plexus, heart, throat, brow, crown, and basic chakras."[23]

---

18. "Seest" is a translation of the Greek word (*blepo*) that sometimes means to see mentally or to understand, as in Matt. 13:13–14.

19. Verse 11 is the first of 12 verses in which there is a command to write. Here, "write" signifies the application, or expression, of words or thoughts, as in James 1:22: "But be ye doers of the word, and not hearers only, deceiving your own selves." H. P. Blavatsky, *Collected Writings*, vol. 6 (Wheaton, IL: Theosophical Society of America, 2002), p. 336, makes a similar point, "Right thought is a good thing, but thought alone does not count for much unless it is translated into action."

20. Books have been used to record history (2 Chron. 25:26). The book in verse 11 is taken as the personality, consisting of the mental, emotional, vital, and physical bodies, because these bodies constitute a record of the decisions that one has made in one's life. Aivanhov, *The Book of Revelations*, p. 113, explains: "everything we do is recorded and our actions, sentiments and thoughts all leave traces, not only on our surroundings but also and above all on us."

21. "Church" is a translation of the Greek word (*ecclesia*) that means an assembly or gathering. Although most commentators interpret the seven churches literally, several writers take them as the seven chakras of Indian philosophy, because the latter are centers where diverse energies are assembled. Both Swami Yukteswar, *The Holy Science* (1894; reprint; Los Angeles: Self-Realization Fellowship, 1977), pp. 71–72, and Paramahansa Yogananda, *The Second Coming of Christ: The Resurrection of the Christ Within You* (Los Angeles: Self-Realization Fellowship, 2004), p. 109, give this interpretation, but do not indicate the church that corresponds to each chakra.

22. "Asia" is a translation of the Greek word (*Asia*) that can mean Orient or the East. C. Fillmore, *The Metaphysical Bible Dictionary* (1931; reprint; Unity Village, MO: Unity School of Christianity, 1995), p. 73, says, "The East always refers to the within, the hidden, the spiritual. . . . Asia therefore must signify the inner, the spiritual, in individual consciousness."

23. For each chakra, Table 1 lists the English, Sanskrit, and Greek names of the associated church, and its approximate location. Both J. M. Pryse, *The Apocalypse Unsealed* (1910; reprint; Kila, MT: Kessinger Publishing Company, 1997), pp. 37–38, and B. Condron, *Kundalini Rising* (Windyville, MO: SOM Publishing, 1992), pp. 145–147, associate the churches with the chakras according to their spatial order. In particular, they associate the first-mentioned church, Ephesus, with the chakra at the base of the spine, and the seventh-mentioned church, Laodicea, with the crown chakra at the top of the head. In Table 1, however, the order of the associated chakras is the same as the order in which they are transformed on the spiritual journey, as discussed in more detail in chapters 2 and 3.

12. And I turned to see the voice that spake with me. And being turned, I saw seven golden candlesticks;

12. The aspirant reflects upon this guidance to understand its content and source. Through this reflection, he senses his seven chakras as centers of energy associated with specific areas of his physical body,[24]

---

24. According to verse 20, a candlestick and a church are equivalent symbols, and so they must stand for the same thing—namely, a chakra. In verse 12, "saw" is a translation of the Greek word (*eido*) that can mean to perceive by any of the senses. K. Wilbur, "Are the Chakras Real?" in J. White (ed.), *Kundalini, Evolution and Enlightenment* (St. Paul, MN: Paragon House, 1990), p. 127, describes how we can sense the chakras: "Different feelings and cognitions are 'located,' or best contained in, certain well-defined segments of the body: one feels stability and groundedness in the legs and feet . . . ; orgasmic ecstasy in the genitals; joy-vitality-laughter in the gut; openness-affirmation-love in the chest; intellection-insight in the eyes and head; and spirituality at the crown. . . . This, then, is the basis of the chakra system as presented in terms of feelings, vibrations, or *energetics.*"

13. And in the midst of the seven candle-sticks *one* like unto the Son of man, clothed with a garment down to the foot, and girt about the paps with a golden girdle.

13. and realizes that the source of his intuitions, often called the soul,[25] is in the midst of his seven chakras and is analogous to Jesus.[26] The aspirant cannot directly perceive the soul, but can discover its nature by observing its effects in his life.[27] One such effect is righteous action.[28]

14. His head and *his* hairs *were* white like wool, as white as snow; and his eyes *were* as a flame of fire;

14. Other effects are wisdom and penetrating insights;[29]

---

25. *A Commentary on the Book of the Revelation*, p. 129, considers the instructor in verses 11 through 20 to be the "Overself," defined as "the self-conscious, individualized portion of God, which is the unchanging core of each entity, the superconscious mind." A. A. Bailey, *Esoteric Psychology*, vol. II (1942; reprint; New York: Lucis Publishing Company, 1981), pp. 439, 491–492, and *Discipleship in the New Age*, vol. I (1944; reprint; New York: Lucis Publishing Company, 1976), p. 14, uses the following terms as synonyms: soul, super-conscious self, inner divinity, inner divine voice, voice of the inner God, and Voice of the Silence. The Bible (e.g., Luke 2:26–27) uses Holy Ghost or Spirit to denote the inner divine voice. This commentary uses the word soul, because it is more widely used by diverse writers than the other synonyms.

26. The New Testament often uses the title "Son of man" to designate Jesus (e.g., Matt. 9:6, 11:19), and so many commentators interpret the instructor in verses 11 through 20 as being Jesus. But verse 13 says only that this instructor is "like unto the Son of man." Here, the word "*like*" is a translation of the Greek word (*homoios*) that means "similar" or "resembling." Thus, verse 13 is interpreted as saying that the soul is similar to Jesus.

27. Job 37:22–23 (RSV) states: "God is clothed with terrible majesty. The Almighty—we cannot find him." In verse 13, the full-length garment indicates that the majestic effects of the soul can be seen, but not the soul itself. *ACIM*, vol. I, p. 173, asks: "How can you become increasingly aware of the Holy Spirit in you except by His effects?" *The Impersonal Life* (1941; reprint; San Gabriel, CA: C. A. Willing, 1971), p. 22, which is written from the point of view of the soul, makes a similar point: "when you have tasted of My Power, harkened to My Wisdom, and know the ecstasy of My all-embracing Love, . . . you *KNOW* I AM *within*."

28. A girdle can be a symbol of righteousness, as in Isa. 11:5, "And righteousness shall be the girdle of his loins."

29. Job 12:12 associates old age with wisdom. With regard to verse 14, *A Commentary on the Book of the Revelation*, p. 129, takes white hair to mean "wisdom," and Mounce, *The Book of Revelation*, p. 59, takes the flaming eyes to mean "penetrating insight." Bailey, *Discipleship in the New Age*, vol. I, p. 223, speaks of an "inflow of soul wisdom."

15. And his feet like unto fine brass, as if they burned in a furnace; and his voice as the sound of many waters.

15. and understanding,[30] which brings strength and stability to the intellect,[31] and spiritual feelings like peace, joy, and fulfillment.[32]

16. And he had in his right hand seven stars: and out of his mouth went a sharp twoedged sword: and his countenance *was* as the sun shineth in his strength.

16. Still other effects of the soul are liberating energies for the seven chakras,[33] intuitions that discriminate between truth and illusion,[34] and selfless and radiant love.[35]

---

30. Verse 15 is based on Dan. 10:6, which describes "feet like in colour to polished brass." Mounce, *The Book of Revelation*, p. 59, says that "the shining, bronzelike feet portray strength and stability." *A Commentary on the Book of the Revelation*, p. 129, interprets these feet as "understanding." Bailey, *Discipleship in the New Age*, vol. I, p. 537, speaks of "the intuitive understanding which the soul possesses."
31. A furnace is an enclosed fire. Bailey, *A Treatise on White Magic*, p. 250, says, "Fire is the symbol of the intellect."
32. Verse 15 is also based on Ezek. 43:2, which says that God's "voice *was* like a noise of many waters." Bailey, *A Treatise on White Magic*, p. 250, says, "Water is the symbol of the emotional nature." The Bible describes God-given waters that bring inner peace (Psal. 23:2), joy (Isa. 12:3), mercy (Isa. 49:10), fulfillment (Isa. 55:1), and salvation (Ezek. 36:25), all of which could be characterized as spiritual feelings. Verse 15 is interpreted as treating such feelings as an effect of the soul's voice. J. S. Goldsmith, *The Infinite Way* (1947; reprint; San Gabriel, CA: Willing Publishing Company, 1971), p. 89, makes a similar point: "The song of the Soul is freedom, joy, and eternal bliss."
33. Verse 20 indicates that the seven stars in verse 16 are related to the seven candlesticks in verse 12. A distinction can be made between the candlestick and the flame that the candlestick supports. Each candlestick is a chakra (see verse 12), and so each star is taken as an energy that activates, or is conducted by, the associated chakra. The Bible sometimes uses the right hand to represent salvation or liberation, as in Psal. 60:5: "That thy beloved may be delivered; save *with* thy right hand, and hear me." See also Acts 2:33. Thus, the first phrase in verse 16 depicts the soul as holding liberating energies for the seven chakras.
34. Paul, in Eph. 6:17, refers to "the sword of the Spirit, which is the word of God." If the sword in verse 16 is the sword of Spirit, then it represents the word of God, which in turn is an intuition (see verse 2). Bailey, *Discipleship in the New Age*, vol. I, p. 476, refers to "the intuitions which are sent to you from your soul."
35. Matt. 17:2 describes Jesus when he was transfigured: "his face did shine as the sun." O. M. Aivanhov, *Cosmic Moral Law* (third edition, Los Angeles: Prosveta, 1989), pp. 22–23, explains this simile: "I learned that the sun's face was so bright and luminous because it thinks of nothing but how to give, help, vivify, warm and resuscitate others. When I see someone's face light up I think to myself, 'Ah, he's planning something magnificent.'. . . And when I see someone's face becoming darker, clouding over, as it were, I say to myself, 'He's got some evil plan in mind.'. . . If a person's face does not shine with the brilliance of the sun it is because the good he has in mind is not strong enough to produce so much light." Thus, a face shining like the sun indicates the presence of selfless, or spiritual, love.

17. And when I saw him, I fell at his feet as dead. And he laid his right hand upon me, saying unto me, Fear not; I am the first and the last:

18. I *am* he that liveth, and was dead; and, behold, I am alive for evermore, Amen; and have the keys of hell and of death.

17. After learning about the soul,[36] the aspirant becomes frightened and expects the soul to condemn him for the same reasons that he has condemned himself.[37] The soul responds with reassurance, saying, "Give up your fear, for my help will always be available.[38]

18. I am the presence whose effects you have observed; although I seem to have been buried by your life in the physical world, I live forever within eternity, as you can verify;[39] and I have the teachings that can bring freedom from guilt[40] and limitation.[41]

---

36. In verse 17, "saw" is a translation of the Greek word (*eido*) that can mean to get knowledge of, or to understand, as in John 21:15 or Rom. 8:28.

37. A. A. Watson, *Through Fear to Love* (West Sedona, AZ: The Circle of Atonement, 1994), p. 32, says: "Because of our own insanity, we project insanity onto Him as well, and expect Him to withdraw from us as we have withdrawn from Him. Because of our guilt we fear His approach."

38. Being touched by the right hand represents reassurance, as shown in Psal. 139:9–10: "*If* I take the wings of the morning, *and* dwell in the uttermost parts of the sea; Even there shall thy hand lead me, and thy right hand shall hold me."

39. Plato states in *Cratylus*, p. 400c: "For some say that the body is the grave of the soul which may be thought to be buried in our present life." This text is taken from E. Hamilton and H. Cairns (eds.), *The Collected Dialogues of Plato* (Princeton, NJ: Princeton University Press, 1989). Paramahansa Yogananda, *Autobiography of a Yogi* (1946; reprint; Los Angeles: Self-Realization Fellowship,1969), p. 170, says, "The soul is ever-free; it is deathless because birthless."

40. Luke 11:52 mentions the "key of knowledge," so the "keys" in verse 18 are taken as teachings. Hell is often thought of as an afterlife realm where sinners are punished and separated from God; e.g., Luke 16:23. Hell is interpreted as guilt, because this emotion is a form of self-punishment in which one feels separated from God. *ACIM*, vol. II, p. 60, also equates hell to guilt: "Your holiness means the end of guilt, and therefore the end of hell."

41. Death could be thought of as a symbol of lack or limitation, because something dead lacks life and death is a limit on life. In fact, *ACIM*, vol. I, p. 618, states, "lack *is* death," and A. A. Bailey, *Esoteric Astrology* (1951; reprint; New York: Lucis Publishing Company, 1979), p. 615, states, "Death and limitation are synonymous terms." In verse 18, death is taken as lack or limitation.

19. Write the things which thou hast seen, and the things which are, and the things which shall be hereafter;

20. The mystery of the seven stars which thou sawest in my right hand, and the seven golden candlesticks. The seven stars are the angels of the seven churches: and the seven candlesticks which thou sawest are the seven churches.

19. Apply what you have learned, so that the present teachings will lead you to more advanced teachings in the future.[42]

20. You presently do not know how to transform the energies within your seven chakras.[43] All that you can now do is observe how the energies of your seven chakras convey messages about yourself, and how your seven chakras are centers for energies gathered from different parts of yourself."[44]

---

42. Bailey, *A Treatise on White Magic*, pp. 84–85, says, "in obedience to the next duty and adherence to the highest known form of truth lies the path of further revelation."

43. In verse 20, the stars, angels, candlesticks, and churches represent energies, messengers, chakras, and gatherings, respectively (see verses 16, 1, 12, 11).

44. Bailey, *A Treatise on White Magic*, pp. 165–166, describes the preliminary stage of learning about the seven chakras: "The disciple becomes aware of capacities and powers which are not as yet intelligently under his control. . . . Within his etheric body, he senses active forces. Sometimes he can localise them, and in any case he admits theoretically that there is awakening into conscious activity, a sevenfold structure, which is symbolic in form, and potent when employed. He cannot as yet control it and he is quite incapable of calling it into intelligent co-operation with his purposes and ideas, no matter how hard he tries. All that he can do is to register such phenomena and keep a record of these experiences, bearing always in mind that in the early stages of his unfoldment only the coarsest and most material of the vibrations will be registered on his brain consciousness."

CHAPTER 2

SACRAL, SOLAR-PLEXUS, HEART, AND THROAT CHAKRAS

The spiritual journey is divided into seven stages, each corresponding to one of the seven chakras and symbolized by one of the seven churches. The soul gives instruction for the first four stages: the sacral, solar-plexus, heart, and throat chakras.

KING JAMES VERSION	PSYCHOLOGICAL INTERPRETATION
1. Unto the angel of the church of Ephesus write; These things saith he that holdeth the seven stars in his right hand, who walketh in the midst of the seven golden candlesticks;	1. With regard to the motives of your sacral chakra,[1] apply these instructions, because they come from the one who holds liberating energies for all seven chakras and who abides in the midst of those chakras.[2]

---

1. The church in Ephesus symbolizes one of the seven chakras (see Rev. 1:11, 20). Except for the name Jesus, all proper names appearing in John's visions are interpreted according to their connotative meanings, rather than taken as denoting persons or things in the external world. Table 2 lists the connotative meanings of the Greek church names, according to which Ephesus means "desirable" or "appealing." Bailey, *Discipleship in the New Age*, vol. II, p. 747, says, "In the sacral centre lie the ancient racial fears and deep-seated personal desires." A. A. Bailey, *The Rays and the Initiations* (1960; reprint; New York: Lucis Publishing Company, 1976), p. 669, also says that "the energy of the sacral centre (the centre most implicated and active at the time of the first initiation) has to be transmuted," suggesting that the sacral chakra is the first chakra to be mastered on the spiritual journey. Thus, the first-mentioned church, Ephesus, is taken as the sacral chakra and the angel of that church as deep-seated personal desires, or motives.
2. *A Commentary on the Book of Revelation*, pp. 131, 139, interprets the instructor in chapters 2 and 3 to be the "Overself," just as it does in Rev. 1:13. Overself is regarded as a synonym for soul. To write

2. I know thy works, and thy labour, and thy patience, and how thou canst not bear them which are evil: and thou hast tried them which say they are apostles, and are not, and hast found them liars:	2. "I know your motives and your past efforts to look carefully at them,[3] and how you were disgusted by the selfishness and hypocrisy that you saw within yourself.[4]
3. And hast borne, and hast patience, and for my name's sake hast laboured, and hast not fainted.	3. After bearing the disgust that came from observing your base motives, you cultivated higher ones—such as charity, love, and mercy—that embody my nature,[5] and you are still acting on those higher motives.[6]
4. Nevertheless I have *somewhat* against thee, because thou hast left thy first love.	4. Nevertheless, you have failed to some extent, because you are no longer looking carefully at your motives.

---

means to apply, the seven stars held in the right hand signify liberating energies for the seven chakras, and the seven candlesticks are the seven chakras (see Rev. 1:11, 16, 12).

3. Biblical patience is a self-imposed restraint in face of opposition or oppression. For example, God is said to be "slow to anger" (Neh. 9:17; Psal. 103:8). In the context of self-observation, patience is taken as a self-imposed restraint on all reactions, such as fear or pride, that could interfere with self-inquiry. Paul, in 2 Cor. 13:5, International Children's Bible (ICB), encourages this kind of observation: "Look closely at yourselves." The discipline of looking closely at motives implements the instruction given in Rev. 1:20.

4. "Them which are evil" are taken as selfish motives, and "them which say they are apostles, and are not" are taken as hypocritical motives.

5. J. L. McKenzie, *Dictionary of the Bible* (1965; reprint; New York: Simon and Schuster, 1995), p. 603, says, "It is a widespread cultural phenomenon that the name is considered to be more than an artificial tag which distinguishes one person from another . . . but it is thought to tell something of the kind of person he is." The Bible often uses a personal name as an indication of the bearer's nature. For example, 1 Sam. 25:25 states: "for as his name *is*, so *is* he." A change in the personal name often indicates a change in the person, such as the change from Abram to Abraham (Gen. 17:5). Consistent with such usage, *A Commentary on the Book of Revelation*, p. 141, interprets "name" as "nature." Thus, the soul's name in verse 3 refers to the soul's nature.

6. H. P. Blavatsky, *The Voice of the Silence* (1889; reprint; Wheaton, IL: Theosophical Publishing House, 1968), characterizes the spiritual journey as "the sevenfold Path" (p. 91) and gives instruction for each stage of the path that matches fairly well with the instruction given in the *Revelation* for each of the seven chakras. Concerning the first stage, she says: "Armed with the key of charity, of love and tender mercy thou are secure before the . . . gate that standeth at the entrance of the PATH" (p. 79). Here, the first "gate" is the sacral chakra.

5. Remember therefore from whence thou art fallen, and repent, and do the first works; or else I will come unto thee quickly, and will remove thy candlestick out of his place, except thou repent.

5. Therefore, remember the discipline from which you have fallen, return to it, and resume your careful observation, because the development of right motive is a progressive effort. For otherwise, I will respond quickly and remove your crown chakra from its position of receiving new insights, unless you change.[7]

6. But this thou hast, that thou hatest the deeds of the Nicolaitans, which I also hate.

6. But you have already received a key insight: there is no justification for behaving in selfish and hypocritical ways, which I am also against.[8]

---

7. Bailey, *A Treatise on White Magic*, p. 203, says, "The development of right motive is a progressive effort, and constantly one shifts the focus of one's incentive when one discovers himself, as the Light shines ever more steadily upon one's way, and constantly a newer and higher motive emerges." Here, Light refers to insight about oneself. In verse 5, the candlestick is taken as the crown chakra, which can receive insights from the soul; see Rev. 2:10 and 3:7–8.

8. Nicolaitans means "followers of Nicolas." According to Acts 6:5, Nicolas of Antioch converted to Judaism and later converted to Christianity. Multiple conversions may indicate that Nicolas was a ritualist in the sense that he was involved with outer rather than inner changes. W. N. Mackay, "Another look at the Nicolaitans," *The Evangelical Quarterly*, vol. 45, 1973, pp. 111–115, also argues for "a probable identity of Nicolaitans with ritualists." Paul, in 2 Tim. 3:2–5, is critical of ritualists, speaking of them as "having a form of godliness, but denying the power thereof," and says that they are "lovers of their own selves" and "unholy." Accordingly, in verse 6, the "deeds of the Nicolaitans" are taken as selfish or hypocritical behavior.

7. He that hath an ear, let him hear what the Spirit saith unto the churches; To him that overcometh will I give to eat of the tree of life, which is in the midst of the paradise of God.

7. If you are attentive to your inner listening ear, which is your crown chakra, you can hear my instructions regarding your chakras.[9] When you have overcome the barriers within yourself, I will give you access to the plane of divine ideas, which lies within the mind of God."[10]

8. And unto the angel of the church in Smyrna write; These things saith the first and the last, which was dead, and is alive;

8. With regard to the emotions of your solar-plexus chakra,[11] apply these instructions, because they come from the one whose help is always present, who seems to have been buried by your life in the physical world, but lives within eternity.

---

9. The exhortation to "hear what the Spirit saith" occurs seven times in the *Revelation*; it introduces a promise in each message to the first three churches, and it follows a promise in each message to the last four churches. This seven-fold repetition calls attention to the importance of the exhortation. In the Gospels (e.g., Luke 2:26–27), Spirit is an abbreviated term for Holy Spirit, or Holy Ghost, which is interpreted as the soul. M. Collins, *Light on the Path* (1888; reprint; Pasadena, CA: Theosophical University Press, 1976), p. 24, says, "to be able to hear is to have opened the doors of the soul." Receptive meditation enables us to open the doors of the soul and receive its guidance. Chapter 4 gives instructions for practicing receptive meditation, and chapter 5 describes the effects of practicing this form of meditation.

10. The Tree of Life often appears in Jewish portrayals of paradise: in Gen. 3:22, the fruits of this tree enable one to "live for ever"; in 2 Esdras 8:49 (RSV), this tree is available only if "you have humbled yourself"; and in 2 Enoch 8:3–4, this tree is "more beautiful than any (other) created thing that exists" and has "the form of fire." The text for 2 Enoch comes from Charlesworth, *The Old Testament Pseudepigrapha,* vol. I. According to Theosophy, our solar system consists of seven worlds that are often called "planes." Taking the Tree of Life as the plane of divine ideas is consistent with these quotations, because fire is a symbol of the mind (see Rev. 1:15), divine ideas can be received only with humility, and such ideas convey the realization of immortality. Chapter 10 gives more information about the plane of divine ideas.

11. As is shown in Table 2, the Greek name *Smyrna* has such meanings as "gall, sorrow, lamentation, bitterness, and rebellion," which are various kinds of emotions. A. A. Bailey, *Esoteric Healing* (1953; reprint; New York: Lucis Publishing Company, 1978), pp. 169–170, says, the "*Solar Plexus Centre* . . . is the outlet—if such a word can be used—of the astral body into the outer world, and the instrument through which emotional energy flows." Sri Aurobindo, in M. P. Pandit, *Sri Aurobindo on the Tantra* (1967; reprint; Pondicherry, India: Dipti Publications, 1999), p. 18, speaks of the solar-plexus chakra as "commanding the larger life-forces and passions and larger desire-movements." Thus, Smyrna is taken as the solar-plexus chakra, and the angel of that church as emotions.

9. I know thy works, and tribulation, and poverty, (but thou art rich) and *I know* the blasphemy of them which say they are Jews, and are not, but *are* the synagogue of Satan.

9. "I know your desires, sorrow, and ignorance (even though you have access to unlimited divine wisdom)[12] and I know your arrogance when you have feelings of religious superiority,[13] which shows that such feelings are hypocritical and based on illusion.[14]

---

12. Plato, in the *Republic* (Book VII, p. 521a), speaks of people "who are really rich, not in gold, but in the wealth that makes happiness—a good and wise life." This text is taken from Hamilton and Cairns (eds.), *The Collected Dialogues of Plato*. Prov. 16:16 makes a similar statement: "How much better *is it* to get wisdom than gold!" Accordingly, rich is interpreted as wise, so poverty is ignorance.

13. Blasphemy is a translation of the Greek word (*blasphemia*) that means slander, verbal abuse, or evil speaking. Although the English word means "contempt for God," the original Greek word is not necessarily concerned with God. In verse 9, blasphemy is taken as arrogance. Paul, in Rom. 2:28–29, writes: "For he is not a Jew, which is one outwardly; neither *is that* circumcision, which is outward in the flesh: But he *is* a Jew, which is one inwardly; and circumcision *is that* of the heart, in the spirit, *and* not in the letter; whose praise *is* not of men, but of God." Accordingly, in verse 9, Jewishness signifies religious superiority.

14. The original Hebrew word for Satan means "adversary," which is the translation used in Num. 22:22. Fillmore, *The Metaphysical Bible Dictionary*, p. 575, interprets Satan to mean "the deceiving phase of mind in man that has fixed ideas in opposition to Truth." In verse 9, Satan is taken as illusion, which is the aggregate of false beliefs accepted by the mind. Illusion is considered in more detail in chapter 12.

10. Fear none of those things which thou shalt suffer: behold, the devil shall cast *some* of you into prison, that ye may be tried; and ye shall have tribulation ten days: be thou faithful unto death, and I will give thee a crown of life.

10. Fear none of the emotions that cause you to suffer—by that I mean observe them with detachment.[15] As you can see, illusion[16] may cause you to feel imprisoned by such an emotion, so that you are tempted to resist or suppress it, and you will feel afflicted for as long as that emotion lasts.[17] If you can observe that emotion with detachment until it ends,[18] I will give you an insight, via your crown chakra, that brings freedom.[19]

---

15. Blavatsky, *The Voice of the Silence*, p. 81, gives the following instruction for the second stage of the spiritual journey: "Beware of fear that spreadeth, like the black and soundless wings of midnight bat, between the moonlight of thy Soul and thy great goal that loometh in the distance far away. Fear, O disciple, kills the will and stays all action." The first part of verse 10 also counsels against fear.

16. Devil and Satan are used interchangeably in the Bible, such as in Matt. 4:8–11. Both devil and Satan are taken as synonyms for illusion.

17. Table 3 summarizes the symbolic meanings of the numbers used in the *Revelation*. Ten Patriarchs are mentioned before the Flood (Gen. 5), the Egyptians were visited with ten plagues (Exod. 7–12), there are ten commandments (Exod. 34:28), there are ten powers that cannot separate one from the love of God (Rom. 8:38–39), and there are ten sins that can exclude one from the Kingdom of God (1 Cor. 6:9–10). The *New Bible Dictionary* (third edition; Downers Grove, IL: Intervarsity Press, 1996), p. 834, concludes: "The number 10, therefore, also signifies completeness."

18. The Buddha taught the way of mindfulness, referring to the bare, or detached, observation of what is happening to us or in us. N. Thera, *The Heart of Buddhist Meditation* (York Beach, ME: Samuel Weiser, 1962), p. 28, explains: "Right Mindfulness is fourfold with regard to its *objects*. It is directed (1) towards the body, (2) the feelings, (3) the state of mind, i.e. the general condition of consciousness at a given moment, (4) mental contents, i.e. the definite contents, or objects, of consciousness at that given moment." In the *Revelation*, the discipline for the solar-plexus chakra is equivalent to right mindfulness of feelings.

19. The last part of verse 10 is similar to James 1:12: "Blessed *is* the man that endureth temptation: for when he is tried, he shall receive the crown of life, which the Lord hath promised to them that love him." In verse 10, "crown of life" is taken as the crown chakra when it is filled with life-freeing insights. Thera, *The Heart of Buddhist Meditation*, p. 44, explains: "It is the intrinsic nature of *Insight* that it produces a growing detachment and an increasing freedom from craving, culminating in the final deliverance of the mind from all that causes its enslavement to the world of suffering."

11. He that hath an ear, let him hear what the Spirit saith unto the churches; He that overcometh shall not be hurt of the second death.

11. Through inner listening, you can hear my instructions about transforming your chakras. When you have completed this process of inner transformation, you will no longer suffer from the second death, which is the progressive elimination of selfishness."[20]

12. And to the angel of the church in Pergamos write; These things saith he which hath the sharp sword with two edges;

12. With regard to the spiritual love of your heart chakra,[21] apply these instructions because they come from the one who transmits intuitions that discriminate between truth and illusion.[22]

---

20. The loss of physical life is the first kind of death, because it is the first kind mentioned in the Bible, namely in Gen. 3:19. Paul, however, refers to a second kind of death when he says, "I die daily" (1 Cor. 15:31). This second kind is the progressive elimination of selfishness, and it occurs on a daily basis until the process of self-purification has been completed. M. P. Hall, *The Apocalypse Attributed to St. John* (Los Angeles: The Philosophical Research Society, 1981), p. 63, has a similar perspective: "The first or natural death is a separation from the world. The second or philosophical death is a separation of the soul from worldliness by initiation into the Mysteries." Other references to the second, or philosophical, death can be found in Rev. 14:13, 20:6, 20:14, and 21:8.
21. As is shown in Table 2, the Greek name *Pergamos* has such meanings as "elevated," "strongly united," and "closely knit." Paul, in Phil. 2:1–2 (New American Standard Bible (NASB)), speaks of spiritual love: "if there is any consolation of love, if there is any fellowship of the Spirit, if any affection and compassion, make my joy complete by being of the same mind, maintaining the same love, united in spirit, intent on one purpose." The point is that spiritual love can elevate our consciousness so that we are united in spirit with our minds closely knit together. Bailey, *Esoteric Healing*, p. 159, says that the "heart centre becomes the agent for spiritual love." Accordingly, Pergamos is taken as the heart chakra, and the angel of that church as spiritual love.
22. The two-edged sword symbolizes the soul's intuitions (see Rev. 1:16).

13. I know thy works, and where thou dwellest, *even* where Satan's seat *is*: and thou holdest fast my name, and hast not denied my faith, even in those days wherein Antipas *was* my faithful martyr, who was slain among you, where Satan dwelleth.

13. "I know when you express spiritual love, which overcomes even the belief of separateness that supports illusion,[23] and which you express by holding fast to my nature and perceiving the presence of God within other people.[24] You have made this effort even when your self-image, which is a faithful witness of how you perceive everyone else,[25] felt separated from others because of false judgments that you held about them.[26]

---

23. Paul, in Eph. 4:25, speaks of the essential unity of human beings: "Wherefore putting away lying, speak every man truth with his neighbour: for we are members one of another." Blavatsky, *Collected Writings*, vol. 10, p. 327, writes: "It is this sense of separateness which is the root of all evil." Moreover, Bailey, *A Treatise on White Magic*, p. 195, says, "the heart centre . . . when awakened, leads to that expansion of consciousness which . . . loses the sense of separateness." In verse 13, Satan's seat is the fundamental belief that underlies or supports illusion, since Satan is illusion (see verse 9). According to these quotations, Satan's seat is the belief of separateness, which can be overcome through the awakening of the heart chakra.

24. The soul's name represents the soul's nature (see verse 3). In the New Testament, faith refers to belief in God (e.g., 1 Cor. 2:5). The soul's faith is taken as the soul's knowledge of the divinity that is within all human beings. Accordingly, holding fast the soul's name and not denying its faith is interpreted as making the effort to live as the soul and to perceive the presence of God within other people. J. S. Goldsmith, *The Gift of Love* (New York: Harper and Row, 1975), p. 16, describes this practice: "When I look at a person, I must not look at his outer human appearance and love that. I must look through him and realize that in the midst of him God is, and that God is living his life." Sri Aurobindo, *The Synthesis of Yoga* (Pondicherry, India: Sri Aurobindo Ashram, 1957), p. 844, connects this practice to spiritual, or universal, love: "The universal love has to be founded on the heart's sight and psychical and emotional sense of the one Divine, the one Self in all existence."

25. Other than verse 13, the name Antipas does not appear in the Bible. Charles, *The Revelation of St. John*, vol. I, p. 62, reports, "Nothing is really known beyond this reference of the martyr Antipas." The word martyr in the KJV is the translation of the Greek word (*martus*) that simply means "witness," which is how this word appears in most modern translations (e.g., RSV). Thus, verse 13 says that Antipas is a faithful witness. Fillmore, *Metaphysical Bible Dictionary*, R. D. Hitchcock, *Hitchcock's Complete Analysis of the Holy Bible* (New York: A. J. Johnson, 1874), and C. A. Potts, *Dictionary of Bible Proper Names* (New York: The Abingdom Press, 1922), all state that one meaning of the Greek name Antipas is "against all." Antipas is interpreted as one's self-image or self-concept, because this image competes against all images that one has of everyone else, yet one's self-image is a faithful witness of how one perceives everyone

14. But I have a few things against thee, because thou hast there them that hold the doctrine of Balaam, who taught Balac to cast a stumbling block before the children of Israel, to eat things sacrificed unto idols, and to commit fornication.

14. But you need to make some additional efforts, because you have discordant thoughts that corrupted your desires,[27] which in turn led your personality[28] astray through greed for material things[29] and lust.[30]

---

else. *ACIM,* vol. I, p. 142, makes a similar point: "When you meet anyone, remember it is a holy encounter. As you see him you will see yourself."

26. Blavatsky, *The Voice of the Silence,* pp. 82–83, speaks of the fleeting nature of the aspirant's achievement in the third stage of the spiritual journey: "For as the lingering sunbeam, that on the top of some tall mountain shines, is followed by black night when out it fades, so is heart-light. When out it goes, a dark and threatening shade will fall from thine own heart upon the path, and root thy feet in terror to the spot. Beware, disciple, of that lethal shade." Here, "heart-light" is spiritual love, in the absence of which fear arises from the belief of separateness.

27. Balaam was a soothsayer (Josh. 13:22) and Balak was the King of Moab (Josh. 24:9). Balaam taught Balak the way by which the Israelites might be led into sin (Num. 31:16). In particular, Balaam taught how to beguile the Israelites so that they would participate in illicit sexual activities, consume pagan food, and worship false gods (Num. 25:1–2). Potts, *Dictionary of Bible Proper Names,* p. 46, says that Balaam is "symbolical of a false teacher" and that the Hebrew name Balak means "one who lays waste." Blavatsky, *Collected Writings,* vol. 12, p. 692, describes the relationship between thought and desire: "What we call the desires of the Body have their origin in thought. Thought arises before desire." In verse 14, the doctrine of Balaam is taken as discordant thoughts and Balak as corrupted desires.

28. Israel is the adopted name of Jacob, and so Gen. 46:8 refers to the descendants of Jacob as "the children of Israel." Potts, *Dictionary of Bible Proper Names,* p. 122, states that Israel means "a prince prevailing with God"; Fillmore, *Metaphysical Bible Dictionary,* and Hitchcock, *Hitchcock's Complete Analysis of the Holy Bible,* give similar meanings. Israel is taken as the soul, because the soul is a ruler with God. The children of Israel, or the Israelites, are taken as the various elements of the personality, because the relationship between parent and child is similar to the relationship between soul and personality.

29. J. S. Goldsmith, *Practicing the Presence* (New York: Harper and Row, 1958), p. 51, provides a broad definition of idolatry: "To give power to anything external to consciousness is idolatry. It is to recognize a power apart from God. We must come to the inner conviction that power does not exist in form—any form, no matter how good the form may be." Accordingly, "to eat things sacrificed unto idols" is interpreted as greed for material things.

30. Swami Nikhilananda, *The Gospel of Sri Ramakrishna* (abridged edition; New York: Ramakrishna-Vivekananda Center, 1958), p. 128, says: "The words 'woman' and 'gold' occur again and again in the teachings of Sri Ramakrishna to designate the chief impediments to spiritual growth. . . . He meant only 'lust' and 'greed,' the baneful influence of which retards the aspirant's spiritual growth." Matt. 5:28 considers lust to be adultery: "That whosoever looketh on a woman to lust after her hath committed adultery with her already in his heart." In verse 14, "to commit fornication" is taken as lust.

15. So hast thou also them that hold the doctrine of the Nicolaitans, which thing I hate.

16. Repent; or else I will come unto thee quickly, and will fight against them with the sword of my mouth.

17. He that hath an ear, let him hear what the Spirit saith unto the churches; To him that overcometh will I give to eat of the hidden manna, and will give him a white stone, and in the stone a new name written, which no man knoweth saving he that receiveth *it*.

15. You also make excuses for behaving in selfish and hypocritical ways, for which there is no valid justification.[31]

16. Thus, you need to make the appropriate changes. For otherwise, you will feel an inner conflict between your separative feelings and my intuitions that discriminate between truth and illusion.[32]

17. By being attentive to inner guidance, you will receive my instructions about your chakras. When you have followed all of these instructions, I will give you an interior heavenly joy[33] and an awareness of your pure divine origin, which provides a sense of identity different from any way you are known in the material world."[34]

---

31. The deeds of the Nicolaitans are selfish and hypocritical activities (see verse 6), and so their doctrine is taken as excuses for behaving in such ways.

32. Blavatsky, *Collected Writings*, vol. 9, p. 159, describes the aspirant's task: "His thoughts must be predominately fixed upon his heart, chasing therefrom every hostile thought to any living being. It (the heart) must be full of the feeling of its non-separateness from the rest of beings as from all in Nature; otherwise no success can follow."

33. Manna, the "bread from heaven," was the chief food of the Israelites during their journey in the wilderness (Exod. 16:4, 35). J. Ruusbroec, *The Spiritual Espousals and Other Works* (New York: Paulist Press, 1985), p. 160, says that the hidden manna in verse 17 signifies "an interior, hidden savor and heavenly joy." Paramahansa Yogananda, *Sayings of Yogananda* (1952; reprint; Los Angeles: Self-Realization Fellowship, 1968), p. 17, says, "The highest experience man can have is to feel that Bliss in which every other aspect of Divinity—love, wisdom, immortality—is fully contained."

34. The last part of verse 17 may be based on Zech. 3:9 (RSV): "upon a single stone with seven facets, I will engrave its inscription, says the LORD of hosts, and I will remove the guilt of this land in a single day." The white stone in verse 17 may be the "pearl of great price," which is said to be worth more than any other possession (Matt. 13:46). White is a symbol of purity (Dan. 12:10) and God is said to be pure (Hab. 1:13). Psal. 82:6 refers to the divine origin of human beings: "Ye *are* gods; and all of you *are* children of the most High." Accordingly, the gift of the white stone in verse 17 is interpreted as the conveyed awareness of one's pure divine origin. St. John of the Cross, *The Complete Works*, vol. III (London: Burns Oates and Washbourne, 1934), pp. 49–50, gives a similar interpretation, saying that the white stone is a "touch of God" and "that it savours of eternal life."

18. And unto the angel of the church in Thyatira write; These things saith the Son of God, who hath his eyes like unto a flame of fire, and his feet *are* like fine brass;

19. I know thy works, and charity, and service, and faith, and thy patience, and thy works; and the last *to be* more than the first.

18. With regard to the thoughts of your throat chakra,[35] apply these instructions, because they come from the soul, which has penetrating insight and deep understanding.[36]

19. "I know that you have used your thoughts to purify your motives, feelings, and perceptions. You are now carefully observing your thoughts, which is more arduous than the earlier disciplines.[37]

---

35. As shown in Table 2 , the meanings of *Thyatira* include "inspired," "frantic," and "rushing headlong." Aurobindo says, "The throat centre, commanding expression and all externalisation of the mind movements and mental forces, is the centre of the physical mind" (quoted in M. P. Pandit, *Sri Aurobindo on the Tantra*, p. 19). A. A. Bailey, *Telepathy and the Etheric Vehicle* (1950; reprint; New York: Lucis Publishing Company, 1975), p. 19, speaks of "the throat centre as the creative formulator of thought." Our thoughts could be inspired, frantic, or rushing by with uncontrolled speed, so Thyatira is taken as the throat chakra and the angel of this church as thoughts.

36. Verse 18 is the only place in the *Revelation* in which the title "the Son of God" is found. Yukteswar, *The Holy Science*, p. 6, explains, "The Holy Ghost, being the manifestation of the Omniscient Nature of the Eternal Father, God, is no other substance than God Himself; and so these reflections of spiritual rays are called the Sons of God." The Holy Ghost, or Spirit, is the soul (see verse 7), and so "the Son of God" denotes the soul. A. A. Bailey, *The Light of the Soul* (1927; reprint; Lucis Publishing Company, 1978), p. 51, also considers "the son of the Father" to be a synonym for the soul. The flaming eyes denote penetrating insight, and the brass feet denote understanding (see Rev. 1:14, 15).

37. The NRSV renders verse 19 as: "I know your works—your love, faith, service, and patient endurance. I know that your last works are greater than the first." Blavatsky, *The Voice of the Silence*, p. 84, provides a clue to the meaning of this verse in her instruction for the fourth stage: "before thine hand is lifted to upraise the fourth gate's latch, thou must have mastered all the mental changes in thy Self and slain the army of the thought sensations that, subtle and insidious, creep unasked within the Soul's bright shrine." Accordingly, "patience" in verse 19 is taken as careful observation of thoughts, just as "patience" in verse 2 is taken as careful observation of motives.

20. Notwithstanding I have a few things against thee, because thou sufferest that woman Jezebel, which calleth herself a prophetess, to teach and to seduce my servants to commit fornication, and to eat things sacrificed unto idols.

20. Nevertheless, I require that you make some changes in your thoughts, because you still believe that sensual pleasure leads to happiness, and you allow this belief to corrupt and mislead your feelings, resulting in lust and greed for material things.[38]

21. And I gave her space to repent of her fornication; and she repented not.

21. I provided the opportunity for transforming this belief in sensual pleasure, and yet it remains.

22. Behold, I will cast her into a bed, and them that commit adultery with her into great tribulation, except they repent of their deeds.

22. As you can observe, I will highlight this belief within your mind, and you will see the pettiness of the thoughts associated with it, until you choose to change them.

23. And I will kill her children with death; and all the churches shall know that I am he which searcheth the reins and hearts: and I will give unto every one of you according to your works.

23. The change in these thoughts will extinguish the feelings of lust and greed. All of your chakras will be affected by the similar way in which I will highlight other thoughts and feelings, and I will bring about a change wherever it is appropriate.[39]

---

38. Jezebel was a Phoenician princess and the wife of Ahab, king of Israel (1 Kings 16:31). She was passionate in her attachment to idolatry and sensual pleasure, and she was also crafty, malicious, and cruel (1 Kings 21). Fillmore, *Metaphysical Bible Dictionary*, p. 352, says that Jezebel represents "unbridled passions of sense consciousness." In verse 20, Jezebel is said to consider herself a prophetess, and so this symbol is taken as the belief that sensual pleasure leads to happiness.

39. Verse 23 is based on Jer. 17:10: "I the LORD search the heart, *I* try the reins, even to give every man according to his ways, *and* according to the fruit of his doings." Heart symbolizes feelings, because it is associated with fear (Gen. 42:28), love (2 Sam. 14:1), pride (Prov. 18:12), and desire (Matt. 5:28). Reins symbolize thoughts, because thoughts guide and control the activities of the personality; in fact, "mind" is used instead of "reins" in the NASB translation of Jer. 17:10. Children symbolize feelings, because the latter are the product of thoughts and beliefs. Blavatsky uses this symbol when referring to "the children of thy thoughts" (*The Voice of the Silence*, p. 84) and says that "wrong thought must therefore be slain, ere desire can be extinguished" (*Collected Writings*, vol. 12, p. 692).

24. But unto you I say, and unto the rest in Thyatira, as many as have not this doctrine, and which have not known the depths of Satan, as they speak; I will put upon you none other burden.

24. But many of your thoughts, which pass through your throat chakra, are not affected by your belief in sensual pleasure, or by any other false belief, and so many of your spoken words are free of error. Thus, I do not require those thoughts and words to be changed.

25. But that which ye have *already* hold fast till I come.

25. Although careful observation of thoughts is difficult, hold that position until I come with new insights.[40]

26. And he that overcometh, and keepeth my works unto the end, to him will I give power over the nations:

26. When you have persevered and followed my instructions for all seven chakras, I will give you power over your thoughts, feelings, and behavior.

27. And he shall rule them with a rod of iron; as the vessels of a potter shall they be broken to shivers: even as I received of my Father.

27. Then you will rule all aspects of your personality by way of awakened kundalini within your spinal column, thereby providing an authority similar to that of a potter over vessels of clay, and even to what I received from God.[41]

---

40. J. Krishnamurti, *Freedom from the Known* (New York: Harper and Row, 1969), pp. 115–116, describes the practice of observing thoughts: "Meditation is to be aware of every thought and of every feeling, never to say it is right or wrong but just to watch it and move with it. In that watching you begin to understand the whole movement of thought and feeling. And out of this awareness comes silence."

41. Verse 27 is based on Psal. 2:9: "Thou shalt break them with a rod of iron; thou shalt dash them in pieces like a potter's vessel." The Old Testament sometimes associates rods with serpents, such as in Exod. 7:10: "Aaron cast down his rod before Pharaoh, and before his servants, and it became a serpent." See also Exod. 4:3, 7:9, 7:12, and Num. 21:9. The Sanskrit word *kundalini* means "serpent." According to yoga philosophy, kundalini is normally dormant; but when kundalini is awakened, it rises up the spinal column and stimulates the seven chakras. Bailey, *A Treatise on White Magic*, p. 572, uses the phrase "Golden Rod of Power" to denote the spinal column after kundalini has been raised in it. The phrase "rod of iron" in verse 27 is taken in the same way. Chapters 8 and 9 describe how this rod of kundalini can be used to gain mastery over the personality.

28. And I will give him the morning star.

28. I will also give you illumination that dispels the darkness of all ignorance.[42]

29. He that hath an ear, let him hear what the Spirit saith unto the churches.

29. Continue your practice of inner listening, so that you can receive my instructions for the remaining chakras."

---

42. Morning star is a name for the planet Venus, which is often visible in the eastern sky before sunrise. 2 Pet. 1:19 (RVS) uses the morning star as a symbol of illumination: "And we have the prophetic word made more sure. You will do well to pay attention to this as to a lamp shining in a dark place, until the day dawns and the morning star rises in your hearts."

CHAPTER 3

BROW, CROWN, AND BASIC CHAKRAS

The soul gives instruction for the last three stages of the spiritual journey—the brow, crown, and basic chakras—which lead to conscious union with the soul.

KING JAMES VERSION	PSYCHOLOGICAL INTERPRETATION
1. And unto the angel of the church in Sardis write; These things saith he that hath the seven Spirits of God, and the seven stars; I know thy works, that thou hast a name that thou livest, and art dead.	1. With regard to the wisdom of your brow chakra,[1] apply these instructions, because they come from the one who can link the seven archangels with your seven chakras.[2] "I know the amount of wisdom that you express, that your nature is alive with wisdom but lacks certain key principles.[3]

---

1. As shown in Table 2, the Greek name *Sardis* has such meanings as "precious stone" and "prince of joy." A principle of wisdom is an ideal that becomes a useful rule after being understood. It is more precious than our mundane thoughts, because it has the power to bring joy into our lives. Prov. 3:13–15 (ICB) makes a similar point: "Happy is the person who finds wisdom. . . . Wisdom is more precious than rubies." Bailey says that "the ajna centre . . . is the recipient of the idealistic intuitional impressions" (*Telepathy*, p. 19) and that "it is the organ of idealism" (*Esoteric Healing*, p. 149). *Ajna* is the Sanskrit name for the brow chakra (see Table 1). Accordingly, Sardis is taken as the brow chakra, and its angel as principles of wisdom.
2. The seven Spirits are the seven archangels, and the seven stars are the energies of the seven chakras (see Rev. 1:4, 16).
3. The name of something is its inner nature (see Rev. 2:3); death is lack or limitation (see Rev. 1:18).

2. Be watchful, and strengthen the things which remain, that are ready to die: for I have not found thy works perfect before God.

3. Remember therefore how thou hast received and heard, and hold fast, and repent. If therefore thou shalt not watch, I will come on thee as a thief, and thou shalt not know what hour I will come upon thee.

2. Learn to watch for repressed feelings, which are on the verge of disappearing, and bring them to the surface of consciousness: for I have not found your self-observation to be satisfactory for your journey to God.[4]

3. Learn, therefore, to remind yourself that self-knowledge and understanding are attained through a self-observant perspective.[5] This cultivated recognition, when held constantly throughout the day, enables you to live from that perspective.[6] If you allow your self-observation to lapse, you may lose an opportunity to receive a new insight from me, because such guidance comes unexpectedly.[7]

---

4. Prov. 28:13 (NIV) states: "He who conceals his sins does not prosper, but whoever confesses and renounces them finds mercy." S. Freud, *Introductory Lectures on Psychoanalysis* (1917; reprint; New York: W. W. Norton, 1977), p. 435, made the conscious recognition of repressed material the keystone of psychoanalytic therapy: "We can express the aim of our efforts in a variety of formulas: making conscious what is unconscious, lifting repressions, filling gaps in the memory—all these amount to the same thing."
5. Collins, *Light on the Path*, p. 25, says, "to have attained to self-knowledge is to have retreated to the inner fortress from whence the personal man can be viewed with impartiality." In verse 3, "heard" is a translation of the Greek word (*akouo*) that sometimes means hear with the ear of the mind, or understand, as in John 8:43, 47 and 1 Cor. 14:2.
6. Bailey, *Discipleship in the New Age*, vol. II, p. 116, says that "a reflective process or cultivated recognition . . . will serve to condition your day's activity. This conditioning attitude should be one of a constant recollection of purpose and objective, and a process of what has been called 'intentional living.'"
7. Verse 3 is related to Matt 24:42: "Watch therefore: for ye know not what hour your Lord doth come." Blavatsky, *The Voice of the Silence*, pp. 92–93, gives instruction for the fifth stage of the spiritual journey: "Ere the gold flame can burn with steady light, the lamp must stand well guarded in a spot free from all wind." If "the gold flame" is insight, "the lamp" is the center of consciousness, and "a spot free from all wind" is a position of detached observation, then this quotation is similar in meaning to the interpretation given for verse 3.

4. Thou hast a few names even in Sardis which have not defiled their garments; and they shall walk with me in white: for they are worthy.

5. He that overcometh, the same shall be clothed in white raiment; and I will not blot out his name out of the book of life, but I will confess his name before my Father, and before his angels.

6. He that hath an ear, let him hear what the Spirit saith unto the churches.

4. You have transformed a few insights into principles of wisdom without distortion.[8] These principles express my guidance in a way that is pure, for they are worthy of being followed.[9]

5. When you complete the remaining stages of your spiritual journey, your personality will be pure, and I will enable you to be aware of your eternal life and your inner relationship with God and the seven archangels.[10]

6. Continue to be attentive for inner guidance, so that you can receive my instructions on how to complete the remaining stages."

---

8. Bailey, *Glamour*, pp. 55–60, describes the corruption of intuitive ideas: "The idea which has emerged in his consciousness, through the partial awakening of his intuition, will be distorted in its descent to his brain consciousness in several ways. . . . Through wrong perception of an idea. . . . Through wrong interpretation. . . . Through wrong appropriation."

9. Table 4 summarizes the symbolic meanings of the colors used in the *Revelation*. The color white symbolizes purity, as in Dan. 12:10: "Many shall be purified, and made white."

10. The last part of verse 5 is based on Psal. 69:28: "Let them be blotted out of the book of the living." In the Old Testament, the book of life generally refers to natural, or physical life (Psal. 139:16); but in the New Testament, the book of life generally refers to eternal life (Phil. 4:3). The angels of God are taken as the seven Spirits of God and therefore as the seven archangels (see verse 1).

7. And to the angel of the church in Philadelphia write; These things saith he that is holy, he that is true, he that hath the key of David, he that openeth, and no man shutteth; and shutteth, and no man openeth;

7. With regard to the spiritual love and insights of your crown chakra,[11] apply these instructions, because they come from the one who transmits both spiritual love and insight.[12] Spiritual love is the key to detached self-observation.[13] When observed with spiritual love, no self-image can block your crown chakra from receiving insights, or act through your sacral chakra to affect your outer behavior.[14]

---

11. As shown in Table 2, the Greek name *Philadelphia* has such meanings as "brotherly love" and "loving as brethren." Bailey says that "the heart centre registers the energy of love," but speaks of "the stage of raising the energy of the heart centre into the head centre" (*Esoteric Healing*, p. 158; *Discipleship in the New Age*, vol. II, p. 131). Philadelphia is taken as the crown, or head, chakra, because this chakra is also associated with spiritual love. An insight is an intuition that is brought forth through careful observation. Rev. 2:10 indicates that the crown chakra is a receiving station for insights. Accordingly, the angel is taken as both spiritual love and insights.

12. In verse 7, "holy" refers to spiritual love, because it is untainted by selfishness; "truth" refers to insights, because they are immediate and direct perceptions of truth.

13. Fillmore, *The Metaphysical Bible Dictionary*, Hitchcock, *Hitchcock's Complete Analysis of the Holy Bible*, and Potts, *Dictionary of Bible Proper Names*, all say that the Hebrew name David means, "beloved" or "well-beloved," and so the "key of David" is spiritual love. David was the second King of Israel, succeeding Saul, and the biblical stories of David in his youth illustrate the power of love. For example, David's music was able to soothe and refresh Saul when the latter was despondent (1 Sam. 16:23), which illustrates the power of love to harmonize the discords created by a willful consciousness.

14. The words of verse 7 are very close to those in Isa. 22:22: "And the key of the house of David will I lay upon his shoulder; so he shall open, and none shall shut; and he shall shut, and none shall open." In verse 7, "man" represents an imagined picture, or concept, of oneself. Paul, in Col. 3:9, uses this word in a similar way: "Lie not one to another, seeing that ye have put off the old man with his deeds."

8. I know thy works: behold, I have set before thee an open door, and no man can shut it: for thou hast a little strength, and hast kept my word, and hast not denied my name.

8. "I know what you have achieved, and so, as you can observe, I have enabled your crown chakra to be open to insights, no matter what self-image is present.[15] You have achieved this status through your directed and controlled aspiration, and through keeping my instruction and expressing my nature.[16]

9. Behold, I will make them of the synagogue of Satan, which say they are Jews, and are not, but do lie; behold, I will make them to come and worship before thy feet, and to know that I have loved thee.

9. As you can observe, I am bringing forth your beliefs of superiority. These are false beliefs, because every human being is essentially equal to every other;[17] and I am transforming these beliefs into new principles of wisdom that enhance your understanding of spiritual love.[18]

---

15. Blavatsky, *The Voice of the Silence*, p. 96, describes the achievement of the sixth stage: "Thou art now on the way that leadeth to the Dhyana haven, the sixth, the Bodhi Portal. The Dhyana gate is like an alabaster vase, white and transparent; within there burns a steady golden fire, the flame of Prajna that radiates from Atman." Here, *Dhyana, Bodhi, Prajna,* and *Atman* are Sanskrit words for meditation, wisdom, spiritual intuition, and soul, respectively.

16. Bailey, *Discipleship in the New Age*, vol. II, p. 115, speaks of "a stage wherein there is a lifting of the energy of the heart centre to the head by means of directed, controlled aspiration—deliberately stimulated, mentally appreciated, and emotionally propelled."

17. *The Impersonal Life*, p. 72, states: "it is *I*, the Infinite, *Impersonal* part of You, abiding always *within*, Who am thus pointing out to you all these illusions of the personality." In verse 9, "make" is a translation of the Greek verb (*didomi*) that can also be translated as "bring forth" (e.g., Matt. 13:8). Satan, Jews, and feet denote illusion, superiority, and understanding, respectively (see Rev. 2:9, 1:15).

18. Rev. 3:9, 6:9, and 14:19 contain the notion that an illusion, or false belief, can be transformed into a new principle of wisdom. N. D. Walsch, *Communion with God* (New York: Penguin Putnam, 2000), p. 109, has a similar perspective: "Yet the illusion *points* to what is real and can give you an experience of it." Bailey, *A Treatise on White Magic*, p. 473, says, "Learn the meaning of illusion, and in its midst locate the golden thread of truth."

10. Because thou hast kept the word of my patience, I also will keep thee from the hour of temptation, which shall come upon all the world, to try them that dwell upon the earth.

11. Behold, I come quickly: hold that fast which thou hast, that no man take thy crown.

10. Because you are keeping my instruction about detached self-observation, I will keep you from failing during the coming trials.[19] These trials will purify your emotional body, especially those feelings that are identified with your physical body.[20]

11. As you can also observe, my insights come frequently. Hold to what you have achieved so that no self-image can diminish the receptivity of your crown chakra.[21]

---

19. Blavatsky, *The Voice of the Silence*, p. 96, says to an aspirant in the sixth stage, "thou art safe."
20. The word "world" appears in seven verses; it consistently refers to the world of emotions, which is the emotional body. Bailey, *A Treatise on White Magic*, p. 215, says, "The elemental of earth . . . is the sum total of the many lives which form the physical body." Similarly, *A Commentary on the Book of the Revelation*, p. 141, considers earth to be a symbol of the "physical body." This meaning is justified by Gen. 2:7 (NRSV), which states that man was formed "from the dust of the ground." Accordingly, "them that dwell upon the earth" refers to feelings that are identified with the physical body.
21. "Crown" refers to the crown chakra (see Rev. 2:10).

12. Him that overcometh will I make a
    pillar in the temple of my God, and
    he shall go no more out: and I will
    write upon him the name of my God,
    and the name of the city of my God,
    which is new Jerusalem, which cometh
    down out of heaven from my God:
    and *I will write upon him* my new
    name.

12. When you have overcome the remain-
    ing impurities within yourself, I will
    make you a pillar, or mainstay, of a
    spiritual community,[22] and you will no
    longer be borne into the physical
    world as part of the cycle of reincarna-
    tion.[23] In addition, I will give you
    unshakable knowledge that your
    nature is divine, that your personality
    is transformed by ideas coming down
    from God,[24] and that my nature is
    your own.[25]

13. He that hath an ear, let him hear what
    the Spirit saith unto the churches.

13. Continue to be attentive to your
    crown chakra, so that you can receive
    my instructions on overcoming your
    remaining impurities."

22. Paul calls the Christian church a "holy temple in the Lord" (Eph. 2:21) and refers to the apostles James and John as "pillars" in this church (Gal. 2:9).
23. W. Q. Judge, *The Ocean of Theosophy* (1893; reprint; Los Angeles: The Theosophy Company, 1987), pp. 63–64, writes: "St. John the Revelator says in Revs. III, 12, he was told in a vision . . . that whosoever should overcome would not be under the necessity of 'going out' any more, that is, would not need to be reincarnated."
24. The Testament of Dan was written in the second century B.C., and it includes an early reference to New Jerusalem: "the righteous shall rejoice in the New Jerusalem, which shall be eternally for the glorification of God" (Dan 5:12). This text comes from Charlesworth, *The Old Testament Pseudepigrapha,* vol. I. A city is a community with many inhabitants. In verse 12, the city is taken as the personality, which is inhabited by many thoughts, feelings, and motives, and New Jerusalem is taken as the spiritually trans-formed personality. Aivanhov, *The Book of Revelations,* p. 175, gives a similar interpretation: "the New Jerusalem is the symbol of a human being who has worked with the power of the spirit to transform his own matter."
25. Yogananda, *Autobiography of a Yogi,* p. 494, says, "For man, truth is unshakable knowledge of his real nature, his Self as soul."

14. And unto the angel of the church of the Laodiceans write; These things saith the Amen, the faithful and true witness, the beginning of the creation of God;

14. With regard to the will aspect of your basic chakra,[26] apply these instructions, because they come from the one who transmits self-validated truths,[27] inner standards of truth,[28] and divine wisdom.[29]

15. I know thy works, that thou art neither cold nor hot: I would thou wert cold or hot.

15. "I know that your motives are both selfish and unselfish.[30] I want you to be unselfish all the time.[31]

16. So then because thou art lukewarm, and neither cold nor hot, I will spue thee out of my mouth.

16. Because you have mixed motives rather than singleness of purpose, you are not yet ready to experience conscious union with me.

---

26. As shown in Table 2, the Greek name *Laodicea* means "justice of the people" or simply "justice." Bailey says that "the most quiescent centre in the body . . . is the basic centre," "the will aspect . . . can arouse the basic centre," and "will or power expresses itself . . . as legislation, legality, justice" (*Esoteric Healing*, pp. 169, 183; *Esoteric Astrology*, p. 244). Thus, the last church, Laodicea, is taken as the basic chakra and its angel as the will aspect.

27. The Hebrew word *Amen* means "firm and faithful." It is used at the end of prayers to confirm the words and invoke the fulfilment of them (Psal. 41:13, 72:19, 89:52). The promises of God are Amen in the sense that they are all true and sure (2 Cor. 1:20). The soul's message is also Amen, because one experiences that message as one's own inner intuitive knowing of truth.

28. A faithful and true witness is taken to mean a standard of truth. The soul's intuitions are standards of truth in that we know an external statement is true when it confirms an intuition from the soul. *The Impersonal Life*, p. 16, says, "*all* that ever appealed to You, coming from some *outward* expression, was but the *confirmation* of My Word already spoken *within*."

29. "The beginning of the creation of God" is taken as divine wisdom. For example, Prov. 8:22 (ICB) states: "I, wisdom, was with God when he began his work. This was before he made anything else long ago." Wisdom of Solomon 7:22–25 (RSV) states: "for wisdom, the fashioner of all things, . . . is a breath of the power of God." See also Prov. 3:19 and Sirach 24.

30. Bailey, *A Treatise on White Magic*, pp. 558–559, writes: "Mixed motive is universal. Pure motive is rare and where it exists there is ever success and achievement. Such pure motive can be entirely selfish and personal, or unselfish and spiritual, and in between, where aspirants are concerned, mixed in varying degree. . . . Singleness of purpose may occasionally be realized in high moments, but it does not abide with us always."

31. Blavatsky, *The Voice of the Silence*, p. 106, describes the effort of the seventh stage: "Thou shalt attain the seventh step and cross the gate of final knowledge but only to wed woe—if thou would'st be Tathagata, follow upon thy predecessor's steps, remain unselfish till the endless end." Here, the Sanskrit word *Tathagata* is a title of the Buddha.

17. Because thou sayest, I am rich, and increased with goods, and have need of nothing; and knowest not that thou art wretched, and miserable, and poor, and blind, and naked:

18. I counsel thee to buy of me gold tried in the fire, that thou mayest be rich; and white raiment, that thou mayest be clothed, and *that* the shame of thy nakedness do not appear; and anoint thine eyes with eyesalve, that thou mayest see.

17. Although you feel wise, take pride in your spiritual accomplishments, and are self-satisfied, you do not know that you are actually deplorable, unhappy, ignorant, unaware, and fearful.[32]

18. I, therefore, counsel you to acquire more lessons from your experiences so that you may be rich in wisdom. I counsel you to clothe yourself with spiritual love so that fear does not appear,[33] and to raise kundalini through your chakras so that you may be aware of what has been previously unrecognized.[34]

---

32. Rich represents wisdom (see Rev. 2:9). Nakedness implies vulnerability, lack of protection, and so naked can mean fearful, as in Amos 2:16 (NIV): "Even the bravest warriors will flee naked on that day, declares the LORD."

33. Isa. 61:10 states: "I will greatly rejoice in the LORD, my soul shall be joyful in my God; for he hath clothed me with the garments of salvation." The garments of salvation represent spiritual love, because the latter provides salvation from fear. In fact, 1 John 4:18 states, "perfect love casteth out fear." In verse 18, the white raiment is taken as the garments of salvation.

34. Bailey, *Esoteric Psychology*, vol. II, p. 432, says, "Through the heightening of vibration, through the swinging into activity of the centres, and through the subsequent and consequent development of the human response apparatus, new avenues of approach to reality, new qualities of awareness, new sensitivity to that which has hitherto been unrecognised, and new powers begin to open up." In verse 18, "eyes" are taken as the chakras, or energy centers, and "eyesalve" as kundalini. Raising kundalini heightens the vibration of the chakras and swings them into greater activity, the effects of which are considered in chapters 8, 9, and 10.

19. As many as I love, I rebuke and chasten: be zealous therefore, and repent.

19. My messages are actually expressions of my love, even though they may seem to rebuke and criticize.[35] Therefore, be zealous in applying these messages and transform yourself.[36]

20. Behold, I stand at the door, and knock: if any man hear my voice, and open the door, I will come in to him, and will sup with him, and he with me.

20. As you can observe, I am revealing the remaining barriers that separate you from me.[37] If you listen to my messages and remove those barriers, you will achieve conscious union with me.[38]

21. To him that overcometh will I grant to sit with me in my throne, even as I also overcame, and am set down with my Father in his throne.

21. By removing the remaining barriers, you will reign with me, just as I already reign with God.[39]

22. He that hath an ear, let him hear what the Spirit saith unto the churches.

22. Continue to listen for inner guidance, so that you can continue to receive my messages about your chakras."

---

35. The idea of divine discipline appears throughout scripture. For example, Prov. 3:11–12 states: "My son, despise not the chastening of the LORD; neither be weary of his correction: For whom the LORD loveth he correcteth; even as a father the son *in whom* he delighteth."

36. Psalm 69:9, New King James Version (NKJV), states: "Because zeal for Your house has eaten me up." Aurobindo, *The Synthesis of Yoga*, p. 65, explains: "It is this zeal for the Lord . . . that devours the ego and breaks up the limitations of its petty and narrow mould."

37. Bailey, *The Rays and the Initiations*, p. 347, writes: "The real meaning underlying the phrase 'door of initiation' is that of obstruction, of something which bars the way, of that which must be opened, or of that which hides or stands between the aspirant and his objective." The door in verse 20 is taken as the "door of initiation," and so it represents the remaining barriers that the aspirant must overcome.

38. St. John of the Cross, *The Complete Works*, considers "Divine union" to be the outcome from having taken "the seven steps of love" (vol. I, p. 107) and interprets verse 20 as describing "the effect of the Divine union" (vol. II, p. 274). Blavatsky, *The Voice of the Silence*, p. 37, gives a similar description of such union: "And now thy *self* is lost in SELF, thyself unto THYSELF, merged in that SELF, from which thou first didst radiate."

39. For verse 21, Yukteswar, *The Holy Science*, p. 23, gives the following interpretation: "Thus, being one with the universal Holy Spirit of God the Father, he becomes unified with the Real Substance, God." Paul refers to both "the judgment seat of God" (Rom. 14:10, RSV) and "the judgment seat of Christ" (2 Cor. 5:10, RSV). Similarly, verse 21 mentions two thrones: the throne of God and throne of the soul. These thrones are taken simply as signifying rulership.

CHAPTER 4

MEDITATION

John has a new vision that shows the effects of practicing the instruction given in the previous one. The first episode depicts the inner constitution of the aspirant and the steps of receptive meditation.

KING JAMES VERSION

KING JAMES VERSION

1. After this I looked, and, behold, a door *was* opened in heaven: and the first voice which I heard *was* as it were of a trumpet talking with me; which said, Come up hither, and I will shew thee things which must be hereafter.

PSYCHOLOGICAL INTERPRETATION

1. After receiving the vision in chapters 2 and 3, which describes disciplines for each stage of the spiritual journey, John realizes that the channel of communication with the spiritual world is still open, and he receives an intuitive message that says, "Raise your consciousness, and I will show you what must occur after the disciplines for each stage are applied."[1]

---

1. Verse 1 is probably based on Ezek. 1:1: "the heavens were opened, and I saw visions of God." The word heaven appears frequently in the *Revelation*; it represents either the spiritual world or something in that world, depending upon the context of the verse in which this word appears. Rev. 10:6 indicates that the spiritual world consists of everything outside the physical and emotional worlds, and so it includes the mind, causal body (which is introduced in verse 4), and soul. The trumpet is the intuitive faculty (see Rev. 1:10).

2. And immediately I was in the spirit: and, behold, a throne was set in heaven, and *one* sat on the throne.

2. John immediately has another vision that begins with an image of the heart of God, which is set in the spiritual world,[2] and of God operating through the divine heart.[3]

3. And he that sat was to look upon like a jasper and a sardine stone: and *there was* a rainbow round about the throne, in sight like unto an emerald.

3. God has three characteristics: divine intelligence, divine love, and divine will.[4] Divine will emanates from the heart of God with seven aspects, or rays—like a rainbow with seven colors.[5]

---

2. In verse 2, the throne symbolizes the heart of God (see Rev. 1:4). In her books, Bailey equates the heart of God with "the centre of pure love," "the centre of all things," and "the inner point of life in all manifested forms" (*The Rays and the Initiations*, p. 399; *The Light of the Soul*, p. 351; and *Esoteric Psychology*, vol. II, p. 396). *ACIM*, vol. II, p. 378, also refers to it: "In your heart the Heart of God is laid."

3. "One sat on the throne" refers to the divine source of all life and consciousness throughout the manifest world. In the Bible, this divine source is referred to as God or Him, as in Acts 17:28 (NKJV): "for in Him we live and move and have our being." In the Hindu Upanishads, the Sanskrit name for this source is Paramatman, which J. M. Tyberg, *The Language of the Gods* (Los Angeles: East-West Cultural Centre, 1970), p. 66, defines as "the Supreme Spirit that ensouls the forms and movements of the Universe."

4. Jasper, sardius (or sardine stone), and emerald were part of the high priest's breast-plate (Exod. 28:17–20) and adorned the king of Tyre (Ezek. 28:12–13). Verse 3 employs these stones to represent the nature of God. Although present-day jasper is opaque, Rev. 21:11 says that jasper is "clear as crystal." The clarity of ancient jasper symbolizes divine intelligence, because the latter does not have any flaws or impediments. Both Charles, *The Revelation of St. John*, vol. I, p. 114, and Mounce, *The Book of Revelation*, p. 120, report that the sardius was a "blood-red" stone. Blood symbolizes love (see Rev. 1:5), so the sardius symbolizes divine love. Because an emerald is a green stone and green symbolizes growth (Job 8:16), the emerald symbolizes divine will.

5. Bailey, *Esoteric Astrology*, p. 605, seems to use the rainbow metaphor to characterize the divine will, because she says that "the divine prototypal will" has the following "seven ray aspects": "Ray I—The will to initiate. Ray II—The will to unify. Ray III—The will to evolve. Ray IV—The will to harmonise or relate. Ray V—The will to act. Ray VI—The will to cause. Ray VII—The will to express."

4. And round about the throne *were* four and twenty seats: and upon the seats I saw four and twenty elders sitting, clothed in white raiment; and they had on their heads crowns of gold.

4. The heart of God is the inner point of life in a subtle repository, often called the causal body,[6] for the wisdom acquired over time.[7] The aspirant reminds himself of the principles of wisdom that he has learned,[8] which are stored within his causal body and are the essence of his pure and noble thoughts and feelings.[9]

---

6. A. E. Powell, *The Causal Body and the Ego* (1928; reprint; Wheaton, IL: Theosophical Publishing House, 1978), p. 89, writes: "The causal body owes its name to the fact that in it reside the causes which manifest themselves as effects in the lower planes. For it is the experiences of past lives, stored in the casual body, which are the *cause* of the general attitude taken up towards life." The Bible refers to the casual body as the "house not made with hands, eternal in the heavens" (2 Cor. 5:1). The notion of the casual body can be found in yoga philosophy, where its Sanskrit name is *Karana Sarira*; *Karana* means "cause" and *Sarira* means "body." For example, Yogananda, *Autobiography of a Yogi*, p. 415, speaks of "the idea, or causal, body," and Aurobindo, *The Synthesis of Yoga*, p. 592, speaks of "our causal body or envelope of gnosis."

7. The number 24 symbolizes the passage of time, because there are 24 hours in a day (John 11:9, Acts 23:23). Bailey, *The Rays and the Initiations*, p. 80, agrees: "The number 24 expresses *time*, and is the key to the great cycle of manifestation." I. K. Taimni, *Self-Culture* (1945; reprint; Adyar, Madras, India: Theosophical Publishing House, 1976), p. 115, associates the causal body with the passage of time: "the Causal body is . . . a repository of the fruits of human evolution." In verse 4, the 24 seats are taken as the causal body, because the latter is the receptacle for the wisdom acquired over time.

8. Job 12:12 (NASB) states: "Wisdom is with aged men, *With* long life is understanding." Powell, *The Causal Body and the Ego*, p. 91, makes a similar statement: "Wisdom is the fruitage of a life's experience, the crowning possession of the aged." In verse 4, each elder symbolizes a principle of wisdom that has been learned.

9. Powell, *The Causal Body and the Ego*, p. 90, says, "The causal body . . . is the receptacle of all that is enduring—i.e., *only* that which is noble and harmonious, and in accordance with the law of the spirit; for every great and noble thought, every pure and lofty emotion, is carried up, and its essence worked into the substance of the causal body." Verse 4 depicts each principle of wisdom as pure and noble, because the white color symbolizes purity (Table 4), and the golden crowns symbolize nobility (2 Chron. 23:11).

5. And out of the throne proceeded lightnings and thunderings and voices: and *there were* seven lamps of fire burning before the throne, which are the seven Spirits of God.

5. Out of the heart of God proceed divine love, divine will, and divine intelligence.[10] These divine qualities are transformed by the seven archangels,[11] who are in the presence of the heart of God, into illumination that is imparted during meditation.[12]

---

10. The Old Testament sometimes uses lightning and thunder to represent the presence of God (Exod. 20:18, Psal. 77:18) and voices to represent divine instruction (Exod. 19:5, Ezek. 1:28). The lightnings, thunderings, and voices in verse 5 are taken as divine love, divine will, and divine intelligence, respectively, corresponding to the three divine characteristics in verse 3.

11. In verse 5, the seven Spirits of God are the seven archangels (see Rev. 1:4). Their function can be inferred from the initial verses of Genesis. There, as Blavatsky, *The Secret Doctrine*, vol. I, pp. 336–337, points out, "'God' commands to *another* 'god,' *who does his bidding*. . . . That which commands is the *eternal Law*, and he who obeys, the *Elohim*." For example, Gen. 1:6 says, "And God said, Let there be a firmament in the midst of the waters"; but Gen. 1:7 says, "And God made the firmament." The God that issues the command in Gen. 1:6 is the Supreme Deity; the God that implements the command in Gen. 1:7 is the Elohim, or, equivalently, the group of seven archangels.

12. A lamp is sometimes used metaphorically to represent mental illumination, as in 2 Sam. 22:29: "For thou *art* my lamp, O LORD: and the LORD will lighten my darkness." See also Psal. 119:105 and Prov. 6:23.

6. And before the throne *there was* a sea of glass like unto crystal: and in the midst of the throne, and round about the throne, *were* four beasts full of eyes before and behind.

6. As the first step in receptive meditation, the emotions become still so they can act as a crystal,[13] transmitting the peace from the heart of God[14] to all four parts of the personality.[15] Those parts receive their life from the heart of God, but are generally agitated by being focused on either the future or the past.[16]

---

13. Throughout the *Revelation*, waters of various kinds represent emotions of various kinds (see Rev. 1:15). For verse 6, *A Commentary on the Book of the Revelation*, p. 145, interprets the sea of glass as "stilled emotions."

14. *ACIM*, vol. II, p. 391, gives this instruction: "I will be still, and let the earth be still along with me. And in that stillness we will find the peace of God." A. E. Powell, *The Astral Body* (1927; reprint; Wheaton, IL: Theosophical Publishing House, 1978), p. 230, makes a similar point: "Grand emotions may be felt, which come from the buddhic level, i.e., from the plane next above the higher mental, and are reflected in the astral body." Here, the buddhic level is the plane of divine ideas (see chapter 10), and the astral body is the emotional body.

15. Verse 6 is based partly on Ezek. 1:5: "Also out of the midst thereof *came* the likeness of four living creatures. And this *was* their appearance; they had the likeness of a man." Both Blavatsky and Bailey use "quaternary" as a synonym for personality, because they regard the personality as having four principal parts; see Blavatsky, *Collected Writings*, vol. 12, p. 692, and A. A. Bailey, *Esoteric Psychology*, vol. I (1936; reprint; New York: Lucis Publishing Company, 1979), p. 162. The personality is the lowest, or animal, portion of a human being, and so the four beasts in verse 6 are taken as symbolizing the four parts of the personality.

16. Bailey, *A Treatise on White Magic*, p. 512, says, "God breathes and His pulsating life emanates from the divine heart and manifests as the vital energy of all forms." This quotation is similar to the last phrase in verse 6, since the divine heart is symbolized by the throne and the forms, or parts, of the personality are symbolized by the beasts.

7. And the first beast *was* like a lion, and the second beast like a calf, and the third beast had a face as a man, and the fourth beast *was* like a flying eagle.

7. The four parts of the personality are the physical body,[17] the vital body,[18] the emotional body,[19] and the mental body.[20]

---

17. Ezek. 1:10 describes four beasts that are similar to those in verse 7, but each of Ezekiel's beasts has four faces: that of a man, a lion, an ox, and an eagle. In John's vision, each beast has it own distinct characteristic, either that of a lion, a calf, a face as a man, or a flying eagle. The lion is the strongest carnivorous animal (Judg. 14:18); it represents the physical body, which is the only part of the personality having physical strength. The physical body includes muscles and bones.

18. The "fatted calf" was regarded as the choicest of animal food (1 Sam. 28:24, Amos 6:4, Luke 15:23); it represents the vital body, which nourishes the physical body. The vital body has been given many other names: "biofield" in alternative medicine; "golden bowl" in the Bible (Eccles. 12:6); and "etheric double" or "etheric body" in Theosophy (A. E. Powell, *The Etheric Double,* Wheaton, IL: Theosophical Publishing House, 1979). The vital body is discussed in several Hindu Upanishads, where its Sanskrit name is *pranamayakosha*, and it is called the "meridians" in Chinese medicine. There is general agreement in the various descriptions of this body given in the Upanishads, Chinese medicine, and clairvoyant investigations (H. Motoyama, *Theories of the Chakras*, Wheaton, IL: Theosophical Publishing House, 1984). The vital body includes the seven chakras of Indian philosophy.

19. The human face reveals character and expresses emotions, as shown in Isa. 3:9 (NRSV): "The look on their faces bears witness against them." Thus, the human face symbolizes the emotional body, which generates our longings, appetites, moods, feelings, and cravings. Theosophical literature often refers to the emotional body as the "astral body"; see Powell, *The Astral Body.*

20. The eagle has swiftness of flight (2 Sam. 1:23) and power of vision (Job 39:27–29), which are also characteristics of thought. Accordingly, the flying eagle represents the mental body, which is sometimes called the "lower mind" or simply the "mind." See A. E. Powell, *The Mental Body* (1927; reprint; Wheaton, IL: Theosophical Publishing House, 1975).

8. And the four beasts had each of them six wings about *him*; and *they were* full of eyes within: and they rest not day and night, saying, Holy, holy, holy, Lord God Almighty, which was, and is, and is to come.

8. As the second step in meditation, the four-fold personality changes its orientation so that it looks for illumination from within, rather than dwelling on the future or past.[21] The personality makes this change by repeatedly affirming: "God is faithful, compassionate, good, all-powerful, and eternal."[22]

9. And when those beasts give glory and honour and thanks to him that sat on the throne, who liveth for ever and ever,

9. When the four-fold personality looks for illumination from within, it gives attention, honor, and gratitude to the inner source of all life, to what is eternal.

---

21. Each of the four beasts is endowed with the six wings of Isaiah's seraphim (Isa. 6:2). These wings symbolize movement, or reorientation. In verse 6, the beasts are "full of eyes before and behind," showing that the four-fold personality is dwelling on the future or past. In verse 8, the beasts are "full of eyes within," showing that the personality changed its orientation, because it is now looking for illumination from within.

22. Verse 8 describes a contemplative approach to meditation. J. S. Goldsmith, *The Contemplative Life* (New Hyde Park, NY: University Books, 1963), p. 95, explains: "You have dwelt in a continuous contemplation of God's allness, God's mightiness, God's grace, God's love; and having come to the end of your thoughts for the moment, you now become quiet and wait for God to speak to you. You keep silent while your ears are open as if the still small voice were about to speak to you."

10. The four and twenty elders fall down before him that sat on the throne, and worship him that liveth for ever and ever, and cast their crowns before the throne, saying,

10. As the final step in meditation, the causal body changes its orientation so that it looks for illumination from the eternal source of life. This change occurs when the causal body realizes its own wisdom is limited and concludes,[23]

11. Thou art worthy, O Lord, to receive glory and honour and power: for thou hast created all things, and for thy pleasure they are and were created.

11. "You are worthy, O Lord, of receiving attention, honor, and faith, for you have created all things and given them their purpose."

---

23. Taimni, *Self-Culture*, p. 110, says, "The first function of the Causal body is that it serves as the organ of abstract thought." Abstract thought includes realizations, expressions of wisdom, philosophical reasoning, and understanding of ideas. In verse 10, the casting of crowns before the throne symbolizes the causal body's realization that its own wisdom is limited. The Bible makes similar points: "Lean not unto thine own understanding" (Prov. 3:5); "Be not wise in thine own eyes" (Prov. 3:7).

CHAPTER 5

GUIDANCE

The aspirant starts to practice meditation, receives guidance from
the soul, and discovers the value of that guidance.

KING JAMES VERSION	PSYCHOLOGICAL INTERPRETATION
1. And I saw in the right hand of him that sat on the throne a book written within and on the backside, sealed with seven seals.	1. Through receptive meditation, the aspirant gains three initial insights: his personality is absolutely dependent upon the power of God;[1] his personality is like a closed book due to his complete lack of self-knowledge;[2] and his personality is imprisoned by his seven chakras.[3]

---

1. F. Schleiermacher, *The Christian Faith* (1821–22; reprint; Edinburgh: T&T Clark, 1999), p. 16, states: "But the self-consciousness which accompanies all our activity, and therefore, since that is never zero, accompanies our whole existence, . . . is itself precisely a consciousness of absolute dependence; for it is the consciousness that the whole of our spontaneous activity comes from a source outside of us." Job 33:4 (RSV) makes a similar point: "The spirit of God has made me, and the breath of the Almighty gives me life." In verse 1, "saw" means understand, "right hand" signifies power, "him that sat on the throne" is God, and "book" symbolizes the personality (see Rev. 1:17, 1:16, 4:2, 1:11).
2. Ezekiel received a book of lamentations that was "written within and without" (Ezek. 2:10). In verse 1, the closed position of the book indicates ignorance about the personality. Blavatsky, *Collected Writings*,

2. And I saw a strong angel proclaiming with a loud voice, Who is worthy to open the book, and to loose the seals thereof?

3. And no man in heaven, nor in earth, neither under the earth, was able to open the book, neither to look thereon.

4. And I wept much, because no man was found worthy to open and to read the book, neither to look thereon.

2. The aspirant becomes intuitively aware of a compelling question: "What source of guidance can lead to self-knowledge and freedom?"[4]

3. The wisdom of the causal body, the knowledge and feelings of the personality, and the instincts of the subconscious nature have all been tried, but none of those guides have led to self-knowledge or freedom.[5]

4. The aspirant passes through a period of suffering, because he is unable to find any form of self-guidance that leads to self-knowledge or freedom.[6]

---

vol. 8, p. 108, says, "The first necessity for obtaining self-knowledge is to become profoundly conscious of ignorance; to feel with every fibre of the heart that one is *ceaselessly* self-deceived."

3. Daniel was told to "seal the book" (Dan. 12:4). When a book had been made secure by affixing a seal, it can be examined and read only when the seal has been broken by an authorized person. Regarding verse 1, Pryse, *The Apocalypse Unsealed*, p. 39, says that the "seals are the seven major *chakras*"; D. H. Lawrence, *Apocalypse* (1931; reprint; New York: Penguin Books, 1995), p. 101, has a similar notion, saying that "the seven seals are . . . the great psychic centres of the human body."

4. An angel is a messenger (see Rev. 1:1). In verse 2, the angel is taken as an intuition, which is a messenger of the soul. *ACIM*, vol. I, p. 298, asks a question that is similar to verse 2 and gives an answer that is similar to verse 3: "How can you, so firmly bound to guilt and committed so to remain, establish for yourself your guiltlessness? That is impossible. But be sure that you are willing to acknowledge that it *is* impossible."

5. Exod. 20:4 and Phil. 2:10 also divide the universe into three parts: heaven, earth, and under the earth. In verse 3, "heaven" is taken as the causal body, which is how this term is used in Matt. 6:20: "But lay up for yourselves treasures in heaven." Bailey, *Esoteric Psychology*, vol. I, p. 327, uses the term "matter aspect" as a synonym for the personality. Similarly, in verse 3, "earth" is taken as the personality, and "under the earth" as the subconscious nature, which lies below the consciousness of the personality.

6. Prov. 20:24 states: "Man's goings *are* of the LORD; how can a man then understand his own way?" *ACIM*, vol. I, p. 299, says, "Whenever you think you know, peace will depart from you, because you have abandoned the Teacher of peace."

5. And one of the elders saith unto me, Weep not: behold, the Lion of the tribe of Juda, the Root of David, hath prevailed to open the book, and to loose the seven seals thereof.

5. Through his abstract reasoning, the aspirant comes to the following conclusion:[7] "Suffering can be eliminated by finding the inner strength that guided the tribe of Juda and King David, because that guide was able to bring enlightenment and freedom in the past."[8]

---

7. Because the elders represent the causal body, speech by an elder signifies abstract reasoning (see Rev. 4:4, 10).
8. Lions represent strength (Judg. 14:18). The tribe of Juda (or Judah) was victorious in its battles when it relied on God's guidance, as shown in 2 Chron. 32:7–8: "Be strong and courageous, be not afraid nor dismayed for the king of Assyria, nor for all the multitude that *is* with him: for *there be* more with us than with him: With him *is* an arm of flesh; but with us *is* the LORD our God to help us, and to fight our battles. And the people rested themselves upon the words of Hezekiah king of Judah." Roots denote inner strength (Prov. 12:3). David wrote many Psalms describing how he relied on God as his inner strength, such as Psal. 28:7: "The LORD *is* my strength and my shield; my heart trusted in him, and I am helped."

6. And I beheld, and, lo, in the midst of the throne and of the four beasts, and in the midst of the elders, stood a Lamb as it had been slain, having seven horns and seven eyes, which are the seven Spirits of God sent forth into all the earth.

6. The aspirant learns to discriminate by looking for a source of inner guidance different from his vitality, knowledge, feelings, instincts, and wisdom.[9] Then, he senses the soul as an inner innocence[10] that has been buried.[11] The soul provides true divine guidance, because it expresses the divine powers and perspectives of the seven archangels that God sent forth for all humanity.[12]

---

9. Bailey, *The Light of the Soul*, p. 357, states: "By learning to discriminate between the true self and the lower personal self he disentangles himself, the light which is in him is seen and he is liberated." In verse 6, the aspirant learns to discriminate between the soul and the other inner voices. The four beasts are the four parts of the personality (see Rev. 4:7).

10. The Bible sometimes uses a lamb to represent innocence (Jer. 11:19, Luke 10:3). *ACIM*, vol. I, p. 37, also considers a lamb to be a symbol of innocence. In his commentary on the *Revelation*, Cayce interprets "the Lamb" as "the mind, spiritual" and as "the Christ-Consciousness," both of which are taken as synonyms for the soul; see J. Van Auken, *Edgar Cayce on the Revelation* (Virginia Beach, VA: A.R.E. Press, 2000), p. 196.

11. Verse 6 depicts the soul as having risen from a slain condition. Blavatsky, *Collected Writings*, vol. 8, p. 173, explains, using Christ as a synonym for soul: "Christ—the true esoteric Savior—is *no man*, but the Divine Principle in every human being. He who strives to resurrect the Spirit *crucified in him by his own terrestrial passions*, and buried deep in the 'sepulchre' of his sinful flesh; he who has the strength to roll back *the stone of matter* from the door of his own *inner* sanctuary, *he has the risen Christ in him.*"

12. Bailey, *Esoteric Psychology*, vol. II, pp. 491–492, writes: "Guidance can come, as you well know, from a man's own soul when through meditation, discipline and service, he has established contact, and there is consequently a direct channel of communication from soul to brain, via the mind. This, when clear and direct, is true divine guidance, coming from the inner divinity." In verse 6, horns are symbols of power and dominion, since they are the chief means of attack and defense for animals endowed with them (Deut. 33:17). The seven eyes symbolize divine vision, as in Zech. 4:10 (NIV): "These seven are the eyes of the LORD, which range throughout the earth." The seven Spirits of God are the seven archangels (see Rev. 1:4, 4:5). Earth refers to humanity, as in Gen. 11:1, Psal. 98:9, and Lam. 2:15.

7. And he came and took the book out of the right hand of him that sat upon the throne.

8. And when he had taken the book, the four beasts and four *and* twenty elders fell down before the Lamb, having every one of them harps, and golden vials full of odours, which are the prayers of saints.

7. The soul becomes apparent through right discrimination and then acts as the intermediary between God and the personality.[13]

8. After the soul has taken control of the personality, the physical, vital, emotional, mental, and causal bodies pay homage to the soul. They enjoy harmony and unity among themselves,[14] and consecrated feelings full of devotion and aspiration that reflect the spiritual understanding of the causal body.[15]

---

13. Bailey, *The Light of the Soul*, p. 411, speaks of "the soul, as the intermediary between spirit and matter." *ACIM*, vol. I, p. 280, also refers to an intermediary: "Your function here is only to decide against deciding what you want, in recognition that you do not know. . . . Leave all decisions to the One Who speaks for God, and for your function as He knows it."

14. Many instruments playing together signify harmony and unity, as in 2 Chron. 5:13: "the trumpeters and singers *were* as one, to make one sound to be heard in praising and thanking the LORD."

15. The phrase "the prayers of the saints" appears in Tobit 12:15 (RSV). In verse 8, the saints are taken as the elders who represent the causal body (see Rev. 4:4). "Golden" can mean "consecrated," because gold was used for the altar, candlestick, and other furnishings within the sacred tent of ancient Israel (Exod. 25, 39). Bailey speaks of "consecrated feeling" (*Telepathy*, p. 9) and says that "the energy of the intuition or spiritual love-wisdom or understanding . . . demonstrates as sensitivity and feeling in the astral body" (*The Rays and the Initiations*, p. 445). In verse 8, the "vials" are taken as feelings, because they can be consecrated and reflect the understanding of the causal body. "Odours," or incense, can symbolize devotion (Psal. 141:2) and religious aspiration (Mal. 1:11), both of which are examples of consecrated feelings.

9. And they sung a new song, saying, Thou art worthy to take the book, and to open the seals thereof: for thou wast slain, and hast redeemed us to God by thy blood out of every kindred, and tongue, and people, and nation;

9. And they display new faith, saying to the soul, "You are worthy to be in charge and to undo all limitations. Although we once ignored you, your spiritual love has related us directly to God, superseding our earlier relationships with family, race, community, and nation;[16]

10. And hast made us unto our God kings and priests: and we shall reign on the earth.

10. and you have made us into a single integrated organism dedicated to serving God,[17] enabling us to bring our inspirations, thoughts, and desires down into physical form."[18]

---

16. "Blood" is a symbol for love (see Rev. 1:5). The blood in verse 9 comes from the Lamb, which symbolizes the soul. Bailey, *A Treatise on White Magic*, p. 40, says, "the soul has outstandingly the quality of love." 1 John 3:1–2 indicates that love can transform a person into a "son of God": "Behold, what manner of love the Father hath bestowed upon us, that we should be called the sons of God. . . . Beloved, now are we the sons of God."

17. Exod. 19:6 states: "And ye shall be unto me a kingdom of priests, and a holy nation." For verse 10, the RSV gives the translation "and hast made them a kingdom and priests to our God, and they shall reign on earth," which is closer to how the promise in Exod. 19:6 is worded. Here, "a kingdom" is interpreted as indicating that the physical, vital, emotional, mental, and causal bodies form a single integrated organism.

18. A. A. Bailey, *Letters on Occult Meditation* (1922; reprint; New York: Lucis Publishing Company, 1974), pp. 1–2, discusses the effects of integrating the personality and causal body: "It is in the aligning of the three vehicles, the physical, the emotional, and the lower mind body, within the causal periphery, and their stabilizing there by an effort of the will, that the real work of the Ego or Higher Self in any particular incarnation can be accomplished. . . . Then the great leaders of the race—those who emotionally and intellectually sway mankind—can be seen working; then the inspirational writers and dreamers can bring down their inspirations and dreams; and then the synthetic and abstract thinkers can transfer their conceptions to the world of form." Here, Ego and Higher Self are synonyms for soul; see Bailey, *A Treatise on Cosmic Fire* (1925; reprint; New York: Lucis Publishing Company, 1973), p. 48. In verse 10, earth refers to physical form (see Rev. 3:10).

11. And I beheld, and I heard the voice of many angels round about the throne and the beasts and the elders: and the number of them was ten thousand times ten thousand, and thousands of thousands;

12. Saying with a loud voice, Worthy is the Lamb that was slain to receive power, and riches, and wisdom, and strength, and honour, and glory, and blessing.

13. And every creature which is in heaven, and on the earth, and under the earth, and such as are in the sea, and all that are in them, heard I saying, Blessing, and honour, and glory, and power, *be* unto him that sitteth upon the throne, and unto the Lamb for ever and ever.

14. And the four beasts said, Amen. And the four *and* twenty elders fell down and worshipped him that liveth for ever and ever.

11. The aspirant practices right discrimination and so receives many intuitions that pass from the heart of God to his personality and causal body. These intuitions are numerous, because diverse kinds of decisions are left to the soul's counsel.[19]

12. These intuitions bring release from every problem addressed, showing that the soul, even though it was once ignored, is worthy to receive faith, devotion, contemplation, obedience, honor, attention, and praise.[20]

13. In all his ways (abstract thoughts, concrete thoughts, instincts, and feelings), the aspirant responds by ascribing happiness, honor, illumination, and power to both God and the soul for all time.[21]

14. The four-fold personality affirms the truth of the lessons it has learned through meditation. The causal body becomes still and waits for guidance from the eternal source of life.

---

19. John 14:26 (NKJV) states: "But the Helper, the Holy Spirit, whom the Father will send in My name, He will teach you all things, and bring to your remembrance all things that I said to you." *ACIM*, vol. I, p. 277, encourages us to "ask the Holy Spirit everything, and leave all decisions to His gentle counsel." Here, the Holy Spirit is a synonym for the soul (see Rev. 2:7). In verse 11, "beheld" refers to right discrimination (see verse 6), and "angels" to intuitions (see verse 2).

20. *ACIM*, vol. I, p. 544, states: "The Holy Spirit offers you release from every problem that you think you have." In verse 12, the "loud voice" is taken as the bringing of such release.

21. Verse 13 is similar to Prov. 3:6: "In all thy ways acknowledge him, and he shall direct thy paths." "Glory" is a translation of the Greek word (*doxa*) that is sometimes translated as brightness (Acts 22:11, NASB); it is taken here to mean illumination. The phrase "be unto" in the KJV can be interpreted in various ways; Weymouth's translation uses "be ascribed to," which means be assigned to a supposed cause or source.

CHAPTER 6

SELF-PURIFICATION

The effects of the instructions previously given are described. These include purification of the four parts of the personality, acquisition of new wisdom, and objective self-observation.

KING JAMES VERSION

1. And I saw when the Lamb opened one of the seals, and I heard, as it were the noise of thunder, one of the four beasts saying, Come and see.

PSYCHOLOGICAL INTERPRETATION

1. The aspirant understands what to do when the soul reveals how to transform the sacral chakra.[1] He is prodded by his vital body, as though it were his will, to observe his motives.[2]

---

1. In verse 1, "saw" means understood and "the Lamb" is the soul (see Rev. 1:17, 5:6). Rev. 5:1 uses a closed seal on a book as a metaphor for a chakra that the aspirant does not know how to transform, because such a chakra imprisons his personality. Verse 1 uses an open seal as metaphor for a chakra that the aspirant does know how to transform, because he can find freedom through it.
2. "The four beasts" are the four parts of the personality (see Rev. 4:7), and "the noise of thunder" symbolizes will (see Rev. 4:5). As in Rev. 2:1, the first seal is the sacral chakra, and the first beast is the vital body.

2. And I saw, and behold a white horse: and he that sat on him had a bow; and a crown was given unto him: and he went forth conquering, and to conquer.

2. The aspirant looks at and purifies his vital body[3] with the aid of a penetrating intelligence that discerns selfishness and hypocrisy.[4] His crown chakra is active with insights showing that such motives are wrong, and so he progressively changes them.[5]

3. And when he had opened the second seal, I heard the second beast say, Come and see.

3. When the soul reveals how to transform the solar-plexus chakra, the aspirant is urged by his emotional body to observe his desires.[6]

4. And there went out another horse *that was* red: and *power* was given to him that sat thereon to take peace from the earth, and that they should kill one another: and there was given unto him a great sword.

4. There is conflict within his emotional body when the aspirant coerces or disciplines a desire, so that one desire tries to overpower another.[7] By detaching himself from his desires, he receives an insight that resolves this inner conflict.[8]

---

3. The "Four Horsemen of the Apocalypse" are widely recognized symbols from the *Revelation*. This imagery seems to have been borrowed from Zech. 6:1–7, which describes various-colored horses pulling four chariots that patrol the earth. In verses 2, 4, 5, and 8, the four horses represent the four parts of the personality, because these parts are vehicles for the aspirant's consciousness, and each rider represents the aspirant after he has understood how to transform the corresponding chakra. In verse 2, the horse symbolizes the vital body, and the white color symbolizes purity (Table 4).
4. A bow symbolizes an intelligence that can penetrate, like an arrow, beneath the surface of behavior and discern the underlying motive. Psal. 38:2 uses a related metaphor: "For thine arrows stick fast in me."
5. A crown represents the crown chakra when it has been awakened with insights (see Rev. 2:10, 3:11). The phrase "conquering, and to conquer" suggests a progressive process of purification.
6. As in Rev. 2:8, the second seal is the solar plexus chakra, and the second beast is the emotional body.
7. J. Krishnamurti, *Commentaries on Living, Third Series* (1960; reprint; Wheaton, IL: Theosophical Publishing House, 1970), p. 294, states: "Desire is energy, and it has to be understood; it cannot merely be suppressed, or made to conform. Any effort to coerce or discipline desire makes for conflict." In verse 4, the earth is the personality (see Rev. 5:3), and the horse is the emotional body. The color red indicates conflict, as in Nah. 2:3: "The shield of his mighty men is made red."
8. A sword symbolizes an intuition (see Rev. 1:16). The word "great" indicates a position of authority (see Rev. 1:10). The "great sword" in the last part of verse 4 is taken as an insight, which is a type of intuition, that resolves the conflict described in the first part of this verse.

5. And when he had opened the third seal, I heard the third beast say, Come and see. And I beheld, and lo a black horse; and he that sat on him had a pair of balances in his hand.

6. And I heard a voice in the midst of the four beasts say, A measure of wheat for a penny, and three measures of barley for a penny; and *see* thou hurt not the oil and the wine.

7. And when he had opened the fourth seal, I heard the voice of the fourth beast say, Come and see.

5. When the soul reveals how to transform the heart chakra, the aspirant regards his physical body as a temple of the soul,[9] which draws his attention to the soul. This orientation enables him to have intuitions that replace materialistic values with justice and fairness.[10]

6. The aspirant hears the soul, which is in the midst of his four-fold personality, say, "Discern the relative value of physical things while maintaining awareness of intuitions and spiritual love."[11]

7. When the soul reveals how to transform the throat chakra, the aspirant is prompted by his mind to observe his thoughts.[12]

---

9. As in Rev. 2:12, the third seal is the heart chakra, and the third beast is the physical body. Paul, in 1 Cor. 6:19, says, "your body is the temple of the Holy Ghost *which is* in you, which ye have of God." See also John 2:21.

10. Black is the color of a mourner's robes (Jer. 14:2) and symbolizes death (Psal. 143:3). The horse represents the physical body, so the black horse symbolizes the death of materialistic values. A pair of balances is a symbol of justice and fairness, as in Job 31:6 (NRSV): "let me be weighed in a just balance, and let God know my integrity!" See also Psal. 62:9 and Prov. 11:1.

11. Olive oil was the usual fuel for lamps (Lev. 24:2, Exod. 27:20), and so it represents intuitions, the source of spiritual illumination. Wine represents spiritual love for two reasons. First, "wine . . . maketh glad the heart of man" (Psal. 104:15), which spiritual love accomplishes when received in the heart chakra; see also Zech. 10:7. Second, wine is sometimes called "blood of the grape" (Gen. 49:11, Deut. 32:14), and blood symbolizes spiritual love (see Rev. 1:5).

12. As in Rev. 2:18, the fourth seal is the throat chakra, and the fourth beast is the mental body.

8. And I looked, and behold a pale horse: and his name that sat on him was Death, and Hell followed with him. And power was given unto them over the fourth part of the earth, to kill with sword, and with hunger, and with death, and with the beasts of the earth.

8. The aspirant looks at and puts away his corrupt and deluded thinking, thereby restoring his buried innocence.[13] He has power over his mind, which is the highest part of his four-fold personality, and can purify it in four ways: by having insights that dispel false beliefs, by refusing to express certain lines of thinking, by refuting false beliefs and prejudices through logical arguments, and by engaging other parts of the personality in altruistic service.[14]

9. And when he had opened the fifth seal, I saw under the altar the souls of them that were slain for the word of God, and for the testimony which they held:

9. When the soul reveals how to transform the brow chakra, the aspirant understands new principles of wisdom, which then become stored within his causal body. These new principles are the transmuted essence of the motives, feelings, and thoughts that were slain for opposing the soul's intuitions and for being based on illusion.[15]

---

13. Paul, in Eph. 4:22–23 (NRSV), captures the meaning of the first part of verse 8: "You were taught to put away your former way of life, your old self, corrupt and deluded by its lusts, and to be renewed in the spirit of your minds." The name of something represents its nature (see Rev. 2:3). The nature of the aspirant in verse 8 is death in that he puts away his corrupt and deluded thinking. The horse is pale, like a sick or dying body, and represents the former mental ways. Hell, which is the place of the dead, follows close behind and represents the renewal of the innocence that had been buried.

14. In verse 8, the four methods of killing are similar to the "four sore judgments" listed in Ezek. 14:21: "the sword, and the famine, and the noisome beast, and the pestilence." "The beasts of the earth" refer to the parts of the personality (see Rev. 4:6–7, 5:3).

15. As in Rev. 3:1, the fifth seal is the brow chakra. The altar in verse 9 refers to the "altar of burnt offering" (Exod. 38:1). The tradition was to "pour all the blood of the bullock at the bottom of the altar of the burnt offering" (Lev. 4:7). In verse 9, the altar is the causal body, which a repository for wisdom (see Rev. 4:4); the souls, which play the role of the blood of the bullock, are principles of wisdom gained by transmuting various impurities (see Rev. 3:9). Words of God are intuitions (see Rev. 1:2) and come from the soul, because the soul acts as the intermediary between God and the personality (see Rev. 5:7).

10. And they cried with a loud voice, saying, How long, O Lord, holy and
true, dost thou not judge and avenge
our blood on them that dwell on the
earth?

11. And white robes were given unto
every one of them; and it was said
unto them, that they should rest yet
for a little season, until their fellowser-
vants also and their brethren, that
should be killed as they *were*, should
be fulfilled.

10. The aspirant's abstract thoughts cry
out to the soul, saying, "How much
time will pass, O Lord, before your
spiritual love and insights[16] judge and
eliminate the principal causes of suffering, which are feelings of identification with the physical body?"[17]

11. Each impurity, after being understood, becomes valued wisdom. An
intuition tells the aspirant to wait a
while longer, until the remaining
impurities are also transmuted into
principles of wisdom.[18]

---

16. In verse 10, "a loud voice" is abstract thinking, because it comes from the causal body (see Rev. 4:10).
"Holy and true" refer to spiritual love and insights, respectively (see Rev. 3:7).

17. Verse 10 refers to an ancient law of retaliation in which "The avenger of blood is the one who shall put
the murderer to death" (Num. 35:19, NRSV). Blood is a symbol with several meanings; in addition to
symbolizing spiritual love (see Rev. 1:5, 5:9), it can also symbolize suffering, as in Hab. 2:12. In verse
10, to "avenge our blood" is interpreted as to eliminate the causes of suffering. "Them that dwell on the
earth" are feelings of identification with the physical body (see Rev. 3:10). D. Ming-Dao, *Chronicles of
Tao* (New York: Harper Collins, 1993), p. 298, considers false identification to be the cause of suffering:
"You suffer because you imagine yourself to be something other than who you actually are."

18. A question similar to the one in verse 10 and an answer similar to the one in verse 11 are given in
4 Ezra 4:35–36: "Did not the souls of the righteous in their chambers ask about these matters, saying,
'How long are we to remain here? And when will come the harvest of our reward?' And Jeremiel the
archangel answered them and said, 'When the number of those like yourselves is completed.'" This text
comes from Charlesworth, *The Old Testament Pseudepigrapha*, vol. I.

12. And I beheld when he had opened the sixth seal, and, lo, there was a great earthquake; and the sun became black as sackcloth of hair, and the moon became as blood;

12. When the soul reveals how to transform the crown chakra, the aspirant observes himself with divine discernment, which brings about a great change in his personality.[19] He is no longer dependent on external teachers and teachings.[20]

13. And the stars of heaven fell unto the earth, even as a fig tree casteth her untimely figs, when she is shaken of a mighty wind.

13. He gives up mental ideals as easily as a fig tree casts off its shriveled figs when blown by a strong wind.[21]

---

19. As in Rev. 3:7, the sixth seal is the crown chakra. An earthquake is a shaking or shifting of the earth's crust. A great earthquake is associated with divine judgment, as in Ezek. 38:19 (NIV): "In my zeal and fiery wrath I declare that at that time there shall be a great earthquake in the land of Israel." See also Isa. 29:6 and Psal. 60:2. In verse 12, a great earthquake is taken as a great change in the personality due to divine discernment.

20. The imagery in the last part of verse 12 comes from Joel 2:31: "The sun shall be turned into darkness, and the moon into blood, before the great and the terrible day of the LORD come." According to Acts 2:20, Peter quoted this passage from Joel on the day of Pentecost, believing that the events of that day fulfilled Joel's prophecy. The sun is an external source of light; it represents an external teacher or authority figure. The moon is an external source of reflected light; it represents an external teaching, such as found in books. On the day of Pentecost, the apostles heard and followed the inner voice, referred to as the Holy Ghost or Spirit, instead of relying on external teachers and teachings. J. Krishnamurti, *Krishnamurti's Journal* (San Francisco: Harper and Row, 1982), p. 28, uses similar imagery: "One has to be a light to oneself. . . . To be a light to oneself is not to follow the light of another, however reasonable, logical, historical, and however convincing."

21. Verse 13 is based on Isa. 34:4 (ICB): "The stars will fall like dead leaves from a vine or dried-up figs from a fig tree." Blavatsky, *Collected Writings*, vol. 11, p. 262, uses a star as a metaphor for an "ideal." With respect to verse 13, *A Commentary on the Book of the Revelation*, p. 149, takes the stars of heaven as "mental ideals." Krishnamurti, *Freedom from the Known*, p. 19, speaks of the need to give up ideals: "Having realised that we can depend on no outside authority in bringing about a total revolution within the structure of our own psyche, there is the immensely greater difficulty of rejecting our own inward authority, the authority of our own particular little experiences and accumulated opinions, knowledge, ideas and ideals."

14. And the heaven departed as a scroll when it is rolled together; and every mountain and island were moved out of their places.

14. He no longer uses the principles of wisdom stored within his causal body as guides for activities.[22] He perceives feelings of pride and separateness differently.[23]

15. And the kings of the earth, and the great men, and the rich men, and the chief captains, and the mighty men, and every bondman, and every free man, hid themselves in the dens and in the rocks of the mountains;

15. Various forms of pride—conceit in power, authority, wisdom, superiority, strength, associations, and independence—try to protect themselves through diverse defenses and excuses.[24]

16. And said to the mountains and rocks, Fall on us, and hide us from the face of him that sitteth on the throne, and from the wrath of the Lamb:

16. They try to hide themselves behind those defenses and excuses, so that they can escape from the light of God's presence and the correction of the soul:[25]

---

22. The first part of verse 14 is also based on Isa. 34:4: "the heavens shall be rolled together as a scroll." A scroll of papyrus was the earliest form of book. In verse 14, heaven is the causal body (see Rev. 5:3). The principles of wisdom stored within this body are like words written in a scroll, so the rolling together of a scroll signifies that those principles are no longer consulted (see Rev. 4:4).

23. Isa. 40:4 states: "Every valley shall be exalted, and every mountain and hill shall be made low." Matt. 23:12 makes a similar statement: "And whosoever shall exalt himself shall be abased; and he that shall humble himself shall be exalted." These two verses show that mountains can be used to represent feelings of pride. The word island can be used metaphorically to represent anything that is separated or isolated. For example, John Donne, the English poet, says, "No man is an island, entire of itself; every man is a piece of the continent" (*Devotions upon Emergent Occasions*, 1624, no. 17). In verse 14, islands are taken as feelings of separateness.

24. Verse 15 is based on Isa. 2:19: "And they shall go into the holes of the rocks, and into the caves of the earth, for fear of the LORD, and for the glory of his majesty, when he ariseth to shake terribly the earth." See also Isa. 2:10, 21. Modern psychologists have described a variety of defensive reactions, or mechanisms, that we use to avoid or allay threats to our self-esteem, such as repression, rationalization, insulation, projection, reaction-formation, fantasy, and withdrawal. In verse 15, the efforts of hiding symbolize these defensive reactions.

25. Verse 16 is based on Hos. 10:8: "and they shall say to the mountains, Cover us; and to the hills, Fall on us." See also Luke 23:30. Gen. 3:8 contains the phrase "the presence of the LORD God" in the KJV, but contains "the face of Jehovah God" in Young's Literal Translation (YLT). Accordingly, in verse 16, "face of him that sitteth on the throne" means presence of God.

17. For the great day of his wrath is come; and who shall be able to stand?

17. For when nearly continuous objective self-observation is present,[26] what forms of pride can remain?[27]

---

26. The "great day of his wrath" is a period of God's judgment that was predicted by the prophets: Joel 2:11, Isa. 13:6, and Zeph. 1:14. It refers to the ongoing period of observing oneself with divine discernment, which began in verse 12.

27. The question asked in verse 17 is similar to those asked in Nah. 1:6: "Who can stand before his indignation? and who can abide in the fierceness of his anger?" See also Mal. 3:2 and Joel 2:11. The context of verse 17 shows that the "who" in this verse refers to the forms of pride hiding in verses 15 and 16.

CHAPTER 7

PREPARATION FOR KUNDALINI

The aspirant realizes that he has completed the preparation neces-
sary to avoid being over-stimulated when kundalini is awakened.

KING JAMES VERSION

1. And after these things I saw four angels standing on the four corners of the earth, holding the four winds of the earth, that the wind should not blow on the earth, nor on the sea, nor on any tree.

PSYCHOLOGICAL INTERPRETATION

1. After enduring the experiences of the previous chapter, the aspirant realizes that an earlier lack of integration in his four-fold personality[1] prevented the energies of four key chakras from uniting,[2] so that kundalini could not be awakened and affect his physical or emotional body, or his nervous systems.[3]

---

1. Angel means messenger (see Rev. 1:1). *A Commentary on the Book of Revelation*, p. 151, says that the four angels in verse 1 are "Controlling intelligences in charge of four elements of body." These angels are taken to be the four parts of the personality (mental, emotional, vital, and physical bodies), because each part has become a messenger for the soul.
2. The Old Testament makes several references to the "four winds" (Jer. 49:36, Ezek. 37:9, Dan. 8:8, and Zech. 2:6) and one reference to the "four corners of the earth" (Isa. 11:12). In verse 1, the "four corners" are key force centers, or chakras, within the vital body, "four winds" are subtle energies that can flow within the vital body, and "the wind" is the blended energy, or awakened kundalini. Bailey explains: "the

2. And I saw another angel ascending from the east, having the seal of the living God: and he cried with a loud voice to the four angels, to whom it was given to hurt the earth and the sea,	2. The aspirant is aware of an intuition coming from the soul[4] that carries divine authority;[5] it gives clear instruction to his four-fold personality, which now has the capacity to awaken kundalini.

---

latent triple kundalini fire . . . is aroused and mounts through the triple spinal channel just as soon as the three major centres (the head, the heart and the throat) form an esoteric triangle, and can thus pass the fiery energy hidden in each centre in circulatory fashion" (*A Treatise on Cosmic Fire*, p. 1129); "The Kundalini Fire . . . is in reality the union of these three fires, which are focussed by an act of the enlightened will, under the impulse of love, in the basic centre" (*Esoteric Healing*, p. 185).

3. The earth is the physical body, and the sea is the emotional body (see Rev. 3:10, 4:6). The phrase "nerve tree" is sometimes used in articles on human anatomy to denote a nervous system, because the latter has the appearance of a tree. J. Bell-Ranske, *The Revelation of Man* (New York: William S. Rhode Company, 1924), p. 190, interprets the two trees in Rev. 11:4 as the "the ganglionic nerve-system." Similarly, "any tree" in verse 1 is taken as any nervous system.

4. The Bible sometimes uses the sun as a symbol for the soul; for example, see Mal. 4:2. The east is the direction from which light rises from the sun, and so it symbolizes the direction from which light comes from the soul. For example, Ezek. 43:2 states, "And, behold, the glory of the God of Israel came from the way of the east." Bailey, *Esoteric Psychology*, vol. I, p. 84, also uses this directional symbol, referring to the soul as "the Master in the east." Accordingly, the angel from the east in verse 2 is an intuition from the soul, which is also how the angel in Rev. 5:2 is interpreted.

5. In ancient times, a seal enabled a document to be regarded as authentic; e.g., 1 Kings 21:8. The title "living God" appears often in the Old Testament; e.g., Josh. 3:10. Mounce, *The Book of Revelation*, p. 157, says, "The title is appropriate wherever God is about to intervene on behalf of his people." The "seal of the living God" in verse 2 is taken as signifying divine authority.

3. Saying, Hurt not the earth, neither the sea, nor the trees, till we have sealed the servants of our God in their foreheads.

3. This intuition says, "Do not hurt the physical body, emotional body, and nervous systems.[6] Before kundalini can be awakened safely, other intuitions must protect the cells throughout the physical body[7] by raising their consciousness."[8]

---

6. Many writers warn that awakening kundalini without adequate preparation could damage the physical body, emotional body, and nervous systems. For example, Swami Rama, "The Awakening of Kundalini" in White (ed.), *Kundalini*, p. 35, advises: "To genuinely awaken kundalini, one must first prepare oneself. Without long and patient practice in purifying oneself and strengthening one's capacity to tolerate and assimilate such a flood of energy, the awakening of this latent power would deeply disturb, disorient, and confuse the student. Even at the physical level such a charge of energy can threaten the integrity of the body."

7. Ezek. 9:4 provides the background for sealing in the forehead: "And the LORD said unto him, Go through the midst of the city, through the midst of Jerusalem, and set a mark upon the foreheads of the men that sigh and that cry for all the abominations that be done in the midst thereof." In this passage, the mark on the forehead serves as protection. *A Commentary on the Book of Revelation*, p. 151, considers the servants of God in verse 3 to be "certain principal cells throughout the body," which is the interpretation used here.

8. Forehead represents mind or consciousness. As an example of a similar usage, the RSV gives the literal translation "hard forehead" in Ezek. 3:7 where the NASB uses "stubborn." See also Jer. 3:3. Yogi Ramacharaka, *The Science of Psychic Healing* (1909; reprint; Chicago: Yogi Publication Society, 1937), pp. 26–27, says that "cell-lifes . . . are really minds of a certain degree of development." Bailey, *Discipleship in the New Age*, vol. I, pp. 263–264, advises: "the cells of the physical body need more rapid sensitising and this through the bringing in of energy and not through diets or other physical plane means." Accordingly, sealing the servants in their foreheads is taken as raising the consciousness of cells through the bringing in of intuitions from the soul.

4. And I heard the number of them which were sealed: *and there were* sealed an hundred *and* forty *and* four thousand of all the tribes of the children of Israel.

4. Eventually, the aspirant receives an intuition saying that the cellular consciousness has been raised[9] within the twelve major parts[10] of his physical body.[11]

5. Of the tribe of Juda *were* sealed twelve thousand. Of the tribe of Reuben *were* sealed twelve thousand. Of the tribe of Gad *were* sealed twelve thousand.

5. The head has three major parts: the brain, the eyes, and the pineal, pituitary, and carotid glands. The cellular consciousness within these parts has been raised.[12]

---

9. Cayce answered "correct" to the question, "Are we correct in interpreting the 144,000 who were sealed as being spiritualized cellular structure of the 12 major divisions of the body?" (Van Auken, *Edgar Cayce on the Revelation*, p. 170). C. Fillmore, *Jesus Christ Heals* (Unity Village, MO: Unity School of Christianity, 1996), p. 152, makes a similar interpretation: "The number sealed is twelve thousand out of the twelve tribes. This is all symbolical and should not be taken literally. Man has twelve faculties, represented by the twelve tribes of Israel. When the consciousness in the forehead is illumined by Spirit, all twelve centers in the body automatically respond."

10. The number 12 represents the divine pattern or organization. For example, the year was divided into 12 months (1 Kings 4:7), the day into 12 hours (John 11:9), the people of Israel into 12 tribes (Gen. 49:28), and 12 apostles were chosen by Jesus (Matt. 10:1). The *New Bible Dictionary*, p. 834, concludes, "Twelve is therefore linked with the elective purposes of God." The number 10 signifies completeness (see Rev. 2:10), and so the number 1000 (which is 10 cubed) represents completeness with respect to multiple criteria. The number 12,000, which is 12 times 1000, represents the fulfillment of the divine pattern. The number 144,000, which is 12 times 12,000, represents the fulfillment of the divine pattern within each of the 12 major parts of the physical body.

11. Table 5 associates the twelve tribes with parts of the physical body. *A Commentary on the Book of Revelation*, p. 38, makes similar associations but without matching well with the meanings of the Hebrew names listed in Table 5. C. Fillmore, *The Twelve Powers of Man* (Unity Village, MO: Unity School of Christianity, 1995), p. 16, describes twelve centers in the physical body and associates them with the twelve apostles of Jesus but not with the twelve tribes. The twelve physical parts given in Table 5 come from Bailey, *A Treatise on White Magic*, p. 43, who says: "There are other organs, but those enumerated are those which have an esoteric significance of greater value than the other parts." Although Bailey did not associate her twelve parts with the twelve tribes, Table 5 shows that they can be associated in such a way that they match reasonably well with the meanings of the Hebrew names or related biblical passages.

12. Regarding verses 5 through 8, Charles, *The Revelation of St. John*, vol. I, p. 207, says that "the tribes are enumerated in a wholly unintelligible order." Table 5, however, shows that the tribes have an intelligible order, because the associated organs in each verse form a natural grouping. For example, the organs associated with the three tribes mentioned in verse 5 are parts of the head. In articles on human anatomy, the carotid gland is often called the "carotid body."

6. Of the tribe of Aser *were* sealed twelve thousand. Of the tribe of Nepthalim *were* sealed twelve thousand. Of the tribe of Manasses *were* sealed twelve thousand.

7. Of the tribe of Simeon *were* sealed twelve thousand. Of the tribe of Levi *were* sealed twelve thousand. Of the tribe of Issachar *were* sealed twelve thousand.

8. Of the tribe of Zabulon *were* sealed twelve thousand. Of the tribe of Joseph *were* sealed twelve thousand. Of the tribe of Benjamin *were* sealed twelve thousand.

9. After this I beheld, and, lo, a great multitude, which no man could number, of all nations, and kindreds, and people, and tongues, stood before the throne, and before the Lamb, clothed with white robes, and palms in their hands;

6. The upper body has three major parts: the heart, lungs, and throat. The cellular consciousness within these parts has been raised.

7. The lower body has three major parts: the sex organs, stomach, and spleen. The cellular consciousness within these parts has been raised.

8. The body as a whole has three major parts: the skin and bony structure, the three-fold nervous system (central, sympathetic, and parasympathetic), and the circulatory system. The cellular consciousness within these parts has also been raised.

9. After receiving this intuition, the aspirant carefully observes his experiences and has the following insights. A vast number of physical cells, belonging to all tissues, organs, regions, and systems, have been brought into alignment with the heart of God and with the soul. They have been purified of negative influences and are thriving[13]

---

13. Cayce answered "This is correct" to the question, "Is the multitude before the throne as described in Ch. 7 the rest of the cellular structure in process of spiritualization?" (Van Auken, *Edgar Cayce on the Revelation*, p. 170). The throne, Lamb, and white denote the heart of God, soul, and purity, respectively (see Rev. 1:4, 5:6, 2:17). A standing position indicates spiritual alignment, as in Rom. 11:20, "thou standest by faith." Clothing symbolizes the nature of the wearer, as shown in Zech. 3:4: "Behold, I have caused thine iniquity to pass from thee, and I will clothe thee with change of raiment." A palm represents prosperity, as in Psal. 92:12, "The righteous shall flourish like the palm tree."

10. And cried with a loud voice, saying, Salvation to our God which sitteth upon the throne, and unto the Lamb.

11. And all the angels stood round about the throne, and *about* the elders and the four beasts, and fell before the throne on their faces, and worshipped God,

12. Saying, Amen: Blessing, and glory, and wisdom, and thanksgiving, and honour, and power, and might, *be* unto our God for ever and ever. Amen.

13. And one of the elders answered, saying unto me, What are these which are arrayed in white robes? and whence came they?

10. because their consciousness has been transformed by intuitions that emanate from the heart of God and pass through the soul.[14]

11. All of these intuitions connect the heart of God to the causal body and the four-fold personality.[15] They emphasize the unity of life and the importance of God,

12. revealing this self-validated truth: "Happiness, illumination, wisdom, gratitude, honor, virtue, and strength have God as their ultimate source at all times."[16]

13. Next, with his abstract reasoning, the aspirant responds to these insights by asking himself: "What is the nature of the physical cells that have been purified? And from what source are they being influenced?"[17]

---

14. Psal. 36:9 uses light as a metaphor for the intuition: "in thy light shall we see light." Bailey, *Glamour*, pp. 5–6, uses this metaphor to describe the transformation of the bodily cells: "The nucleus of every cell in the body is a point of light, and when the light of the intuition is sensed, it is this cell-light which will immediately respond. The continuance of the inflow of the light of the intuition will draw forth, esoterically speaking, into the light of day every cell which is so constituted that it will respond."

15. In verse 11, the elders and beasts are the causal body and four-fold personality, respectively (see Rev. 4:4, 4:7).

16. The double use of Amen indicates a self-validated truth (see Rev. 3:14). "Power" is the translation of the Greek word (*dunamis*) that is sometimes rendered as "virtue" (Mark 5:30).

17. Verse 13 may be based on Josh. 9:8, "And Joshua said unto them, Who *are* ye? and from whence come ye?" Speech of an elder represents the abstract thoughts of the causal body (see Rev. 5:5). In verses 9 through 12, the aspirant has insights. In verses 13 through 17, he contemplates those insights with his abstract reasoning, thereby converting them into new understanding. A. A. Bailey, *Initiation, Human and Solar* (1922; reprint; New York: Lucis Publishing Company, 1974), p. 12, says, "*The understanding* may be defined as the faculty of the Thinker in Time to appropriate knowledge as the foundation for wisdom, that which enables him to adapt the things of form to the life of spirit, and to take the flashes of inspiration that come to him . . . and link them to the facts."

14. And I said unto him, Sir, thou knowest. And he said to me, These are they which came out of great tribulation, and have washed their robes, and made them white in the blood of the Lamb.

15. Therefore are they before the throne of God, and serve him day and night in his temple: and he that sitteth on the throne shall dwell among them.

16. They shall hunger no more, neither thirst any more; neither shall the sun light on them, nor any heat.

14. The aspirant has confidence in his abstract reasoning, which comes to the following conclusions. "These physical cells were once affected by discordant thoughts and feelings, but have been purified by the spiritual love of the soul.[18]

15. Therefore, these cells are connected to the heart of God and form a channel for God, because the life and love of God will manifest through them.[19]

16. These cells will no longer be impure or unfulfilled;[20] the soul will not hurt them,[21] nor will any heat from kundalini.[22]

---

18. The notion that blood can cleanse or purify can be found in Lev. 14:52, Heb. 9:14, and 1 John 1:7. The blood of the Lamb is the spiritual love of the soul (see Rev. 1:5, 5:9).

19. Verse 15 is based on the Old Testament promises that God will dwell in the midst of his people (Ezek. 37:27, Zech. 2:10). Bailey, *A Treatise on White Magic*, p. 321, says that the "love of God" is a "stream of living energy" that emanates from the "Heart of the Sun." Bailey, *The Light of the Soul*, p. 417, also describes how "the physical, emotional and mental bodies form simply a channel for the divine light, and constitute the vehicle through which the life and love of God may manifest."

20. Verses 16 are 17 are based on Isa. 49:10, "They shall not hunger nor thirst; neither shall the heat nor sun smite them: for he that hath mercy on them shall lead them, even by the springs of water shall he guide them." In verse 16, hunger and thirst are taken as the lack of purity and fulfillment, as in Matt. 5:6: "Blessed *are* they which do hunger and thirst after righteousness: for they shall be filled."

21. The sun is taken as a metaphor for the soul, as in Mal. 4:2: "But unto you that fear my name shall the Sun of righteousness arise with healing in his wings; and ye shall go forth, and grow up as calves of the stall." Interpreting the sun as the soul is consistent with how verse 2 is interpreted. Moreover, Bailey, *Discipleship in the New Age*, vol. I, p. 462, speaks of "the soul, the inner sun."

22. Bailey, *A Treatise on Cosmic Fire*, p. 124, associates kundalini with heat: "The fire of kundalini produces the heat of the centre, and its intense radiance and brilliance." Here, centre is a synonym for chakra (Bailey, *A Treatise on White Magic*, p. 362). Accordingly, in verse 16, heat is taken as an effect of awakened kundalini.

17. For the Lamb which is in the midst of the throne shall feed them, and shall lead them unto living fountains of waters: and God shall wipe away all tears from their eyes.

17. For the soul is an intermediary within the living stream that extends from the heart of God to these physical cells. While the soul is conveying spiritual love to them, God is wiping away all discord from their consciousness."[23]

---

23. Bailey, *Telepathy*, pp. 9, 20, distinguishes between emotions associated with the solar plexus chakra, such as "fear, hate, disgust, love, desire and many other purely astral reactions," and emotions associated with the heart chakra, such as "high and consecrated feeling, devotion, aspiration and love." Two kinds of water appear in chapter 7: "the sea" in verse 1, which has a relatively low altitude; and "fountains of water" in verse 17, which have a higher altitude. The lower waters represent the lower, or solar plexus, emotions, as in Psal. 69:2: "I sink in deep mire, where *there is* no standing: I am come into deep waters, where the floods overflow me." The higher waters represent the higher, or heart, emotions, as in Psal. 36:8–9: "thou shalt make them drink of the river of thy pleasures. For with thee *is* the fountain of life."

CHAPTER 8

AWAKENING KUNDALINI

The aspirant invokes the spiritual will and awakens kundalini,
which rises up his spinal column and acts on each of his chakras
sequentially.

KING JAMES VERSION

1. And when he had opened the seventh seal, there was silence in heaven about the space of half an hour.

PSYCHOLOGICAL INTERPRETATION

1. When the soul reveals how to transform the basic chakra,[1] the aspirant achieves mental silence[2] and invokes the spiritual will.[3]

---

1. As in Rev. 3:14, the seventh seal, or chakra, is the basic.
2. Bailey, *The Rays and the Initiations*, p. 517, considers the step of achieving "mental silence" to be equivalent to achieving "the necessary focal point of silence" and becoming "simply a point of intelligent concentration."
3. The spiritual will is the will of God in us. Sri Aurobindo, *The Life Divine* (1949; Pondicherry, India: Sri Aurobindo Ashram, 1990), p. 414, says, "The will of God in us [is] to transcend evil and suffering, to transform imperfection into perfection, to rise into a higher law of Divine Nature." Regarding the spiritual will, Bailey, *Esoteric Astrology*, p. 584, says, "This Will *must* be invoked and evoked." Invocation is the act of petitioning for help or support from a greater entity; evocation is the subsequent response of help. In verse 1, "half an hour" is taken as a reference to invoking the spiritual will, which is the first half of the entire process of invocation and evocation. The evocative half of the process is the subsequent response of the soul; it is covered in verses 3 through 5.

2. And I saw the seven angels which stood before God; and to them were given seven trumpets.

2. The aspirant realizes that the energies of his seven chakras, which are aligned with the heart of God due to the previous preparation, can be stimulated by kundalini as it rises up his spinal column.[4]

3. And another angel came and stood at the altar, having a golden censer; and there was given unto him much incense, that he should offer *it* with the prayers of all saints upon the golden altar which was before the throne.

3. The soul responds to the aspirant's invocation and becomes ready to work with both the aspirant's causal body[5] and his crown chakra.[6] The soul receives the spiritual will from the heart of God and offers it to the abstract thoughts in the causal body.[7]

---

4. Verse 2 is similar to Josh. 6:4: "And seven priests shall bear before the ark seven trumpets of rams' horns." In verse 2, the seven angels are the energies within the seven chakras (see Rev. 1:20), their standing position symbolizes alignment (see Rev. 7:9), and their possession of seven trumpets depicts the readiness of the chakras to be stimulated by kundalini.

5. The altar in verse 3 refers to the "altar of incense," sometimes called the "golden altar" (Exod. 40:5, RSV), which is the term used in this verse. Exod. 30:6 (ICB) states: "Put the altar of incense in front of the curtain. This curtain is in front of the Box of the Agreement. Put the altar in front of the lid that covers that Holy Box. There I will meet with you." Thus, the altar of incense is a place where a human being can meet with God. Bailey speaks of "the causal body, the karana sarira, the spiritual body of the soul, standing as the intermediary between Spirit and matter" (*A Treatise on White Magic*, p. 247), and considers soul and Solar Angel to be synonymous terms (*A Treatise on Cosmic Fire*, p. 48). Accordingly, the altar in verse 3 is taken as the causal body, and the angel, who is standing at this altar, is taken as the soul.

6. Bailey mentions "the soul working through the first or highest head centre" (*Esoteric Astrology*, p. 301) and says that "the head centre becomes the point of contact for the spiritual will" (*Esoteric Healing*, p. 159). A censer is a vessel for burning incense (2 Chron. 26:19). The golden censer in verse 3 is taken as the highest head center, which is the crown chakra, because the soul can work with it and because it can be a vessel for the spiritual will.

7. The incense of verse 3 is interpreted as the spiritual will, because of the effect described in verse 4. In addition, the throne and prayers of the saints are the heart of God and abstract thoughts (see Rev. 1:4, 5:8).

4. And the smoke of the incense, *which came* with the prayers of the saints, ascended up before God out of the angel's hand.

5. And the angel took the censer, and filled it with fire of the altar, and cast *it* into the earth: and there were voices, and thunderings, and lightnings, and an earthquake.

6. And the seven angels which had the seven trumpets prepared themselves to sound.

4. By sharing a common purpose, the abstract thoughts become unified with God through the mediation of the soul.[8]

5. The soul fills the crown chakra with the spiritual will from the causal body, and casts this will down the spinal column into the basic chakra.[9] Here, the vital energies of the throat, crown, and heart chakras unite,[10] which awakens kundalini.[11]

6. Kundalini rises up the spinal column and acts sequentially on each of the seven chakras.[12]

---

8. *ACIM*, vol. I, p. 498, speaks of the unifying power of a common purpose: "Only a purpose unifies, and those who share a purpose have a mind as one."

9. Bailey describes "the awakening of the seventh centre, the centre at the base of the spine, by the soul working through the first or highest head centre and producing (as a consequence) the surging upwards of the kundalini fire" (*Esoteric Astrology*, p. 301), mentions "the descent of the fire of will to the base of the spine" (*Esoteric Psychology*, vol. II, p. 388), and refers to "the physical material form with its centre at the base of the spine" (*A Treatise on White Magic*, p. 106). Accordingly, in verse 5, the angel, censer, fire, and earth are taken as the soul, crown chakra, spiritual will, and basic chakra, respectively.

10. In Rev. 4:5, "lightnings and thunderings and voices" represent divine love, divine will, and divine intelligence, respectively. Similarly, in verse 5, "voices, and thunderings, and lightnings" are taken as the vital energies of the throat, crown, and heart chakras, respectively, as they are the centers through which intelligence, will, and love are expressed.

11. H. Hotema, *Awaken the World Within* (Pomeroy, WA: Health Research, 1962), uses "Serpentine Fire" as a synonym for kundalini (p. 299) and interprets the earthquake in verse 5 as the arousal of kundalini: "Then with a shock (earthquake) the Serpentine Fire starts flowing" (p. 132). The arousal of kundalini occurs by uniting the energies of the throat, crown, and heart chakras within the basic chakra (see the footnotes for Rev. 7:1). The aspirant in Rev. 7:2 had the capacity of uniting these energies, but waits until verse 5 of this chapter before doing so.

12. Swami Vivekananda, *The Yogas and Other Works* (second edition, New York: Ramakrishna-Vivekananda Center, 1953), p. 602, describes the effect of kundalini on the chakras: "If this coiled-up energy is roused and made active and then consciously made to travel up the Sushumna canal, as it acts upon centre and centre, a tremendous reaction will set in." Here, Sushumna is the Sanskrit word for spinal column.

7. The first angel sounded, and there followed hail and fire mingled with blood, and they were cast upon the earth: and the third part of trees was burnt up, and all green grass was burnt up.

7. When kundalini reaches the sacral chakra,[13] the aspirant acquires a heightened sensitivity to motives, spiritual ideals, and their influence on behavior.[14] This sensitivity derives from the stimulation of the parasympathetic nervous system, which is one part of the three-fold nervous system,[15] and the stimulation of the nadis[16] throughout the vital body.[17]

---

13. The sounding angels, or chakras, are enumerated according to Table 2, so that the first angel to sound is the sacral chakra, which is the first chakra above the basic chakra.

14. Verse 7 is similar to Exod. 9:23: "the LORD sent thunder and hail, and the fire ran along upon the ground." C. W. Leadbeater, *The Chakras* (1927; reprint; Wheaton, IL: Theosophical Publishing House, 1977), p. 83, states that the "unfoldment of higher aspects of kundalini . . . intensifies everything in the man's nature." A person's nature includes motives, ideals, and behavior. A motive is the result of transforming an emotion into vital energy. In verse 7, "hail" symbolizes motives, because it is the result of transforming liquid water, representing emotions (see Rev. 1:15), into a solid. "Fire mingled with blood" symbolizes mental ideals based upon spiritual love, because fire and blood represent intellect and spiritual love (see Rev. 1:15, 1:5). "Earth" represents the physical body (see Rev. 3:10).

15. Trees symbolize the human nervous systems (see Rev. 7:1, 3), which are organized into three main parts: central, sympathetic, and parasympathetic. The parasympathetic nerves originate in the cranial (base of the brain) and sacral (near the bottom) regions of the spinal column. The sacral parasympathetic nerves affect the urinary and genital organs, which is the area of the physical body that Motoyama, *Theories of the Chakras*, p. 24, says is controlled by the sacral chakra.

16. Bailey, *Esoteric Healing*, pp. 197–198, says, "When the centres are awakened throughout the body, there will then be present a highly electric nervous system, responsive with immediacy to the energy carried by the nadis." This quotation describes an effect of kundalini, because *Esoteric Healing*, p. 185, also says, "The kundalini fire will be raised . . . *when* all the centres are awakened." Here, the Sanskrit word *nadis* denotes an extensive and intricate network of energy channels in the vital body. A single nadi is a thin channel of force, so its form is similar to that of a blade of grass. Several Hindu *Upanishads* claim that there are 72,000 nadis in the vital body (see Motoyama, *Theories of the Chakras*, p. 135). Similarly, a lawn has many blades of grass. Accordingly, "grass" in verse 7 is taken as the nadis.

17. The Old Testament uses the color green to represent vitality and growth, as in Job 8:16, "He *is* green before the sun, and his branch shooteth forth in his garden." See also Psal. 37:35, Isa. 15:6, and Jer. 17:8. In verse 7, "green" refers to the vital body.

8. And the second angel sounded, and as it were a great mountain burning with fire was cast into the sea: and the third part of the sea became blood;

8. When kundalini reaches the solar-plexus chakra, the mind becomes a powerful force that dominates the emotional body.[18] The spiritual will, acting through the mind, transforms many emotions into spiritual love,[19]

9. And the third part of the creatures which were in the sea, and had life, died; and the third part of the ships were destroyed.

9. and eliminates many images, fantasies, prejudices, and motives.[20]

10. And the third angel sounded, and there fell a great star from heaven, burning as it were a lamp, and it fell upon the third part of the rivers, and upon the fountains of waters;

10. When kundalini reaches the heart chakra, it brings an intuitive recognition of reality that resolves all differentiated parts into a unity and produces illumination. The spiritual will, acting through the illumined mind, strengthens higher emotions such as devotion and aspiration.[21]

---

18. Leadbeater, *The Chakras*, p. 83, says, "kundalini . . . would be likely to bring with it a great intensification of the power of intellect." In verse 8, "great" indicates authority (see Rev. 1:10), and "fire" symbolizes the intellect (see verse 7), so "a great mountain burning with fire" symbolizes a dominating mind. In addition, "sea" and "blood" denote emotions and spiritual love, respectively (see Rev. 4:6, 1:5).

19. On "the third day," God was to come down to Mount Sinai (Exod. 19:11), would raise up his people (Hos. 6:2), delivered Jonah (Jonah 1:17), and raised Jesus from the dead (1 Cor. 15:4). The *New Bible Dictionary*, p. 831, concludes: "The number 3 is also associated with certain of God's mighty acts." Ezek. 5:2 states: "Thou shalt burn with fire a third part in the midst of the city, when the days of the siege are fulfilled: and thou shalt take a third part, *and* smite about it with a knife: and a third part thou shalt scatter in the wind." In this passage, "third part" is associated with an act performed by a spiritual man who is cooperating with the plan and purpose of God. See Neh. 10:32 for a similar example. The spiritual will is the will of God in a human being. Accordingly, in verse 8, "third part" is interpreted as indicating a direct act of the spiritual will and an indirect act of God.

20. In verse 9, "the creatures which were in the sea" include images, fantasies, and prejudices, because they are part of emotional experiences. Ships are physical vessels that move on the sea; they represent motives, which are vital impulses based on emotions.

21. Bailey, *Esoteric Psychology*, vol. II, p. 417, speaks of "the intuitive recognition of reality, which resolves the differentiated parts into a unit, producing illumination." In verse 10, the falling "star" is taken as this intuitive recognition. In addition, "lamp" symbolizes mental illumination (see Rev. 4:5), and "rivers" and "fountains of waters" represent the higher emotions associated with the heart chakra (see Rev. 7:17). Devotion and aspiration are examples of both higher emotions and consecrated feelings (see Rev. 5:8).

11. And the name of the star is called Wormwood: and the third part of the waters became wormwood; and many men died of the waters, because they were made bitter.

11. This new illumination, like wormwood, makes separative feelings, which are incompatible with the spiritual will, exceedingly bitter. Many prideful self-images disappear, because they become too distasteful.[22]

12. And the fourth angel sounded, and the third part of the sun was smitten, and the third part of the moon, and the third part of the stars; so as the third part of them was darkened, and the day shone not for a third part of it, and the night likewise.

12. When kundalini reaches the throat chakra, the spiritual will throws the mind back upon itself,[23] spurning external teachers, external teachings, and ideals. The aspirant no longer consults those guides on how to be illumined or overcome ignorance.[24]

13. And I beheld, and heard an angel flying through the midst of heaven, saying with a loud voice, Woe, woe, woe, to the inhabiters of the earth by reason of the other voices of the trumpet of the three angels, which are yet to sound!

13. Instead, the aspirant looks for guidance from within and receives a clear intuitive message: "There are still physical attachments that must be purified through the response of the three remaining chakras, which are not yet fully active."[25]

---

22. Wormwood (Artemisia absinthium) is a shrublike plant found in many parts of the world. Its leaves are noted for their intense bitterness, as in the phrase "bitter as wormwood" from Prov. 5:4. In verse 11, the name of something represents its nature (see Rev. 2:3), and men symbolize self-images (see Rev. 3:7).

23. Isa. 45:3 uses the metaphor of darkness in a way similar to verse 12: "I will give thee the treasures of darkness." Bailey, *The Rays and the Initiations*, p. 198, explains: "The disciple is thrown back upon himself. All he can see is his problem, his tiny field of experience, and his—to him—feeble and limited equipment. It is to this stage that the prophet Isaiah refers when he speaks of giving to the struggling aspirant 'the treasures of darkness.' The beauty of the immediate, the glory of the present opportunity and the need to focus upon the task and service of the moment are the rewards of moving forward into the apparently impenetrable darkness."

24. The sun, moon, and stars are external teachers, external teachings, and ideals, respectively (see Rev. 6:12–13). Day and night denote illumination and ignorance, respectively, as in Rom. 13:12–13: "The night is far spent, the day is at hand: let us therefore cast off the works of darkness, and let us put on the armour of light. Let us walk honestly, as in the day; not in rioting and drunkenness, not in chambering and wantonness, not in strife and envying."

25. In verse 13, "beheld" refers to looking for inner guidance (see Rev. 5:6), and the flying angel is an intuition (see Rev. 5:2). "The inhabiters of the earth" are feelings of identification with the physical body (see Rev. 3:10).

Chapter 9

Guilt and Fear

Long-repressed feelings of guilt rise to the level of consciousness and lead to new insights. The aspirant progressively eliminates self-images based on fear.

King James Version	Psychological Interpretation
1. And the fifth angel sounded, and I saw a star fall from heaven unto the earth: and to him was given the key of the bottomless pit.	1. When kundalini reaches his brow chakra,[1] the aspirant observes his personality from the vantage point of his causal body.[2] This detached observation is the key to opening the subconscious nature,[3] because any resistance to the emergence of a subconscious feeling can be observed and removed, allowing the feeling to move up to the level of consciousness.[4]

1. Nikhilananda, *The Gospel of Sri Ramakrisna*, p. 581, describes kundalini's effect on the brow chakra: "During this upward journey of the Kundalini, the jiva is not quite released from the relative state till it reaches the sixth centre or plane, which is the 'opening' for the experience of Reality. At this sixth centre (the two-petalled white lotus located at the junction of the eyebrows) the jiva sheds its ego and burns the seed of duality, and its higher self rises from the ashes of its lower self." The Sanskrit word *jiva* literally means "living being."
2. If heaven and earth symbolize the causal body and personality (see Rev. 5:3), and if the falling star is

2. And he opened the bottomless pit; and there arose a smoke out of the pit, as the smoke of a great furnace; and the sun and the air were darkened by reason of the smoke of the pit.

3. And there came out of the smoke locusts upon the earth: and unto them was given power, as the scorpions of the earth have power.

2. After detached observation has opened the subconscious nature, confusion arises out that nature, like the smoke of a great furnace; and the soul and its intuitions are blocked by the emerging confusion.[5]

3. Long-repressed guilt feelings come out of the confusion into the personality. These feelings, like locusts, can devour inner peace and contentment.[6] They have the power, like that of scorpions, to poison or corrupt thoughts and feelings.[7]

interpreted as the light of self-observation, verse 1 indicates that the aspirant's center of consciousness has shifted from the personality to the causal body. Bailey, *Letters on Occult Meditation*, p. 96, speaks of this shift: "The student having withdrawn his consciousness on to the mental plane at some point within the brain, . . . let him then raise his vibration as high as may be, and aim next at lifting it clear of the mental body into the causal." Bailey refers to polarization within the causal body as "causal consciousness" or as "the full consciousness of the higher Self" (pp. 28, 292, 340).

3. The bottomless pit, or the abyss, is mentioned in Luke 8:31, Rom. 10:7, and 1 Enoch 88:1. *A Commentary on the Book of the Revelation*, p. 155, interprets the bottomless pit in verse 1 as the "subconscious mind" or "area of repression." Bailey, *Esoteric Psychology*, vol. II, p. 440, uses a similar image to depict the subconscious nature: "The subconscious nature is like a deep pool from which a man can draw almost anything from his past experience, if he so desires, and which can be stirred up until it becomes a boiling cauldron, causing much distress."

4. Motoyama, *Theories of the Chakras*, p. 216, describes how kundalini affects the subconscious: "When the kundalini awakens as the result of yoga practice or other spiritual disciplines, there is an explosive gushing forth from the realm of the unconscious. It is like an earthquake, in which things hidden underground are pushed to the surface."

5. *A Commentary on the Book of the Revelation*, p. 155, interprets smoke as "obscurity" or "confusion." Sun represents the soul (see Rev. 7:16). Bailey, *A Treatise on Cosmic Fire*, pp. 82, 269, uses air as a symbol of intuitions.

6. Verse 3 is based on Exod. 10:1–20, which describes a plague of locusts that devours all vegetation within Egypt. Locusts are large migratory grasshoppers that cause great damage to crops wherever they swarm, and they are used as symbols of destruction throughout the Old Testament; e.g., Deut. 28:42, 1 Kings 8:37, and Psal. 78:46. *A Commentary on the Book of the Revelation*, p. 155, interprets the locusts as "repressed negative emotions," including "old regrets and guilt feelings."

7. Scorpions are common in the wilderness through which the people of Israel journeyed (Deut. 8:15). This animal is about 4 to 6 inches long, with two claws and eight legs; its slender tail is usually curved

4. And it was commanded them that they should not hurt the grass of the earth, neither any green thing, neither any tree; but only those men which have not the seal of God in their foreheads.

5. And to them it was given that they should not kill them, but that they should be tormented five months: and their torment *was* as the torment of a scorpion, when he striketh a man.

4. Detached observation keeps the emergent guilt feelings from operating through the nadis and chakras of the vital body, or through any nervous system of the physical body, so that these feelings cannot affect outer behavior.[8] Instead, these feelings can hurt only self-images based on illusion.[9]

5. Emergent guilt feelings do not destroy the self-images with which they conflict. Instead, the feelings cause torment for as long as the mind defends those images.[10] This emotional torment is similar to the physical swelling that occurs from a scorpion's sting, because the mind responds to the guilt feelings with a flurry of excuses and justifications.

---

upward and forward over its back and holds a venomous stinger. The sting of most scorpion species produces pain and swelling in human beings. The Old Testament figuratively uses scorpions to represent enemies (Ezek. 2:6) and cruelty (1 Kings 12:11, 14).

8. In verse 4, the "grass of the earth" are the nadis (see Rev. 8:7). Green refers to the vital body (see Rev. 8:7), and so "any green thing" is any part of the vital body, such as a chakra. "Any tree" is any nervous system (see Rev. 7:1; 8:7). Both verse 4 and Rev. 3:7 contain the notion that detached observation prevents an observed feeling from being actualized through outer behavior.

9. In verse 4, men and forehead represent self-images and consciousness (see Rev. 3:7, 7:3). Thus, "those men who have not the seal of God in their foreheads" represent self-images based on pride, vanity, or some other form of illusion.

10. Verse 5 states that the torment will last five months. W. Smith, *A Dictionary of the Bible* (Hartford, CT: J. B. Burr and Hyde, 1873), p. 465, says, "*Five* appears in the table of punishments, of legal requirements." For example, Exod. 22:1 states, "he shall restore five oxen for an ox." See also Lev. 5:16, 22:14, 27:15. In verse 5, this number represents the length of time that the aspirant is tormented by his own folly. The Wisdom of Solomon (12:23, RSV) speaks of this torment: "Therefore those who in folly of life lived unrighteously thou didst torment through their own abominations."

6. And in those days shall men seek death, and shall not find it; and shall desire to die, and death shall flee from them.

6. The aspirant is aware of his desire to repress his guilty memories, but his self-observation prevents him from doing so. Although he has a desire to repress, he has a stronger desire to continue his observation and gain the following insights.[11]

7. And the shapes of the locusts *were* like unto horses prepared unto battle; and on their heads *were* as it were crowns like gold, and their faces *were* as the faces of men.

7. A guilt feeling is always ready for battle, either to defend itself or to affix blame.[12] Projecting guilt onto other people in the form of blame or judgment makes the aspirant feel superior, like a king wearing a crown.[13] Guilt is projected resentment, because, within every guilt feeling, is a picture of someone whom the aspirant has harmed and whom he believes still resents him.[14]

---

11. *ACIM*, vol. II, p. 309, says, "Death is a thought that takes on (. . .) all forms in which the wish to be as you are not may come to tempt you." Repression denotes the forgetting process by which unacceptable ideas are prevented from entering the conscious mind. Death in verse 6 is interpreted as repression, because the latter is a wish to be as one is not.

12. Job 39:19–24 describes a horse prepared for battle: "Hast thou given the horse strength? hast thou clothed his neck with thunder? . . . He paweth in the valley, and rejoiceth in *his* strength: he goeth on to meet the armed men. . . . He swalloweth the ground with fierceness and rage." A guilt feeling is like a horse prepared for battle, because it is always ready to attack. *ACIM*, vol. I, p. 260, makes a similar point: "The guilty always condemn."

13. In Jungian psychology, the term "shadow" denotes the sum of those personal characteristics that we wish to hide from ourselves. C. J. Jung, *Analytic Psychology: Its Theory and Practice* (New York: Random House, 1970), p. 179, explains: "When [the patient] projects negative qualities and therefore hates and loathes the object, he has to discover that he is projecting his own inferior side, his shadow, as it were, because he prefers to have an optimistic and one-sided image of himself." A crown of gold is a symbol of royalty (2 Sam. 12:30). In verse 7, the crown represents the optimistic and one-sided self-image that a person obtains by projecting his or her shadow onto someone else.

14. F. S. Perls, *Gestalt Therapy Verbatim* (1969; reprint; New York: Bantam Books, 1976), p. 51, says, "We see guilt as projected *resentment*."

8. And they had hair as the hair of women, and their teeth were as *the teeth* of lions.

9. And they had breastplates, as it were breastplates of iron; and the sound of their wings *was* as the sound of chariots of many horses running to battle.

10. And they had tails like unto scorpions, and there were stings in their tails: and their power *was* to hurt men five months.

8. Guilt is seductive in that the aspirant has willingly increased it in himself by resenting or intimidating other people.[15] A guilt feeling has the power to rip apart the aspirant's facade of self-righteousness and expose his underlying hypocrisy.[16]

9. A guilt feeling is impervious to all weapons that the personality may use against it—struggle, repression, projection, distraction, or argumentation. The various guilt feelings strengthen each other and attack together.[17]

10. A guilt feeling stings like a scorpion, because the aspirant condemns himself with the same judgment used to condemn other people. A particular guilt feeling has power for only a limited time, because it will eventually disappear if the aspirant refrains from struggling with it.[18]

---

15. 1 Peter 3:3 (NRSV) instructs Christian women, saying, "Do not adorn yourselves outwardly by braiding your hair." This exhortation acknowledges that the hair of women has the potential of being seductive. *ACIM*, vol. I, p. 415, alludes to the seductive aspect of guilt: "Who would send messages of hatred and attack if he but understood he sends them to himself? Who would accuse, make guilty and condemn himself?"
16. The teeth of lions symbolize destructive power, as in Joel 1:6: "For a nation is come up upon my land, strong, and without number, whose teeth *are* the teeth of a lion."
17. A breastplate is a symbol of protection, as in Isa. 59:17, Eph. 6:14, and 1 Thess. 5:8. Iron is a symbol of strength, as in Jer. 1:18 and Job 40:18.
18. Psal. 32:5 (NIV) states: "Then I acknowledged my sin to you and did not cover up my iniquity. I said, 'I will confess my transgressions to the LORD'—and you forgave the guilt of my sin." J. Krishnamurti, *Last Talks at Saanen 1985* (San Francisco: Harper and Row, 1986), p. 123, makes a similar point: "All the implications of guilt, all the implications of its subtlety, where it hides, is like a flower blooming. And if you let it bloom, not act, not say, 'I must do or must not do', then it begins to wither away and die."

11. And they had a king over them, *which is* the angel of the bottomless pit, whose name in the Hebrew tongue *is* Abaddon, but in the Greek tongue hath *his* name Apollyon.

12. One woe is past; *and*, behold, there come two woes more hereafter.

13. And the sixth angel sounded, and I heard a voice from the four horns of the golden altar which is before God,

11. Finally, all guilt feelings are essentially caused by the same belief—namely, that human beings are separate entities. This belief is powerful, active, and destructive.[19]

12. These insights into the nature of guilt complete another experience with kundalini, but two more experiences remain.

13. When kundalini reaches the crown chakra, the causal body gains a four-fold power over the personality. The aspirant uses the abstract thoughts of his causal body, which are still unified with God by sharing the spiritual will,[20]

---

19. The Hebrew word *Abaddon* is used in the Old Testament to mean destruction (Job 31:12), place of destruction (Job 26:6), or personification of destruction (Job 28:22). The Greek word *Apollyon* means destroyer. Either word is taken as symbolizing the belief in separation. *ACIM*, vol. I, p. 50, has a similar perspective: "The mind can make the belief in separation very real and very fearful, and this belief *is* the 'devil.' It is powerful, active, destructive and clearly in opposition to God." For more information about this key belief, see Rev. 2:13 and 11:4.

20. In verse 13, the golden altar is the causal body (see Rev. 8:3), so the voice that comes from the altar consists of abstract thoughts (see Rev. 4:10). The horns represent powers (see Rev. 5:6), and they are taken as new powers because they have not been mentioned before. The phrase "golden altar which is before God" refers to Rev. 8:4, in which the abstract thoughts of the causal body become unified with God by sharing a common purpose.

14. Saying to the sixth angel which had the trumpet, Loose the four angels which are bound in the great river Euphrates.

15. And the four angels were loosed, which were prepared for an hour, and a day, and a month, and a year, for to slay the third part of men.

16. And the number of the army of the horsemen *were* two hundred thousand thousand: and I heard the number of them.

14. saying to his crown chakra, "Release the four parts of the personality,[21] which are bound by the pervasive emotion of fear."[22]

15. The four-fold personality, which was prepared for this moment by earlier efforts on the spiritual journey, is released from being afraid to inquire into any sudden fear that arises, so it can fulfill the spiritual will's purpose of eliminating all fearful self-images.[23]

16. The number of inquiries needed to root out all fearful self-images is quite large, as the aspirant realizes.[24]

---

21. In verse 14, the sixth angel is the crown chakra (see verse 13), and the four angels are the four parts of the personality (see Rev. 7:1).

22. The Euphrates is the largest river of western Asia and formed the northeast boundary of the land that the Israelites were intended to occupy (Gen. 15:18). Isa. 8:6–8 uses the symbolic inundation of this land by the Euphrates to represent the invading armies of Assyria. Water is a symbol for emotions (see Rev. 1:15), and the Israelites represent the personality (see Rev. 2:14). The Assyrian armies were an object of great fear for the Israelites, so the Euphrates is taken as symbolizing the pervasive emotion of fear within the personality. Just as the Kingdom of Israel needed to be liberated from the Assyrian empire, the personality needs to be freed from all traces of fear.

23. Prov. 3:25 advises: "Be not afraid of sudden fear." In verse 15, the "third part" indicates the activity of the spiritual will (see Rev. 8:8), and "men" represents self-images (see verse 4).

24. J. Krishnamurti, *Krishnamurti on Education* (New Delhi: Orient Longman, 1974), p. 35, says: "So, when I face fear it goes away. But to face fear, I have to enquire." In verse 16, a horseman is taken as an inquiry into fear, because such an inquiry goes to the area of the personality that requires attention. The number of the horsemen is two hundred million, which is two myriads of myriads (twice 10,000 times 10,000); it simply represents an indefinitely large number. This number may be a reference to Psal. 68:17, American Standard Version (ASV): "The chariots of God are twenty thousand, even thousands upon thousands."

17. And thus I saw the horses in the vision, and them that sat on them, having breastplates of fire, and of jacinth, and brimstone: and the heads of the horses *were* as the heads of lions; and out of their mouths issued fire and smoke and brimstone.

17. The aspirant understands the nature of these inquiries and directs them with his causal body. His abstract thinking provides sufficient clarity, poise, and incentive to overcome any resistance that a fearful self-image may offer, like excuses, denials, and distractions.[25] Once an inquiry examines a particular fearful self-image, it fastens onto that image until the fear is resolved.[26] Each resolution is accomplished through the purified thoughts, feelings, and motives that issue from the chakras.[27]

18. By these three was the third part of men killed, by the fire, and by the smoke, and by the brimstone, which issued out of their mouths.

18. The spiritual will, acting through the purified thoughts, feelings, and motives that pass through the chakras, progressively eliminates all fearful self-images.[28]

---

25. Jacinth (hyacinth) can refer to a precious stone, a flowering plant, or a color. Smith, *A Dictionary of the Bible*, p. 267, states: "The expression in Rev. ix. 17, 'of jacinth,' applied to the breastplate, is descriptive simply of a hyacinthine, i.e. dark-purple color." Jacinth is taken as perfect poise, signifying dominion over the emotional (or astral) body, because purple is associated with royalty and majesty (Judg. 8:26, Dan. 5:29). Bailey, *Esoteric Healing*, pp. 672–673, says, "*Perfect Poise* indicates complete control of the astral body, so that emotional upheavals are overcome, or at least are greatly minimised in the life of the disciple."

26. Lions symbolize strength, so "heads of lions" indicate that the inquiries cannot be dislodged from remaining focused on their subjects until completion.

27. Verse 17 may be based on Gen. 19:24, which describes fire and brimstone destroying the decadent cities of Sodom and Gomorrah, and on Job 41:19–21, which describes fire coming out of the mouth and smoke out of the nose of the monster Leviathan. Fire is taken as purified thoughts (see Rev. 1:15). Smoke can refer to watery mist, so it is taken as purified feelings (see Rev. 1:15). Brimstone, or sulphur, ignites easily and burns with an almost invisible smoke; it is interpreted as purified motives that display almost no selfishness. An opened mouth has the shape of a wheel, which is the form that a chakra is said to have; see Powell, *The Etheric Double*, p. 22. In fact, the Sanskrit word chakra means "wheel." Accordingly, a mouth is taken as a chakra.

28. *ACIM*, vol. II, p. 161, says, "Your image of yourself cannot withstand the Will of God."

19. For their power is in their mouth, and in their tails: for their tails *were* like unto serpents, and had heads, and with them they do hurt.

20. And the rest of the men which were not killed by these plagues yet repented not of the works of their hands, that they should not worship devils, and idols of gold, and silver, and brass, and stone, and of wood: which neither can see, nor hear, nor walk:

21. Neither repented they of their murders, nor of their sorceries, nor of their fornication, nor of their thefts.

19. For the power of the inquiries lies in the chakras and in kundalini, which rises through the spinal column from one chakra to another, thereby providing authority over the personality.[29]

20. Nevertheless, self-images still remain that take pride in personal accomplishments, are attached to false concepts of God, or yearn for physical possessions—like those made of gold, silver, brass, stone, or wood, which do not even have any life of their own.[30]

21. Those self-images bring about hatred, confusion, lust, and envy.[31]

---

29. The tail is taken as the spinal column, because the latter has the shape of a tail. The heads are interpreted as the chakras that are arranged along the spinal column. The serpent is interpreted as kundalini flowing through the spinal column, because the Sanskrit word *kundalini* means "serpent." Accordingly, verse 19 fulfills the promise made in Rev. 2:27.

30. Devil is a translation of the Greek word (*daimonion*) that is sometimes used to denote an inferior pagan deity (Acts 17:18, 1 Cor. 10:20). In verse 20, devils are taken as false concepts of God. An idol is taken as any physical possession that has been given power and importance (see Rev. 2:14).

31. In verse 21, murder is taken as hatred, as in 1 John 3:15: "Whosoever hateth his brother is a murderer." Fornication is taken as lust (see Rev. 2:14). Similarly, theft is taken as envy, because envy desires to deprive another of what he or she has. Sorcery is taken as bewitchment or confusion, as in Gal. 3:1: "O foolish Galatians, who hath bewitched you, that ye should not obey the truth, before whose eyes Jesus Christ hath been evidently set forth, crucified among you?"

CHAPTER 10

THE PLANE OF
DIVINE IDEAS

*The aspirant refuses to be distracted by new paranormal abilities
and instead receives a series of divine ideas.*

1. And I saw another mighty angel come down from heaven, clothed with a cloud: and a rainbow *was* upon his head, and his face *was* as it were the sun, and his feet as pillars of fire:

1. The aspirant realizes that the soul is approaching from the spiritual world.[1] Although he cannot directly perceive it, he recognizes its presence as the source of three kinds of intuitions:[2] spiritual will, which operates through his crown chakra;[3] spiritual love, which radiates through his emotional body; and spiritual understanding, which enlightens his causal body and mind.[4]

---

1. James 4:8 (NRSV) states: "Draw near to God, and he will draw near to you." Bailey, *Esoteric Psychology*, vol. II, p. 269, speaks of a stage in which the soul approaches the aspirant: "This stage is called the '*Touch of Enlightenment*,' and through the bringing together of the forces of the purified personality and those of the 'approaching' soul, a 'light is engendered which fadeth not away.'" In verse 1, heaven is the spiritual world (see Rev. 4:1). "Another mighty angel" is taken as the soul, because its characteristics are similar to those in Rev. 1:13–16 and because "another angel" in Rev. 8:3 also denotes the soul.

2. Verse 1 may be based on Exod 13:21: "And the LORD went before them by day in a pillar of a cloud,

2. And he had in his hand a little book open: and he set his right foot upon the sea, and *his* left *foot* on the earth,

2. The soul is conscious of the plane of divine ideas and can convey those ideas;[5] it also understands the emotional and physical worlds,[6]

---

to lead them the way; and by night in a pillar of fire, to give them light; to go by day and night." Clouds symbolize the conveyance of intuitions (see Rev. 1:7). In verse 1, "clothed with a cloud" means that the soul cannot be perceived directly but can be inferred as the source of intuitions (see Rev. 1:13). Aurobindo, *The Synthesis of Yoga*, p. 70, makes a similar point: "We recognise this divine leading . . . in the molding of our thoughts by a transcendental Seer, of our will and actions by an all-embracing Power, of our emotional life by an all-attracting and all-assimilating Bliss and Love."

3. Bailey, *A Treatise on White Magic*, p. 39, describes the relationship between the spiritual will and the divine, or universal, will: "The spiritual will—that quota of the universal will which any one soul can express, and which is adequate for the purpose of enabling the spiritual man to co-operate in the plan and purpose of the great life in which he has his being." The rainbow surrounding the throne of God in Rev. 4:3 symbolizes the divine will; but the rainbow upon the angel's head in verse 1 symbolizes the spiritual will, which acts through the crown chakra (see Rev. 8:5).

4. A face like the sun indicates spiritual love (see Rev. 1:16). Feet and fire symbolize understanding and intellect, respectively (see Rev. 1:15).

5. Bailey, *A Treatise on White Magic*, pp. 456–457, says, "the soul is consciously aware . . . of the thoughts of God" and it is "possible for the soul to act as the intermediary between the plane of divine ideas and the mental plane." Here, plane is a synonym for world. In verse 2, the "little book" is taken as the plane of divine ideas, which is how the "tree of life" is interpreted in Rev. 2:7. This plane is sometimes called the "buddhic plane," "archetypal plane," "plane of the intuition," or "world of ideas" (Taimni, *Self-Culture*, pp. 7–9; Bailey, *A Treatise on White Magic*, pp. 456–458). The plane of divine ideas is "little" in the sense that it is more subtle, or less dense, than the physical, emotional, and mental planes. The book in verse 2 is open and in the hand of the angel, indicating that the soul is aware of the divine ideas and can convey them.

6. The sea and earth are the emotional and physical worlds, respectively (see Rev. 4:6, 3:10), and feet signifies understanding (see Rev. 1:15). In fact, *A Commentary on the Book of the Revelation*, p. 157, interprets "right foot upon the sea" to mean "understanding of emotional nature," and "left foot on the earth" to mean "understanding of physical nature."

3. And cried with a loud voice, as *when* a lion roareth: and when he had cried, seven thunders uttered their voices.

3. and can use a Word of Power, which is sound enunciated with the full purpose of the will, to raise kundalini.[7] When the soul does so, the aspirant's seven chakras, energized by kundalini, yield new paranormal powers that can be used for egotistical purposes.[8]

4. And when the seven thunders had uttered their voices, I was about to write: and I heard a voice from heaven saying unto me, Seal up those things which the seven thunders uttered, and write them not.

4. After sensing his new paranormal powers, the aspirant is tempted to apply them. But he hears an abstract thought from his causal body that says,[9] "Ignore those new powers, since their application would hinder further spiritual growth."[10]

---

7. Bailey, *Initiation, Human and Solar*, p. 150, defines a Word of Power as "enunciated sound . . . with the full purpose of the will behind it." The lion is a symbol of power (see Rev. 5:5; 9:8). In verse 3, calling out like a lion is taken as using a Word of Power. Bailey, *Esoteric Healing*, p. 185, describes how kundalini can be raised in this way: "This unified fire is then raised by the use of a Word of Power (sent forth by the will of the Monad) and by the united authority of the soul and personality, integrated and alive." Here, Monad is a synonym for Divine Self (Bailey, *A Treatise on Cosmic Fire*, p. 48).

8. In verse 3, the seven thunders are taken as the seven chakras after being energized by kundalini, and their voices as new paranormal powers. Motoyama, *Theories of the Chakras*, pp. 217, 227, 231, and 233, lists the paranormal powers that kundalini is said to yield by acting on the chakras: telepathy, clairvoyance, clairaudience, psychic healing, psychokinetic powers, ability to see the body from within, and ability to locate hidden treasures.

9. To write means to apply to oneself (see Rev. 1:11). Verse 8 indicates that the "voice from heaven" is different from the angel of verse 1. The "voice from heaven" is taken as the abstract thinking of the causal body, which is how the voices in Rev. 4:10 and 9:13 are interpreted.

10. Patanjali, the founder of the system of raja yoga, warned against turning spiritual powers into a hindrance (*Yoga Sutras*, Book III, verse 37). C. Johnson, *The Yoga Sutras of Patanjali* (1949; reprint; London: Stuart and Watkins, 1968), p. 82, comments on this warning: "The divine man is destined to supersede the spiritual man, as the spiritual man supersedes the natural man. . . . The opened powers of the spiritual man, spiritual vision, hearing, and touch, stand, therefore, in contradistinction to the higher divine power above them, and must in no wise be regarded as the end of the way. . . . So that, if the spiritual powers we have been considering are regarded as in any sense final, they are a hindrance, a barrier to the far higher powers of the divine man. But viewed from below, from the standpoint of normal physical experience, they are powers truly magical."

5. And the angel which I saw stand upon the sea and upon the earth lifted up his hand to heaven,

6. And sware by him that liveth for ever and ever, who created heaven, and the things that therein are, and the earth, and the things that therein are, and the sea, and the things which are therein, that there should be time no longer:

5. The soul, which helped the aspirant to understand his physical and emotional natures,[11] now encourages him to learn about the divine source of life.[12]

6. The soul, serving as a link with God—the creator of the spiritual, physical, and emotional worlds and of all things within those worlds—declares, "There should be no more delay in learning about God;[13]

---

11. Verses 5 and 6 are based on Dan. 12:7: "And I heard the man clothed in linen, which *was* upon the waters of the river, when he held up his right hand and his left hand unto heaven, and sware by him that liveth for ever that *it shall be* for a time, times, and an half."

12. Kundalini has reached the crown chakra, as shown by Rev. 9:13 and verse 3. Nikhilananda, *The Gospel of Ramakrnishna*, p. 582, describes the consequence: "Finally, the Kundalini rises to the lotus at the cerebrum and becomes united with Siva, or the Absolute; and the aspirant realizes, in the transcendental consciousness, his union with Siva-Sakti." Here, the lotus at the cerebrum is the crown chakra, Siva is a name for God, and Siva-Sakti is the creative power of God. This quotation seems to suggest that divine realization occurs automatically after kundalini rises to the crown chakra. In contrast, verses 4 and 5 indicate that divine realization is possible only if the aspirant refuses to be sidetracked by lower paranormal powers.

13. Verse 6 uses heaven, earth, and sea as though they cover all possibilities. Heaven, earth, and sea represent the spiritual, physical, and emotional worlds, and so the spiritual world must include everything outside the physical and emotional worlds, including the mind, causal body, soul, and plane of divine ideas. Most modern translations of the Bible use the word "delay" instead of "time" in this verse. In the RSV, for example, the last part of verse 6 appears as "there should be no more delay."

7. But in the days of the voice of the seventh angel, when he shall begin to sound, the mystery of God should be finished, as he hath declared to his servants the prophets.

8. And the voice which I heard from heaven spake unto me again, and said, Go *and* take the little book which is open in the hand of the angel which standeth upon the sea and upon the earth.

9. And I went unto the angel, and said unto him, Give me the little book. And he said unto me, Take *it*, and eat it up; and it shall make thy belly bitter, but it shall be in thy mouth sweet as honey.

7. For in the days of the basic chakra, when that chakra is brought into full expression, the hidden nature of God must already have been unveiled by the revelation that God gives to his servants who speak for him."[14]

8. Another abstract thought tells the aspirant, "Go and take the divine ideas from the soul, because it has already proven itself by bringing understanding of the emotional and physical worlds."

9. And so the aspirant achieves alignment with the soul and invokes the divine ideas. The soul says, "Take in and think about these ideas; they are difficult to apply, but pleasant to contemplate."[15]

---

14. Verse 7 is based on Amos 3:7: "he revealeth his secret unto his servants the prophets." The word prophet can simply mean spokesman, or one who speaks for another, as shown by Exod. 7:1–2. In the Old Testament, God provides the revelation that transforms a person into a prophet, who then stands before other human beings as a person who has stood before God. For examples, see Isa. 6:1, Ezek. 1:1, and 1 Kings 22:19. The basic chakra is the seventh chakra listed in Table 2, because it is the last one to be transformed on the spiritual journey.

15. Verses 9 and 10 are based on Ezek. 3:3: "And he said unto me, Son of man, cause thy belly to eat, and fill thy bowels with this roll that I give thee. Then did I eat *it*; and it was in my mouth as honey for sweetness." Eating up the ideas means thinking about them, as in Jer. 15:16: "Thy words were found, and I did eat them." *A Commentary on the Book of the Revelation*, p. 157, interprets "it shall make thy belly bitter" to mean "difficult in experience as it is digested in application," and "in thy mouth sweet" to mean "pleasing to hear about—to contemplate."

10. And I took the little book out of the angel's hand, and ate it up; and it was in my mouth sweet as honey: and as soon as I had eaten it, my belly was bitter.

11. And he said unto me, Thou must prophesy again before many peoples, and nations, and tongues, and kings.

10. The aspirant receives a series of divine ideas from the soul and thinks about them,[16] discovering that they are pleasant to contemplate, but difficult to apply.[17]

11. Nevertheless, the soul tells the aspirant, "You must apply these ideas to all peoples, nations, communities, and rulers of the world."[18]

---

16. The metaphor of the book in verse 10 suggests that the divine ideas are received and grasped progressively and serially. Bailey, *Glamour*, pp. 135–136, describes this series of ideas: "Through the intuition, progressive understanding of the ways of God in the world and on behalf of humanity are revealed; through the intuition, the transcendence and the immanence of God is sequentially grasped and man can enter into that pure knowledge, that inspired reason, which will enable him to comprehend not only the processes of nature in its fivefold divine expression but also the underlying causes of these processes."

17. The divine ideas affirm the unity of all life. These ideas are pleasant to contemplate on an abstract or philosophical level, because they provide an underlying meaning and significance to all events and circumstances. Nevertheless, these ideas are difficult to apply on a practical level, because their application entails giving up all sense of separation, judgment, and pride.

18. *A Commentary on the Book of the Revelation*, p. 157, interprets verse 11 to mean: "He is now told that he must apply that which he has learned to all peoples, in all conditions."

CHAPTER 11

JUDGMENT

The aspirant learns about judgment, eliminates all judgments of
unworthiness, and achieves conscious union with the soul.

KING JAMES VERSION

1. And there was given me a reed like unto a rod: and the angel stood, saying, Rise, and measure the temple of God, and the altar, and them that worship therein.

PSYCHOLOGICAL INTERPRETATION

1. The aspirant has a mental standard that he believes can be used to judge the worth of other people.[1] The soul tells the aspirant, "Raise your consciousness into your causal body[2] and use your mental standard to identify the people who are worthy of receiving the blessings of God,[3]

---

1. Verse 1 is probably based on Ezek. 40–42, in which a man with a reed carefully measures each part of the temple of God. In this verse, the reed is interpreted as a mental standard of judgment.
2. The angel is the soul, because the events in chapter 11 are a continuation of those in chapter 10. Just as ordinary waking consciousness cannot be maintained indefinitely but must alternate with periods of sleep, Bailey, *Letters on Occult Meditation*, p. 292, indicates that causal consciousness may last only for "a brief moment." In Rev. 9:1, the aspirant achieves causal consciousness. In verse 1 of this chapter, "rise" is taken as telling the aspirant to raise the polarization of his consciousness, once again, into his causal body.
3. Cayce comments on verse 1: "Ye, your own souls as individuals, who will you put in your heaven? Ye of a denomination, ye of a certain creed, ye of a certain measurement, with what measure ye mete it is

2. But the court which is without the
temple leave out, and measure it not;
for it is given unto the Gentiles: and
the holy city shall they tread under
foot forty *and* two months.

2. and judge everyone else, without
explicitly having to consider them, as
unworthy. Your disdainful concepts[4]
about these other people will cause
your own personality to be perturbed[5]
as long as you maintain your judgment about them.[6]

---

measured to thee again. . . . Those that will measure then, those that will set metes and bounds—how
has it been given oft? When ye name a name, or when ye give metes and bounds, ye forget that God's
force, God's power is *infinite!*" (Van Auken, *Edgar Cayce on the Revelation*, pp. 183–184). *ACIM*, vol. I,
p. 284, has a similar notion: "Each one you see you place within the holy circle of Atonement or leave
outside, judging him fit for crucifixion or for redemption." In verse 1, the temple is taken to be what
Cayce calls "your heaven" or what *ACIM* calls "the holy circle of Atonement."

4. The word *gentile* generally means "any nation except the Jews." In the course of time, the Jews began to
pride themselves on their peculiar privileges, and so this word became a term of contempt. By the time
of Jesus, according to Matt. 18:17 (RSV), "a Gentile and a tax collector" were comparable in opprobri-
um. In verse 2, the Gentiles are taken as disdainful concepts of other people.

5. J. S. Goldsmith, *The Thunder of Silence* (New York: Harper and Row, 1961), p. 173, describes how we
are perturbed by our concepts of other people: "If we continue to be perturbed about someone, it is
because we are entertaining a concept of him, and it is that concept that is causing the conflict within
us. If we are disturbed about a person, we may be quite certain that our concept of him is entirely
wrong." In verse 2, the city is the personality (see Rev. 3:12), so the treading of the city symbolizes the
disturbance that the personality feels as a result of its wrong concepts of others.

6. Verse 2 says that the conflict lasts 42 months, which is also the period during which the beast has
authority in Rev. 13:5. This period of three and a half years is equivalent to the "time, and times, and
half a time" that the woman is nourished in Rev. 12:14, and also to the three and a half days mentioned
in verses 9 and 11 in this chapter. If each month lasts exactly thirty days, the same period is equivalent
to the 1260 days that the witnesses prophesy in verse 3 and that the woman is nourished in Rev. 12:6.
This period has its origin in Dan. 7:25, in which the power of evil is said to last "until a time and times
and the dividing of time." Mounce, *The Book of Revelation*, p. 215, says, "The temporal designation of
42 months . . . became a standard symbol for that limited period of time during which evil would be
allowed free rein." In verse 2, this period symbolizes the length of time during which a judgment of
unworthiness is maintained.

3. And I will give *power* unto my two witnesses, and they shall prophesy a thousand two hundred *and* threescore days, clothed in sackcloth.

3. I will give power to your emotional and vital bodies so they witness or reflect your judgment of unworthiness. These bodies will express your mental judgment as long as you hold it, but they will do so while bereft of their spiritual qualities."[7]

4. These are the two olive trees, and the two candlesticks standing before the God of the earth.

4. The activity within the sympathetic and parasympathetic nervous systems reflects the activity within the solar-plexus and sacral chakras, which reflects the activity within the emotional and vital bodies, which in turn reflects any mental judgment of unworthiness.[8] Judgments of unworthiness are based on the belief of separateness, which can be called the God of the earth, because it controls the vast majority of people.[9]

---

7. The "two witnesses" are taken as the vital and emotional bodies. Cayce gives a similar interpretation: "These then are the witnesses. The innate and the emotional." (Van Auken, *Edgar Cayce on the Revelation*, p. 186). As explained in the preceding footnote, 1,230 days symbolize the length of time that a judgment of unworthiness is maintained. Sackcloth is a symbol of loss or mourning; for examples, see Isa. 15:3 and Jer. 4:8.

8. Verse 4 is based on Zech. 4:2–3, which describes a single golden candlestick flanked by two olive trees. Trees are nervous systems (see Rev. 7:1). In verse 4, the two trees are the sympathetic and parasympathetic nervous systems, which are the two branches of the autonomic nervous system. Bell-Ranske, *The Revelation of Man*, p. 190, also interprets the two trees in this verse as "the ganglionic nerve-system." The two candlesticks are the sacral and solar plexus chakras (see Rev. 1:12). The sacral parasympathetic nerves are connected to the vital body via the sacral chakra (see Rev. 8:7). Bailey, *A Treatise on White Magic*, p. 284, describes a similar role for the solar-plexus chakra: "The sympathetic nervous system, that marvellous apparatus of sensation, is closely related to the emotional or astral body. The contact is made via the solar plexus."

9. Paul, in 2 Cor. 4:4, says, "the god of this world hath blinded the minds of them which believe not." In verse 4, earth refers to humanity (see Rev. 5:6), and so "God of the earth" is taken as the belief of separateness, because the latter distorts the perceptions of most people (see Rev. 2:13, 9:11). For example, Bailey, *Esoteric Psychology*, vol. I, p. 378, says, "our race is controlled by the great heresy of separativeness."

5. And if any man will hurt them, fire proceedeth out of their mouth, and devoureth their enemies: and if any man will hurt them, he must in this manner be killed.

6. These have power to shut heaven, that it rain not in the days of their prophecy: and have power over waters to turn them to blood, and to smite the earth with all plagues, as often as they will.

7. And when they shall have finished their testimony, the beast that ascendeth out of the bottomless pit shall make war against them, and shall overcome them, and kill them.

5. Perturbed by unworthy people, the emotional and vital bodies respond with angry feelings and behavior, and try to hurt those people just as they believe they have been hurt.[10]

6. The emotional and vital bodies have power to block the influence of the spiritual world, thus stopping the flow of righteousness. They can create conflict on the emotional level and project that conflict, in the form of disease, into the physical body, over and over again.[11]

7. The act of judging others causes guilt to emerge from the subconscious nature, attack the emotional and vital bodies, and overcome them.[12] A guilt feeling also brings death in a spiritual sense: it extinguishes spiritual love from the emotional body and spiritual will from the vital body.

---

10. Krishnamurti, *Last Talks At Saanen*, p. 35, describes how subjective division leads to conflict: "But if we create subjectively a division—I belong to this and you belong to that, I am a Catholic, you are a Protestant, I am a Jew and you are an Arab—then there is conflict." Fire can be a symbol of anger, as in Isa. 30:27: "Behold, the name of the LORD cometh from far, burning *with* his anger, and the burden *thereof is* heavy: his lips are full of indignation, and his tongue as a devouring fire." In verse 5, the fire represents the anger arising from the subjective division brought about by judgment.

11. Rain can be a symbol of righteousness, as in Hos. 10:12 (NASB): "For it is time to seek the Lord Until He comes to rain righteousness on you." See also Isa. 45:8. In verse 6, heaven, waters, blood, and earth symbolize the spiritual world, emotional body, conflict, and physical body, respectively (see Rev. 4.1, 1:15, 6:10, 3:10). Bailey, *Esoteric Healing*, p. 112, says, "Ninety percent of the causes of disease are to be found in the etheric and astral bodies." Here, etheric and astral are synonyms for vital and emotional. The power "to smite the earth with all plagues" is taken as the power to project disease into the physical body.

12. The bottomless pit is the subconscious nature, and the beast that emerges from this pit is a guilt feeling (see Rev. 9:1–3).

8. And their dead bodies *shall lie* in the street of the great city, which spiritually is called Sodom and Egypt, where also our Lord was crucified.

9. And they of the people and kindreds and tongues and nations shall see their dead bodies three days and an half, and shall not suffer their dead bodies to be put in graves.

10. And they that dwell upon the earth shall rejoice over them, and make merry, and shall send gifts one to another; because these two prophets tormented them that dwelt on the earth.

8. The emotional and vital bodies transmit their pain via internal communication channels to the rest of the personality, resulting in a pervasive sense of sin, bondage, and suffering.[13]

9. All elements of the personality focus on painful memories of past emotional and physical experiences as long as a judgment of unworthiness persists, and they maintain those memories.[14]

10. The unredeemed parts of the personality, which are identified with the physical form, use this suffering to justify, support, and strengthen each other, because they had been superseded by the spiritual love and spiritual will that the emotional and vital bodies had previously displayed.[15]

---

13. The city is the personality (see verse 2), and the street of the city consists of the internal communication channels that were alluded to in verse 4. Sodom was a place of moral degradation (Gen. 19:4–11), and Egypt kept the Israelites in bondage (Exod. 1:13–14). Fillmore, *Metaphysical Bible Dictionary*, pp. 183, 624, says that "Sodom symbolizes the lowest form of sense desire," and that "Egypt signifies the darkness of ignorance."

14. J. Krishnamurti, *Commentaries on Living, First Series* (1956; reprint; Wheaton, IL: Theosophical Publishing House, 1970), pp. 242–243, states: "What we know is the dead past, not the living. To be aware of the living, we must bury the dead in ourselves." In verse 9, "dead bodies" are memories of past experiences, and "to be put in graves" means to forget those memories. As explained in a footnote for verse 2, "three days and an half" symbolize the length of time that a judgment of unworthiness is maintained.

15. "They that dwell upon the earth" are thoughts, feelings, and motives that are identified with the physical body (see Rev. 3:10).

11. And after three days and an half the Spirit of life from God entered into them, and they stood upon their feet; and great fear fell upon them which saw them.

11. After gaining the insights set forth in verses 4 through 10, the aspirant remembers the ideas from God, which show that the belief of separateness is unreal. His emotional and vital bodies start to recover, and his unredeemed parts can no longer justify themselves.[16]

12. And they heard a great voice from heaven saying unto them, Come up hither. And they ascended up to heaven in a cloud; and their enemies beheld them.

12. The causal body, which understands the divine ideas, calls upon the emotional and vital bodies to rise in consciousness, which they do in spite of the unredeemed parts.[17]

---

16. After being asked the question "What is signified by the revival of these witnesses?," Cayce gave the following answer: "How hath He given? 'If ye meditate on these things, I will bring to thy remembrance all things.' The reviving, the renewing, by the abilities of the soul to take hold upon the witnesses of the life itself! And what is life? God!" (Van Auken, *Edgar Cayce on the Revelation*, p. 187). In verse 11, "the Spirit of life from God" is taken as the ideas from God that were received in Rev. 10:10.

17. The "voice from heaven" is the causal body (see Rev. 10:4). The word "great" indicates authority (see Rev. 1:10) and represents the understanding that was gained through the contemplation of the divine ideas in Rev. 10:10.

13. And the same hour was there a great earthquake, and the tenth part of the city fell, and in the earthquake were slain of men seven thousand: and the remnant were affrighted, and gave glory to the God of heaven.

13. Soon afterward, the aspirant's application of the divine ideas eliminates all mental judgments of unworthiness because they are based on the belief of separateness,[18] all separative feelings because they are based on judgments of unworthiness, and all egotistical activities because they are based on separate feelings. The remaining activities of the personality reflect the ideas from the God of heaven rather than that of the earth.[19]

14. The second woe is past; *and*, behold, the third woe cometh quickly.

14. When these changes are accomplished, only one more step in the purification process remains, and it comes quickly.

---

18. Matt. 7:1 states: "Judge not, that ye be not judged." Goldsmith, *The Infinite Way*, p. 156, explains: "In the spiritual life, you place no labels on the world. You do not judge as to good or evil, sick or well, rich or poor." A great earthquake symbolizes a great change in the personality due to divine discernment (see Rev. 6:12). The great change in verse 13 is taken as the elimination of all judgments of unworthiness due to the application of divine ideas.

19. Gen. 2:2–3 states: "And on the seventh day God ended his work which he had made; and he rested on the seventh day from all his work which he had made. And God blessed the seventh day, and sanctified it." The *New Bible Dictionary*, p. 834, concludes, "*seven* . . . is associated with completion, fulfilment and perfection." Ten represents completeness (see Rev. 2:10), and so the loss of a tenth of the city is taken as the loss of all separative feelings. One thousand represents completeness with respect to three criteria (see Rev. 7:4). In the context of verse 13, seven thousand refers to the perfection that is achieved in the personality through the elimination of all egotistical activities on mental, emotional, and physical levels.

15. And the seventh angel sounded; and there were great voices in heaven, saying, The kingdoms of this world are become *the kingdoms* of our Lord, and of his Christ; and he shall reign for ever and ever.

15. The basic chakra is brought into full expression.[20] The aspirant, who is still polarized in his causal body, concludes that his personality is no longer ruled by his emotional body,[21] but answers instead to the power of God and the soul. This power will overcome any resistance.[22]

16. And the four and twenty elders, which sat before God on their seats, fell upon their faces, and worshipped God,

16. The aspirant's abstract thoughts, which have been aligned with God, recognize their own limitations and acknowledge God's role,[23]

17. Saying, We give thee thanks, O Lord God Almighty, which art, and wast, and art to come; because thou hast taken to thee thy great power, and hast reigned.

17. saying, "We give you thanks, O Lord God, all powerful and eternal, because your power is governing the personality.

---

20. Bailey, *Esoteric Healing*, p. 216, describes "the stage of energising the entire man, via the basic centre thus bringing: a. The head centre and the basic centre, b. These two and the ajna centre, c. All the three, simultaneously and consciously, into rhythmic, coordinated expression." Step (a) occurs when kundalini from the basic chakra reaches the crown chakra; it corresponds to the sounding of the sixth angel in Rev. 9:13. Step (b) occurs when the wisdom of the causal body is expressed through the brow (or ajna) chakra; it corresponds to verses 11 through 13. Step (c) occurs when all activities reflect the ideas from God; it corresponds to the sounding of the seventh angel in verse 15.

21. In verse 15, the world is the emotional body (see Rev. 3:10).

22. Christ is a translation of the Greek word (*Christos*) that means "anointed" or "Messiah." It is a title applied to Jesus (Matt. 16:16, Acts 17:3). Fillmore, *Metaphysical Bible Dictionary*, p. 150, says that this title also applies to our higher self: "This Christ, or perfect-man idea existing eternally in Divine Mind, is the true, spiritual, higher self of every individual. Each of us has within him the Christ, just as Jesus had, and we must look within to recognize and realize our sonship, our divine origin and birth, even as He did. By continually unifying ourselves with the Highest by our thoughts and words, we too shall become sons of God, manifest." In verse 15, Christ is taken as a synonym for soul, or higher self. Cayce, Blavatsky, and Goldsmith use the term Christ in similar ways; see the footnotes for Rev. 5:6, 12:10, and 20:4.

23. The sayings of the 24 elders represent the abstract thoughts of the causal body (see Rev. 4:4, 10). Alignment of these thoughts with God occurred in Rev. 8:4 and was mentioned again in Rev. 9:13.

18. And the nations were angry, and thy wrath is come, and the time of the dead, that they should be judged, and that thou shouldest give reward unto thy servants the prophets, and to the saints, and them that fear thy name, small and great; and shouldest destroy them which destroy the earth.

18. The personality was once filled with anger, but your correction is come. Now is the time to observe any thoughts, feelings, and images about the past, so that they can be compared with your ideas. Through this kind of judgment, you give reward to the emotional and vital bodies, to the causal body,[24] and to the activities aligned with your nature, both small and great. You also destroy the factors that cause disease and suffering."[25]

---

24. The wrath of God is correction or punishment for unrighteousness, as shown in Rom. 1:18: "For the wrath of God is revealed from heaven against all ungodliness and unrighteousness of men, who hold the truth in unrighteousness." In verse 18, the "dead" are memories (see verse 9). "Thy servants the prophets" are "my two witnesses" that prophesy in verse 3, which in turn are the emotional and vital bodies. The "saints" are principles of wisdom stored in the causal body (see Rev. 5:8).

25. Verse 18 is based partly on Psalm 115:13: "He will bless them that fear the LORD, *both* small and great." Fear is a translation of the Greek word (*phobeo*) that sometimes means to treat with reverential obedience (Eph. 5:33), or more simply, to be aligned with. The last part of verse 18 answers the question posed in Rev. 6:10.

19. And the temple of God was opened in heaven, and there was seen in his temple the ark of his testament: and there were lightnings, and voices, and thunderings, and an earthquake, and great hail.

19. The foregoing acknowledgment of the presence and power of God[26] creates an opening in the aspirant's causal body through which his consciousness rises into the soul.[27] He looks down upon his causal body and sees that its accumulated wisdom contains evidence of God's will, love, and intelligence.[28] The aspirant, who is now an adept, discovers that he is a point of divine will, focused within the soul's love and arriving at the awareness of Being through the use of form.[29]

---

26. Acknowledging the presence and power of God is sometimes called "practicing the presence of God"; see Brother Lawrence, *The Practice of the Presence of God* (1692; reprint; Grand Rapids, MI: Fleming H. Revell Company, 1989). The *Revelation* prescribes this practice as the means for achieving the final step in the spiritual journey, which is union with the soul. Chapter 19 gives more information about this practice.

27. Bailey, *A Treatise on White Magic*, p. 264, says that "*the Causal Body* . . . is the vehicle of the higher consciousness, the temple of the indwelling God*." Accordingly, the temple of God in verse 19 is taken as the causal body. Bailey, *Letters on Occult Meditation*, p. 95, speaks of two shifts in consciousness: "the mental body becomes the centre of consciousness and then later—through practice—it becomes the point of departure for the transference of the polarisation into a higher body, first the causal and later into the Triad." The first shift results in causal consciousness and is described in chapters 9 and 16. The second shift results in union with the soul, because Triad is a synonym for soul (Bailey, *A Treatise on Cosmic Fire*, p. 48); this shift is described in verse 19 and chapter 19.

28. In the Old Testament, the sacred ark is called the "ark of the testimony" (Exod. 30:6), "ark of the covenant" (Num. 10:33), and "ark of God" (1 Sam. 3:3). This ark was a box covered with gold, and it contained the two tablets of the Ten Commandments, the golden pot that had manna, and Aaron's rod (Heb. 9:4). In verse 19, the ark of God's testament is taken as accumulated wisdom that contains evidence of God's will, love, and intelligence.

29. Bailey, *The Rays and the Initiations*, p. 107, describes the aspirant's ultimate discovery of self-identity: "The disciple . . . begins to realise himself as the soul. Then, later, comes the awful 'moment in time' when, pendant in space, he discovers that he is not the soul. What then is he? A point of divine dynamic will, focussed in the soul and arriving at awareness of Being through the use of form." *ACIM*, vol. I, p. 129, makes a similar statement: "You *are* the Will of God." In verse 19, "lightnings, and voices, and thunderings, and an earthquake" symbolize awakened kundalini, which is the result of expressing the spiritual will through physical form (see Rev. 8:5). "Great hail" symbolizes spiritual love expressed through physical form (see Rev. 8:7).

CHAPTER 12

ILLUSION

John has another vision that depicts the spiritual journey from beginning to end, but with a different perspective and emphasis. In this vision, the aspirant calls for guidance, becomes aware of illusion, and learns how to cast it out.

KING JAMES VERSION

1. And there appeared a great wonder in heaven; a woman clothed with the sun, and the moon under her feet, and upon her head a crown of twelve stars:

PSYCHOLOGICAL INTERPRETATION

1. At the beginning of the spiritual journey, the aspirant's mind is receptive to the divine,[1] because it is influenced by external teachers, understands external teachings, and aspires toward mental ideals of spiritual development.[2]

---

1. Heaven is the spiritual world and includes the mind (see Rev. 10:6). The personality consists of the mental, emotional, vital, and physical bodies (see Rev. 4:7). In verse 1, the woman is taken as the mental body, or mind, because it is the only portion of the personality that is part of the spiritual world. The feminine form is a symbol of receptivity. For example, Isa. 54:5 states, "For thy Maker *is* thine husband," indicating that a human being ought to have a feminine, or receptive, relationship to the divine. See also Isa. 62:5. The "great wonder in heaven" depicted in verse 1 is that the aspirant's mind has developed this receptivity.

2. Paul, in Rom. 10:17 (RSV), states: "So faith comes from what is heard, and what is heard comes by the preaching of Christ." As in Rev. 6:12 and 8:12, the sun represents an external teacher or authority figure, and the moon represents an external teaching, such as found in books. Clothing symbolizes the nature of the wearer (see Rev. 7:9), and so "clothed by the sun" indicates a nature influenced by external teachers. Feet signify understanding (see Rev. 1:15, 10:2), and so "moon under her feet" indicates an

2. And she being with child cried, travailing in birth, and pained to be delivered.

3. And there appeared another wonder in heaven; and behold a great red dragon, having seven heads and ten horns, and seven crowns upon his heads.

2. The aspirant's mind, receptive to the soul, calls for its guidance and is distressed by seeing what is revealed.[3]

3. The fact of illusion is revealed.[4] Illusion appears as a great adversary responsible for all conflicts.[5] It controls the seven chakras and all desires,[6] gives paramount importance to the outer form,[7] and deludes through the passage of time.[8]

---

understanding of external teachings. Stars are mental ideals and twelve indicates a divine pattern (see Rev. 6:13, 7:4). Accordingly, "a crown of twelve stars" symbolizes mental ideals of spiritual development.

3. Verse 2 is based on Isa. 26:17: "Like as a woman with child, *that* draweth near the time of her delivery, is in pain, *and* crieth out in her pangs; so have we been in thy sight, O LORD." In verse 2, the woman, child, cry, and pain of childbirth represent the mind (see verse 1), soul (see Rev. 2:18), call for the soul's guidance, and distress from receiving the soul's light, respectively. Bailey, *Discipleship in the New Age*, vol. I, p. 727, gives the reason for this distress: "The searchlight of the soul reveals faults in character, limitations in expression and inadequacies in conduct. These must be intelligently corrected."

4. Bailey, *Esoteric Healing*, p. 11, writes, "The best minds of this age are only just beginning to see the first dim ray of light which is . . . serving first of all to reveal the fact of illusion." Illusion is the aggregate of false beliefs accepted by the mind. Without the light of the soul, the mind cannot even recognize the presence of illusion within itself. In verse 3, the great red dragon is taken as illusion, because verse 9 equates this dragon with the Devil or Satan, both of which denote illusion (see Rev. 2:9–10).

5. The dragon's red color indicates that illusion engenders conflict, because red symbolizes conflict (see Rev. 6:4). Indeed, *ACIM*, vol. II, p. 130, says, "Without illusions conflict is impossible." John 8:44 makes a similar point: "the devil . . . was a murderer from the beginning."

6. The seven heads are the seven chakras (see Rev. 9:19). The ten horns symbolize the full range of desires, because ten and horn signify completeness and power (see Rev. 2:10, 5:6).

7. Bailey, *Esoteric Psychology*, vol. II, p. 434, says, "The vital or etheric body . . . is an exact replica or counterpart of the outer form." As shown in Table 1, the seven chakras, which are centers of energy within the vital body, determine the profile of the physical body, or outer form. The crowns on these chakras are taken to mean that illusion gives paramount importance to the outer form. Paul, in Rom. 8:7 (RSV), expresses a similar idea: "For the mind that is set on the flesh is hostile to God; it does not submit to God's law, indeed it cannot."

8. Twenty-four features of the dragon are mentioned: 7 heads, 10 horns, and 7 crowns. This number indicates that illusion is closely related to time, because 24 symbolizes the passage of time (see Rev. 4:4). J. Krishnamurti, *Krishnamurti's Notebook* (New York: Harper and Row, 1976), p. 153, makes a similar point: "Time is illusion." In addition, Collins, *Light on the Path*, p. 31, speaks of "Time, the great deluder."

4. And his tail drew the third part of the stars of heaven, and did cast them to the earth: and the dragon stood before the woman which was ready to be delivered, for to devour her child as soon as it was born.

4. The chakras in the spinal column, which are controlled by illusion, have corrupted some of the mental ideals,[9] turning them into false beliefs, emotional reactions, and compulsions.[10] Illusion, operating on the mental level, is ready to fight against any guidance from the soul as soon as the mind has received it.

5. And she brought forth a man child, who was to rule all nations with a rod of iron: and her child was caught up unto God, and *to* his throne.

5. Eventually, the mind brings forth the guidance of the soul, which combines the wisdom of maturity with a still small voice. The soul will rule all aspects of the personality by way of awakened kundalini in the spinal column. It acts as the intermediary for God and is aligned with the heart of God.[11]

---

9. Verse 4 may be based on Dan. 8:10 (NIV): "It grew until it reached the host of the heavens, and it threw some of the starry host down to the earth and trampled on them." In verse 4, the tail is the spinal column (see Rev. 9:19), which contains the five lowest chakras. The "third part" is interpreted simply as meaning "some," which is consistent with how Dan. 8:10 is worded.

10. Wrong perception, interpretation, or appropriation of an ideal creates a false belief on the mental level (see Rev. 3:4). Combining a false belief with desire produces a reaction on the emotional level, such as pride or anger. Combining an emotional reaction with vital energy produces a compulsion on the physical level. A compulsion is an impulse to perform an irrational act, such as a persistent habit, sexual fetish, or compulsive gambling. The earth is the physical body (see Rev. 3:10), and so casting mental ideals into the physical body is taken as transforming them into false beliefs, emotional reactions, and then compulsions.

11. The man child is the soul, because the soul has wisdom, which is associated "with the aged" (Job 12:12, RSV), but speaks with "a still small voice" (1 Kings 19:12, RSV). The mind brings forth the guidance of the soul through right discrimination (see Rev. 5:6). The rod of iron is awakened kundalini in the spinal column (see Rev. 2:27). The throne of God is the heart of God (see Rev. 1:4). "Caught up unto God" could be translated as "pulled to God" (Jude 23), and it refers to acting as the intermediary between the personality and God (see Rev. 5:7).

6. And the woman fled into the wilderness, where she hath a place prepared of God, that they should feed her there a thousand two hundred *and* threescore days.

7. And there was war in heaven: Michael and his angels fought against the dragon; and the dragon fought and his angels,

6. Through the practice of meditation, the mind becomes detached from the external world[12] and abides in an inner sanctuary,[13] remaining there until inner peace comes.[14]

7. During meditation, a war takes place within the mind. Intuitions from the soul oppose the beliefs that illusion fosters; illusion fights back through its judgments, doubts, and projections.[15]

---

12. Verses 6 through 8 are equivalent to the first step of receptive meditation that is described in Rev. 4:6. The Bible often considers the wilderness to be a place of refuge and communion with God, as in Hos. 2:14: "I will allure her, and bring her into the wilderness, and speak comfortably unto her." M. Kiddle, *The Revelation of St. John* (London: Hodder and Stoughton, 1940), p. 229, says, "the desert to which the woman fled represents . . . a condition of *spiritual detachment* from the affairs and fortunes of the civilized world."

13. *ACIM*, vol. II, p. 228, states: "In silence, close your eyes upon the world that does not understand forgiveness, and seek sanctuary in the quiet place where thoughts are changed and false beliefs laid by." "The quiet place" in this quotation is taken to be the same as "a place prepared of God" in verse 6.

14. The duration of each meditation session is symbolized by 1260 days, which represents the time before a sense of peace occurs (see the footnotes for Rev. 11:2). J. S. Goldsmith, *Collected Essays of Joel S. Goldsmith* (Marina del Rey, CA: Devorss and Company, 1986), pp. 164–165, speaks of this duration: "It may take five minutes for the peace to descend; it may take fifteen minutes. There are obstinate beliefs in this world, but if we are patient and know what it is we are waiting for—the assurance from within—it will descend. . . . It may take practice, but whenever agitation comes to your thought, find a place to rest and relax and wait for this peace to descend upon you."

15. Verse 7 is related to Dan. 12:1: "And at that time shall Michael stand up, the great prince which standeth for the children of thy people." Bailey, *Glamour*, p. 83, says, "It is the soul itself which dispels illusion, through the use of the faculty of the intuition." In verse 7, Michael fights against the dragon, which symbolizes illusion, and so Bailey's quotation indicates that Michael symbolizes the soul and Michael's angels symbolize intuitions from the soul.

8. And prevailed not; neither was their place found any more in heaven.

8. Eventually, illusion is temporarily vanquished during a moment of illumination in which the mind dwells within the innocence of the present and is no longer identified with the past or future.[16]

9. And the great dragon was cast out, that old serpent, called the Devil, and Satan, which deceiveth the whole world: he was cast out into the earth, and his angels were cast out with him.

9. Even though the great adversary, illusion, is cast out of the mind during a moment of illumination, it is still part of the emotional body in the form of latent reactions; it is still part of the physical body in the form of latent compulsions.[17]

10. And I heard a loud voice saying in heaven, Now is come salvation, and strength, and the kingdom of our God, and the power of his Christ: for the accuser of our brethren is cast down, which accused them before our God day and night.

10. The aspirant comes to the following conclusions with his abstract thinking: "A moment of illumination brings salvation from fear, inner peace, awareness of the divine whole, and the power of the soul, because illusion is cast out of the mind along with its continual judgments that hide the presence of God.[18]

---

16. *ACIM*, vol. I, pp. 301–329, uses the term "holy instant" to denote a moment of illumination. R. Perry, *A Course Glossary* (West Sedona, AZ: The Circle of Atonement, 1996), pp. 35–36, gives the following definition of such a moment: "A moment in which we temporarily set aside the past and enter into the timeless present, in which we momentarily transcend identification with illusions and recognize what is real. We enter the holy instant not by making ourselves holy, but by forgetting our normal frame of reference, with its absorption in the past, the future, the body and our own sinfulness. This allows our minds to be still and shift into another state of mind."
17. Blavatsky, *Collected Writings*, vol. 12, p. 693, states: "When evil tendencies and impulses have been thoroughly impressed on the physical nature, they cannot at once be reversed." In verse 9, the world is the emotional body (see Rev. 3:10).
18. Goldsmith, *Practicing the Presence*, p. 116, writes: "This practice of nowness develops a consciousness which is never pressed from the outside because there is nothing to do except what is at hand this minute. Living in this consciousness, we are never worried about supply, nor about any obligation due tomorrow. . . . Then there develops in us—we do not do it—*It*, the Christ of our being, develops in us a sense of peace." Both the "now" in verse 10 and what Goldsmith calls the "practice of nowness" are taken as referring to a moment of illumination. The voice from heaven is the abstract thinking of the causal body (see Rev. 10:4), and Christ is the soul (see Rev. 11:15).

11. And they overcame him by the blood of the Lamb, and by the word of their testimony; and they loved not their lives unto the death.

11. These spiritual factors overcome illusion through the spiritual love of the soul and related intuitions,[19] which eliminate temporal goals that extinguish awareness of eternal life.[20]

12. Therefore rejoice, *ye* heavens, and ye that dwell in them. Woe to the inhabiters of the earth and of the sea! for the devil is come down unto you, having great wrath, because he knoweth that he hath but a short time.

12. Therefore, happiness comes through dwelling in a moment of illumination.[21] But between such moments, suffering comes from identifying with the physical or emotional body, whereby latent compulsions and emotional reactions become active and can preserve themselves."[22]

13. And when the dragon saw that he was cast unto the earth, he persecuted the woman which brought forth the man *child.*

13. When illusion is active through wrong identification, it can torment the mind, even after it has brought forth the soul's guidance.[23]

---

19. "The blood of the Lamb" is the spiritual love of the soul (see Rev. 5:9); "the word of their testimony" is an intuition (see Rev. 1:2, 6:9). Bailey says that both are factors in overcoming illusion: "If the healer *loves* enough . . . he has achieved a poise which brings negation to the world of illusion and of glamour" (*Esoteric Healing*, p. 675); "Only the intuition can dispel illusion" (*Glamour*, p. 23).

20. The last part of verse 11 is based on John 12:25: "He that loveth his life shall lose it; and he that hateth his life in this world shall keep it unto life eternal." Goldsmith, *The Infinite Way*, pp. 181–182, makes a similar statement: "As long as there remains concern for *personal* good—security, health, or peace of mind—there is that which must 'die daily' in order that one may be 'reborn of the Spirit' into the realization of immortality here and now."

21. L. Wittgenstein, *Notebooks, 1914–1916* (Oxford: Blackwell, 1961), p. 8.7.16, writes: "Only a man who lives not in time but in the present is happy." In verse 12, dwelling in multiple "heavens" is taken as dwelling in a moment of illumination, because the latter involves living within the innocence of the present (see verse 8), within the inner sanctuary (see verse 6), and within the mind (see verse 1).

22. The sea is the emotional body (see Rev. 4:6).

23. Bailey, *Esoteric Healing*, p. 347, says, "Wrong identification is the cause of pain and leads to suffering, distress and various effects."

14. And to the woman were given two wings of a great eagle, that she might fly into the wilderness, into her place, where she is nourished for a time, and times, and half a time, from the face of the serpent.

14. And yet, at any moment, the mind can use the love and intuition of the soul to become detached and dwell in its inner sanctuary until illusion is once again vanquished.[24]

15. And the serpent cast out of his mouth water as a flood after the woman, that he might cause her to be carried away of the flood.

15. Nevertheless, illusion can generate powerful emotional reactions that might cause the mind to forget the soul and the inner sanctuary.[25]

16. And the earth helped the woman, and the earth opened her mouth, and swallowed up the flood which the dragon cast out of his mouth.

16. The physical body helps the mind cope with these emotional reactions fostered by illusion, because any emotional indulgence eventually has to be replaced by efforts to satisfy ordinary physical needs for sleep, food, drink, and shelter.

17. And the dragon was wroth with the woman, and went to make war with the remnant of her seed, which keep the commandments of God, and have the testimony of Jesus Christ.

17. Illusion keeps attacking the mind, and it tries to subvert those parts of the personality that follow the intuitions from the soul and the teachings of Jesus.[26]

---

24. Deut. 32:11–12 likens God's care over his people to that of the eagle in training its young to fly: "As an eagle stirreth up her nest, fluttereth over her young, spreadeth abroad her wings, taketh them, beareth them on her wings: So the LORD alone did lead him, and *there was* no strange god with him." In verse 14, the great eagle is taken as the soul, and the two wings as the two powers of the soul mentioned in verse 11, namely, love and intuition. "A time, and times, and half a time" has the same meaning as the 1260 days in verse 6 (see the footnotes for Rev. 11:2). "Face of the serpent" means presence of illusion (see Rev. 6:16).

25. Water symbolizes emotions (see Rev. 1:15). Cayce interprets the "flood" in verse 15 as "the flood of emotions that make for doubt, fears, tribulation, disturbances, anxieties" (Van Auken, *Edgar Cayce on the Revelation*, p. 190). Psal. 69:2 uses this symbol in a similar way: "I sink in deep mire, where *there is* no standing: I am come into deep waters, where the floods overflow me."

26. The commandments of God are taken as the words of God, which in turn are intuitions from the soul (see Rev. 6:9).

CHAPTER 13

GLAMOUR AND MAYA

The aspirant studies his emotional and physical natures and learns
about glamour and maya.

1. And I stood upon the sand of the sea, and saw a beast rise up out of the sea, having seven heads and ten horns, and upon his horns ten crowns, and upon his heads the name of blasphemy.

1. From a position of detachment,[1] the aspirant studies his emotional nature and learns about glamour, which is the aggregate of his emotional reactions.[2] Glamour controls the seven chakras and the full range of desires.[3] It gives paramount importance to fulfilling desires, and is judgmental in nature.[4]

---

1. *A Commentary on the Book of the Revelation*, p. 163, interprets standing on the sand of the sea to be the "detached state of observation."
2. The beast from the sea is the adversary that the aspirant must eventually face and overcome on the emotional level, because the sea is the emotional body (see Rev. 4:6). *A Commentary on the Book of the Revelation*, p. 163, says that this beast symbolizes "emotional urges for expression of *selfish* desires." Bailey, *Glamour*, p. 241, uses the term glamour to denote the emotional adversary: "*Glamour*, in its turn, veils and hides the truth behind the fogs and mists of feeling and emotional reaction."
3. Regarding this beast, St. John of the Cross, *The Complete Works*, vol. I, p. 107, writes: "Happy the soul that can fight against that beast of the Apocalypse, which has seven heads, set over against these seven

2. And the beast which I saw was like unto a leopard, and his feet were as *the feet* of a bear, and his mouth as the mouth of a lion: and the dragon gave him his power, and his seat, and great authority.

3. And I saw one of his heads as it were wounded to death; and his deadly wound was healed: and all the world wondered after the beast.

2. Glamour is also treacherous, blundering, and boastful.[5] Illusion gives glamour its power of deception, controls the personality via glamour, and makes glamour the authority for judging the worth of whatever is perceived.[6]

3. The aspirant realizes that his solar-plexus chakra, under the influence of glamour, seems wounded by the past,[7] but can also feel redeemed by the present. The emotional body, following the lead of glamour, desires external circumstances that engender this feeling of redemption.[8]

---

steps of love. . . . And undoubtedly if it strive faithfully against each of these heads, and gain the victory, it will deserve to pass from one step to another, . . . leaving the beast vanquished after destroying its seven heads." This quotation is consistent with taking each head as one of the seven chakras (see Rev. 9:19), because chapters 2 and 3 show that each stage on the spiritual journey corresponds to transforming one of the chakras.

4. Paul, in Eph. 2:3 (RSV), says: "Among these we all once lived in the passions of our flesh, following the desires of body and mind, and so we were by nature children of wrath, like the rest of mankind." In verse 1, the ten horns are the full range of desires; having horns with crowns means that fulfilling desires is the paramount goal (see Rev. 12:3). The name of something is its basic nature (see Rev. 2:3). Blasphemy refers to slander, verbal abuse, or evil speaking (see Rev. 2:9).

5. The beast in verse 2 is a composite of the four beasts of Dan. 7:4–7, which also come up from the sea: a winged lion, a bear, a four-headed leopard, and a beast with ten horns. *A Commentary on the Book of the Revelation*, p. 163, interprets the leopard as "treacherous," feet of a bear as "blundering," and mouth of a lion as "boastful."

6. Bailey, *Glamour*, p. 21, says, "*The Problem of Glamour* is found when the mental illusion is intensified by desire. . . . It is illusion on the astral plane." In verse 2, the dragon is illusion (see Rev. 12:3).

7. The solar-plexus chakra transmits feelings from the emotional body to the nervous system (see Rev. 2:8).

8. R. Perry, *Relationships as a Spiritual Journey* (West Sedona, AZ: The Circle of Atonement, 1997), p. 40, describes the false form of redemption offered by feelings: "We feel that the past wounded us and we would desperately like to heal those wounds. But the past is gone. It cannot be changed. What, then, to do? We will bring the past into the present. We will put on a play that re-enacts the past. This time, however, we will change the ending. This time there will be a happy ending. We will be the hero, we will get the love and recognition denied us the first time around. All injustices will be rectified, all wrongs made right, and we will be redeemed." In verse 3, the world is the emotional body (see Rev. 3:10).

4. And they worshipped the dragon which gave power unto the beast: and they worshipped the beast, saying, Who *is* like unto the beast? who is able to make war with him?

5. And there was given unto him a mouth speaking great things and blasphemies; and power was given unto him to continue forty *and* two months.

6. And he opened his mouth in blasphemy against God, to blaspheme his name, and his tabernacle, and them that dwell in heaven.

7. And it was given unto him to make war with the saints, and to overcome them: and power was given him over all kindreds, and tongues, and nations.

4. All desires accept without question the false beliefs that lie behind glamour and give it power. All desires act as though glamour were an infallible guide, rather than something that can or should be overcome.[9]

5. Glamour appears attractive because it offers self-aggrandizement and judgments of others. The aspirant will continue to give glamour its power as long as he believes that it is attractive and worth maintaining.[10]

6. Glamour's boast of privilege is a slanderous attack on God and God's nature, for all human beings are created equal and are spiritually united.[11]

7. Glamour distorts and subverts even the wisdom of the causal body, and it controls all parts of the personality.[12]

---

9. Verse 4 parodies the praise of God found in such passages as Exod. 15:11: "Who *is* like unto thee, O LORD, among the gods?" Bailey, *Glamour*, p. 45, writes, "Many good people today . . . deify their glamours and regard their illusions as their prized and hard won possessions."

10. The period of 42 months represents the length of time that the aspirant suffers from glamour due to his own decisions (see the footnotes for Rev. 11:2).

11. Specialness claims that some people in the world are better than others. *ACIM*, vol. I, p. 501, asks: "For what is specialness but an attack upon the Will of God?" A tabernacle of God is a dwelling-place of God on earth (Exod. 25:8–9). Paul, in 1 Cor. 3:16, indicates that human beings are such dwelling-places: "Know ye not that ye are the temple of God, and *that* the Spirit of God dwelleth in you?"

12. In verse 7, the saints are the principles of wisdom contained within the causal body (see Rev. 5:8).

8. And all that dwell upon the earth shall worship him, whose names are not written in the book of life of the Lamb slain from the foundation of the world.

9. If any man have an ear, let him hear.

10. He that leadeth into captivity shall go into captivity: he that killeth with the sword must be killed with the sword. Here is the patience and the faith of the saints.

8. All feelings of identification with the physical body pay homage to glamour, yet such feelings are based on beliefs that are inconsistent with divine ideas. The soul can convey divine ideas to the aspirant, but the aspirant's beliefs, which are the foundation of his feelings, cause him to ignore or forget about the soul.[13]

9. If the aspirant has the capacity to understand the following key points, let him do so.[14]

10. Whoever is angry with other people will be held captive by guilt. Whoever condemns other people will suffer from self-condemnation. Herein lies the wisdom of being detached from emotions and perceiving the essential divinity within other people.[15]

---

13. Cayce states: "the Book of Life has been eaten. It is in the mouth, sweet; in the belly (or the body), bitter." (Van Auken, *Edgar Cayce on the Revelation*, pp. 185–186). According to this quotation, the book of life is the book of Rev. 10:10, which is the plane of divine ideas. "All that dwell upon the earth" are feelings of identification with the physical body (see Rev. 3:10). The Lamb is the soul (see Rev. 5:6). The name of a feeling is taken as its underlying belief, because that belief determines the nature of the feeling. The foundation of the emotional world is the set of all such beliefs.

14. In verse 17, "hear" means hear with the ear of the mind, or understand (see Rev. 3:3).

15. Killing, patience, and faith refer to condemnation, detached observation, and perception of the divinity within others, respectively (see Rev. 9:21, 2:2, 2:13). The sword in verse 10 is taken to be what *ACIM*, vol. I, p. 664, calls the "sword of judgment." Thus, the message of this verse is similar to that of Luke 6:37: "Judge not, and ye shall not be judged: condemn not, and ye shall not be condemned: forgive, and ye shall be forgiven."

11. And I beheld another beast coming up out of the earth; and he had two horns like a lamb, and he spake as a dragon.

12. And he exerciseth all the power of the first beast before him, and causeth the earth and them which dwell therein to worship the first beast, whose deadly wound was healed.

13. And he doeth great wonders, so that he maketh fire come down from heaven on the earth in the sight of men,

11. Next, the aspirant studies his physical nature and learns about maya, which is the aggregate of his compulsions. Maya is a false prophet with the powers of both glamour and vitality, and it embodies illusion.[16]

12. More specifically, maya has glamour's power of deception, as well as the vital energy that causes the physical body and all self-images that are identified with that body to seek the false form of redemption offered by glamour.[17]

13. Maya has the power of manifestation, because it can make thoughts come down from the mind and appear outwardly as physical behavior.[18]

---

16. The beast from the earth is the adversary that the aspirant must eventually face and overcome on the physical level, because the earth is the physical body (see Rev. 3:10). Bailey, *Glamour*, p. 148, uses the Sanskrit word *maya* to denote this adversary: "Maya is predominantly (for the individual) the aggregate of the forces which control his septenary force centres to the exclusion, I would emphasise, of the controlling energy of the soul." The beast's lamb-like appearance shows that maya is a false prophet in the sense of being a counterfeit version of the soul; its two horns symbolize the two powers of maya (see Rev. 5:6).

17. Bailey, *Glamour*, p. 149, distinguishes between glamour and maya: "In the case of glamour, the forces of a man's nature are seated in the solar plexus. In the case of maya, they are seated in the sacral centre. Glamour is subtle and emotional. Maya is tangible and etheric." Here, etheric is a synonym for the vital body.

18. Bailey, *Glamour*, p. 26, says that maya gives vital energy to mental illusion: "*Maya* is vital in character and is a quality of force. It is essentially the energy of the human being as it swings into activity through the subjective influence of the mental illusion or astral glamour or of both in combination." In verse 13, fire represents thoughts (see Rev. 1:15) and heaven includes the mind (see Rev. 10:6).

14. And deceiveth them that dwell on the earth by *the means of* those miracles which he had power to do in the sight of the beast; saying to them that dwell on the earth, that they should make an image to the beast, which had the wound by a sword, and did live.

15. And he had power to give life unto the image of the beast, that the image of the beast should both speak, and cause that as many as would not worship the image of the beast should be killed.

14. Maya reinforces feelings of identification with the physical body by fulfilling desires fostered by glamour.[19] Maya encourages fantasies of using the physical body for self-glorification. Each of these fantasies contains a dream of retribution for the past.[20]

15. Maya gives vital energy to any strongly felt fantasy, resulting in an impulse to act out that fantasy and to resent anything that blocks its fulfillment.[21]

---

19. Bailey, *Glamour*, p. 242, notes the close relationship between maya and identification with the physical body: "The average man . . . believes himself to be the form, the medium through which he attempts to express his desires and ideas. This complete identification with the transient creation and with the outer appearance is maya."

20. According to Prov. 6:16–18, one of the "six *things* doth the LORD hate" is "An heart that deviseth wicked imaginations." In verse 14, an image of the beast is a fantasy of wish fulfillment. *ACIM,* vol. I, p. 348, says, "There is no fantasy that does not contain the dream of retribution for the past."

21. Baily, *A Treatise on White Magic*, p. 551, says, "Potencies produce precipitation." Thus, a strongly felt fantasy precipitates a glamour from the emotional body down to the vital body, which means that it is transformed into a compulsion. The reference to killing in verse 15 is interpreted as a form of hatred (see Rev. 9:21).

16. And he causeth all, both small and great, rich and poor, free and bond, to receive a mark in their right hand, or in their foreheads:

17. And that no man might buy or sell, save he that had the mark, or the name of the beast, or the number of his name.

16. Maya compels all parts of the physical body—minor or great, healthy or sick, voluntary or involuntary—to use their strength and consciousness to act out strongly felt fantasies.[22]

17. The aspirant would not value external things unless he were affected by maya, or glamour, or illusion.[23]

---

22. *A Commentary on the Book of the Revelation*, p. 163, equates "Mark of Beast" with "Pattern of animalistic behavior shown," which is the same as a compulsion. Hand and forehead symbolize the strength and consciousness of the physical cells and organs (see Rev. 1:16, 7:3).

23. In ancient times it was widely believed that numbers are the essential elements of all things. For example, this doctrine can be found in Plato's *Timaeus* (53b) and in the Wisdom of Solomon (11:20). Bailey, *A Treatise on White Magic*, pp. 455–456, says, "The mathematics which underlie the construction of a bridge . . . are the bridge itself, reduced to its essential terms." Here, the mathematics refer to the numbers that characterize the architectural pattern, or blueprint, of the bridge. In verse 17, the "number" of glamour is taken as illusion, because illusion underlies the construction of glamour and is the essence of glamour. Table 6 summarizes the other symbols used for illusion, glamour, and maya throughout the *Revelation*.

18. Here is wisdom. Let him that hath understanding count the number of the beast: for it is the number of a man; and his number *is* Six hundred threescore *and* six.

18. Here is a key principle of wisdom: illusion operates throughout the personality,[24] pervading the mental body as false beliefs, the emotional body as glamour, and the vital body as maya.[25] Understanding this principle implies deeply distrusting all reactions of the personality to life and circumstance, because illusion cannot even be recognized as illusion without the illumination of the soul.[26]

---

24. Six is a numerical symbol of illusion, which can be arrived at in two ways. First, the dragon in Rev. 12:3 symbolizes illusion and has 24 features: 7 heads, 10 horns, and 7 crowns. According to ancient Greek numerology, the digits of a decimal number can be added together to obtain an equivalent number; see M. P. Hall, *The Secret Teachings of All Ages* (1928; reprint; Los Angeles: The Philosophical Research Society, 1975), p. LXIX. Thus, as Bailey, *The Rays and the Initiations*, p. 79, points out, "the number 24 . . . in its turn equals 6." Second, W. E. Vine, *Vine's Complete Expository Dictionary of Old and New Testament Words* (Nashville, TN: Thomas Nelson, 1985), p. 579, says that "six . . . sometimes suggests incompleteness, in comparison with the perfect number seven." For examples, see Job 5:19 and Prov. 6:16.

25. The number in verse 18 can be written as the sum of the three numbers obtained from its decimal expansion: "Six hundred and sixty and six" (ASV). Here, six represents illusion on the mental level. Sixty (6 times 10) represents glamour, which is the product of illusion and the desire-generating process of the emotional body, because ten signifies completion of a process (Table 3). Similarly, six hundred (6 times 10 times 10) represents maya, which is the product of illusion, the desire-generating process of the emotional body, and the energizing process of the vital body. Bailey, *The Rays and the Initiations*, p. 183, speaks of "the Great Illusion, in its three forms of illusion, glamour and maya." Accordingly, 666 symbolizes the Great Illusion—the composite of illusion, glamour, and maya.

26. Bailey, *Glamour*, p. 82, advises: "A deep distrust of one's reactions to life and circumstance, when such reactions awaken and call forth *criticism, separateness* or *pride*, is of value." Krishnamurti, *Commentaries on Living, First Series*, p. 82, states: "Ignorance of the ways of the self leads to illusion; and once caught in the net of illusion, it is extremely hard to break through it. It is difficult to recognize an illusion, for, having created it, the mind cannot be aware of it."

CHAPTER 14

THE SPIRITUAL KINGDOM

*The aspirant becomes aware of powerful evolutionary forces
coming from the spiritual kingdom that can help overcome the
involutionary forces described in the two preceding chapters.*

KING JAMES VERSION

1. And I looked, and, lo, a Lamb stood on the mount Sion, and with him an hundred forty *and* four thousand, having his Father's name written in their foreheads.

PSYCHOLOGICAL INTERPRETATION

1. The aspirant opens his mental consciousness upward[1] and raises it to its highest possible point,[2] thereby becoming aligned with both the soul[3] and the spiritual kingdom.[4] The members of this kingdom form a vast integrated organization,[5] and are consciously aware of their own divine nature.[6]

---

1. Bailey, *Discipleship in the New Age*, vol. II, p. 490, says that "you can look *outward* upon the world of physical living, *inward* upon the world of emotions or of mental perception, or *upward* towards the soul." Based on the context of verse 1, the aspirant is looking *upward*. Sri Aurobindo, *The Integral Yoga* (Pondicherry, India: Sri Aurobindo Ashram, 1993), p. 152, describes this practice: "One must open the silent mental consciousness upward to all that is above mind. After a time one feels the consciousness rising upward and in the end it rises beyond the lid which has so long kept it tied in the body and finds a centre above the head where it is liberated into the Infinite." This practice is equivalent to the second step of receptive meditation given in Rev. 4:8.
2. Mount Sion, or Zion, is one of the hills on which the ancient city of Jerusalem is built. The Old

2. And I heard a voice from heaven, as the voice of many waters, and as the voice of a great thunder: and I heard the voice of harpers harping with their harps:

2. The aspirant receives subtle impressions from the spiritual kingdom. These come as spiritual feelings, spiritual intentions and inner harmony.[7]

Testament often gives a theological meaning to this hill, as in Psal. 2:6: "Yet have I set my king upon my holy hill of Zion." Mount Sion is interpreted here as the mental body, so "on the mount Sion" symbolizes the highest point of mental consciousness. Bailey, *The Rays and the Initiations*, p. 487, refers to this point: "raise the consciousness to the head centre; hold the consciousness at the highest possible point."

3. The Lamb is the soul, and a standing position indicates spiritual alignment (see Rev. 5:6, 7:9).

4. *A Commentary on the Book of the Revelation*, p. 165, interprets the 144,000 in verse 1 as the "perfected souls of mankind." Leadbeater, *The Masters and the Path*, pp. 3, 5, 256, refers to this group as the "Perfected Men whom we call Masters," "Supermen," or "Hierarchy." Bailey refers to this group as the "spiritual kingdom," "Hierarchy," or "Kingdom of God" (*Telepathy*, p. 194; *Discipleship in the New Age*, vol. II, p. 407). The Bible uses the term "kingdom of heaven" (Matt. 11:11), and this commentary uses the term "spiritual kingdom."

5. Bailey, *Discipleship in the New Age*, vol. II, p. 407, states: "The Kingdom of God is . . . a vast and integrated group of soul-infused persons." Verse 1 uses the number 144,000 to symbolize the spiritual kingdom and Rev. 7:4 uses it to symbolize a physical body that has been transformed by spiritual love, indicating that the organization of the spiritual kingdom—with soul-infused persons as elements—is analogous to the organization of a physical body—with physical cells as elements.

6. The name of anything represents its nature (see Rev. 2:3), so the name of God represents the nature of God. Forehead refers to consciousness (see Rev. 7:3). Both Rev. 2:17 and Rev. 11:19 indicate that the aspirant will become conscious of his divine nature by the end of the spiritual journey.

7. Bailey, *Discipleship in the New Age*, vol. II, pp. 407–408, describes the spiritual kingdom as "radiating love and spiritual intention, motivated by goodwill." In verse 2, hearing "a voice from heaven" is taken as receiving impressions from the spiritual kingdom. Many waters, great thunder, and harps represent spiritual feelings, spiritual intention, and inner harmony, respectively (see Rev. 1:15, 4:5, 5:8).

3. And they sung as it were a new song before the throne, and before the four beasts, and the elders: and no man could learn that song but the hundred *and* forty *and* four thousand, which were redeemed from the earth.

3. The spiritual kingdom also radiates spiritual love from the heart of God to the aspirant's personality and causal body.[8] No one can know spiritual love in its fullness except members of the spiritual kingdom, who have been redeemed from a physical sense of life.[9]

---

8. The members of the spiritual kingdom are sometimes called "Masters." Bailey, *Discipleship in the New Age*, vol. I, p. 755, discusses the radiation of spiritual love by a Master: "The radiation which comes from the plane of buddhi or of the spiritual intuition . . . is an expression of the love nature of the Master and is that which enables Him to be in touch with the Heart of God." The plane of buddhi is the same as the plane of divine ideas (see chapter 10). In verse 3, "song" is taken as spiritual love. The throne, four beasts, elders, and earth are the heart of God, four-fold personality, causal body, and physical body, respectively (see Rev. 1:4, 4:7, 4:4, 3:10).

9. The last part of verse 3 makes a point similar to Collins, *Light on the Path*, p. 11: "Only fragments of the great song come to your ears while yet you are but man."

4. These are they which were not defiled with women; for they are virgins. These are they which follow the Lamb whithersoever he goeth. These were redeemed from among men, *being* the first fruits unto God and to the Lamb.

4. Members of the spiritual kingdom are free of the cycle of reincarnation. They need not be born through women into the physical world,[10] for they are virgins in that their thoughts cannot be led astray.[11] They consistently follow the soul's guidance, and are redeemed from the human kingdom, being the first to achieve the objectives of God and the soul.[12]

5. And in their mouth was found no guile: for they are without fault before the throne of God.

5. Members of the spiritual kingdom convey only truthful messages, for they have been illumined by the heart of God.[13]

---

10. Matt. 11:11 quotes Jesus: "Verily I say unto you, Among them that are born of women there hath not risen a greater than John the Baptist: notwithstanding he that is least in the kingdom of heaven is greater than he." Thus, the members of the spiritual kingdom are not born of women.

11. Paul (2 Cor. 11:2–3, NIV) writes: "I promised you to one husband, to Christ, so that I might present you as a pure virgin to him. But I am afraid that just as Eve was deceived by the serpent's cunning, your minds may somehow be led astray from your sincere and pure devotion to Christ." Here, the serpent is illusion and Christ is the soul (see Rev. 12:9, 11:15); virgin refers to the personality when it is free of illusion, or equivalently, when it cannot be led astray from a sincere and pure devotion to the soul. M. Eckhart, *Meister Eckhart: A Modern Translation* (New York: Harper and Row, 1941), p. 207, gives a similar definition: "A virgin . . . is a person who is free of irrelevant ideas, as free as he was before he existed."

12. Theosophical writers emphasizes that the spiritual kingdom includes the saints and sages of all religions. For example, Leadbeater, *The Masters and the Path*, p. 5, writes: "The records of every great religion show the presence of such Supermen, so full of the Divine Life that again and again They have been taken as the very representatives of God Himself. In every religion, especially at its founding, has such an One appeared, and in many cases more than one."

13. A. Jurriaanse, *Bridges* (Cape, South Africa: Sun Centre, 1980), p. 195, states: "The Masters are members of that group of 'illumined Minds' which is guided by love and understanding, and by deep compassion and inclusiveness towards humanity. They are striving towards a comprehension and translation of the Divine Purpose, and are illumined by knowledge of the Plan."

6. And I saw another angel fly in the midst of heaven, having the everlasting gospel to preach unto them that dwell on the earth, and to every nation, and kindred, and tongue, and people,

7. Saying with a loud voice, Fear God, and give glory to him; for the hour of his judgment is come: and worship him that made heaven, and earth, and the sea, and the fountains of waters.

6. The aspirant becomes aware of an intuitive telepathic message from the spiritual kingdom that conveys the eternal gospel to human beings throughout the world, to every nation, race, language, and community.[14]

7. This message says with clarity, "Be aligned with God and give him your attention, for his illumination is present. So look for illumination from the creator of the spiritual, physical, and emotional worlds—the creator of devotion, aspiration, and spiritual love."[15]

---

14. This commentary includes citations from the works of both Mary Bailey and Alice Bailey. M. Bailey, *A Learning Experience* (New York: Lucis Publishing Company, 1990), pp. 19–20, uses the terms "telepathic communication" and "intuitional suggestion" to characterize messages from the spiritual kingdom. The angel in verse 6 is taken as such a message.

15. To fear God means to be aligned with God (see Rev. 11:18). Heaven, earth, and sea are the spiritual, physical, and emotional worlds (see Rev. 4:1, 3:10, 4:6). Fountains of waters are the higher emotions, such as devotion, aspiration, and spiritual love (see Rev. 7:17, 8:10).

8. And there followed another angel, saying, Babylon is fallen, is fallen, that great city, because she made all nations drink of the wine of the wrath of her fornication.

8. There follows another intuitive message that says, "Your ego, or personal self, is a sense of identity without permanent or independent substance.[16] Your ego only seems like an internal center of authority,[17] because all parts of your personality have accepted its beliefs, which bring suffering from its idolatry."[18]

9. And the third angel followed them, saying with a loud voice, If any man worship the beast and his image, and receive *his* mark in his forehead, or in his hand,

9. A third intuitive message follows that says, "If you are enamored by glamour and fantasies of wish fulfillment, and plan or act to fulfill those fantasies,[19]

16. The first part of verse 8 is based on Isa. 21:9: "Babylon is fallen, is fallen." Babylon is the Greek form of the Hebrew word *Babel,* which in turn means confusion (Gen. 11:9). Here, Babylon is interpreted as the ego, or personal self, because the latter is the principal source of confusion in our minds. Cayce also says that "Babylon symbolizes self" (Van Auken, *Edgar Cayce on the Revelation,* p. 196). The fallen condition indicates that the ego lacks intrinsic substance. *The Shambhala Dictionary of Buddhism and Zen* (Boston: Shambhala Publications, 1991), p. 8, has a similar perspective: "The *anatman* doctrine is one of the central teachings of Buddhism; it says that no self exists in the sense of a permanent, eternal, integral, and independent substance within an individual existent." Chapters 17 and 18 treat the ego in more detail.

17. A city is a center of commerce and laws for the region that surrounds it (Num. 21:25, 35:2). The word "great" indicates a position of authority (see Rev. 1:10), so "great city" is taken as an internal center of authority that promulgates values and edicts to the surrounding personality.

18. The Old Testament sometimes uses a reference to fornication as a metaphor for idolatry. For example, Jer. 3:9 (ICB) states: "She was guilty of adultery. This was because she worshiped idols made of stone and wood." See also Ezek. 16:15, Jer. 3:8, Hos. 1:2, and Hos. 2:1–5. This commentary uses idolatry in a broad sense to mean giving power to external circumstances (see Rev. 2:14). In verse 8, wine, wrath, and fornication are taken as beliefs, suffering, and idolatry, respectively.

19. In verse 9, "the beast and his image" refer to glamour and fantasy (see Rev. 13:1, 13:14).

10. The same shall drink of the wine of the wrath of God, which is poured out without mixture into the cup of his indignation; and he shall be tormented with fire and brimstone in the presence of the holy angels, and in the presence of the Lamb:

11. And the smoke of their torment ascendeth up for ever and ever: and they have no rest day nor night, who worship the beast and his image, and whosoever receiveth the mark of his name.

12. Here is the patience of the saints: here *are* they that keep the commandments of God, and the faith of Jesus.

10. you will feel the presence of the soul through the voice of conscience, which will bring untempered torment to your personality.[20] This torment will arise from thoughts that compare your base motives with the higher way shown by intuitions from the soul.[21]

11. The suffering from this torment constantly increases, without pause day or night, when you are enamored by glamour and fantasy, and controlled by maya."[22]

12. Here is a call to apply three principles of wisdom: observe your personality with detachment; follow intuitions from the soul; cultivate the faith of Jesus, which is the willingness to wait for an intuition to come.[23]

---

20. The wrath of God is correction or punishment for unrighteousness (see Rev. 11:18). The Old Testament sometimes pictures God's wrath as a draft of wine; see Psal. 75:8, Isa. 51:17, and Jer. 25:15. *A Commentary on the Book of the Revelation*, p. 165, takes the "wine of the wrath of God" in verse 10 as the "workings of conscience." Bailey, *Esoteric Healing*, p. 506, explains the relationship between soul and conscience: "The aspect of the soul which is concealed within the sheaths is for a long, long period dominated by the life of those sheaths, only making its presence felt through what is called 'the voice of conscience.'" The personality is denoted as the "sheaths" in this quotation and as the "cup" in verse 10.

21. Fire and brimstone are thoughts and motives, respectively (see Rev. 9:17).

22. In verse 11, "smoke" is taken as suffering, and "mark of his name" is a symbol of maya (see Table 6).

23. The saints are principles of wisdom (see Rev. 5:8), patience is detached observation (see Rev. 2:2), and a commandment of God is an intuition from the soul (see Rev. 12:17). Matt. 26:36–44 describes Jesus as waiting for divine guidance in the Garden of Gethsemane. Many verses in the Bible tell us to cultivate the same faith, saying to "wait on the Lord" (Prov. 20:22).

13. And I heard a voice from heaven saying unto me, Write, Blessed *are* the
dead which die in the Lord from
henceforth: Yea, saith the Spirit, that
they may rest from their labours; and
their works do follow them.

13. The aspirant hears an abstract thought
from his causal body that says to him,
"Apply the following principle of wisdom:[24] Become happy through dying
psychologically, which means purging
your self of whatever is inconsistent
with the soul's truth from now on."[25]
"That is correct," responds the soul,[26]
"because you will rest from your egotistical striving and yet perform valuable service."[27]

---

24. "A voice from heaven" is the abstract thinking of the causal body (see Rev. 10:4). To write means to apply (see Rev. 1:11).
25. Ruusbroec, *The Spiritual Espousals*, p. 170, interprets verse 13 as referring to a psychological death in which we transcend ourselves: "But when we rise above ourselves and in our ascent to God become so unified that bare love can envelop us at that high level where love itself acts, . . . we will then come to nought, dying in God to ourselves and to all that is our own. In this death we become hidden sons of God and discover in ourselves a new life, which is eternal." Paul, in Col. 3:3, refers to the same kind of death: "For ye are dead, and your life is hid with Christ in God." This psychological death is called the "second death" in Rev. 2:11.
26. The soul is denoted as "the Spirit" and is performing the function of an intuitive standard of truth that confirms the conclusions of the causal body (see Rev. 2:7, 3:14).
27. In Hinduism, "karma yoga" is a spiritual discipline based upon the unselfish performance of duty. The meaning of the last part of verse 13 is similar to karma yoga, as described by Vivekananda, *The Yogas and Other Works*, p. 508: "He works best who works without any motive—neither for money, nor for fame, nor for anything else."

14. And I looked, and behold a white cloud, and upon the cloud *one* sat like unto the Son of man, having on his head a golden crown, and in his hand a sharp sickle.

14. The aspirant understands what to do:[28] he detaches himself from his personality while observing it; he emulates the attitude of Jesus by waiting patiently for guidance from above; he is attentive to his crown chakra for such guidance; he is ready to use the sharp, discriminating power of his mind.[29]

15. And another angel came out of the temple, crying with a loud voice to him that sat on the cloud, Thrust in thy sickle, and reap: for the time is come for thee to reap; for the harvest of the earth is ripe.

15. Eventually, the aspirant hears an abstract thought from his causal body clearly saying to him,[30] "Use your mind to uncover the beliefs that underlie your apparent suffering. The time is come for you to take an active role, for your knowledge about the suffering of your personality is sufficiently developed."[31]

---

28. In verse 14, "looked" is a translation of the Greek word (*eido*) that can also mean to get knowledge of, or to understand (see Rev. 1:17). Verses 14 through 19 show how the four principles of wisdom listed in verses 12 and 13 can be applied in a practical, integrated way.

29. In verse 14, the white cloud is detached from the earth, so it represents the position of detached observation. The crown symbolizes the crown chakra (see Rev. 2:10), golden color symbolizes attractive value (Lam. 4:2), hand symbolizes strength (Isa. 28:2), and sharp sickle symbolizes the power of discrimination (Joel 3:13). The Gospels often use the title "Son of man" to designate Jesus (see Rev. 1:13), but verse 14 refers only to "one like unto the Son of man." To overcome glamour or maya, the aspirant must be like unto Jesus, that is, have the faith of Jesus in the sense of being willing to wait for guidance from above (see verse 12).

30. The "temple" is the causal body, so the "angel" coming out of the temple is an abstract thought (see Rev. 11:19, 4:10).

31. Krishnamurti, *Commentaries on Living, First Series*, p. 179, describes the need for acquiring knowledge about suffering: "There is a possibility of being free of suffering only when one observes its process, when one is aware of every phase of it, cognizant of its whole structure." In verse 15, the "earth" is the personality (see Rev. 5:3), so its "harvest" is taken as suffering, because the latter is produced by the personality and corresponds to the "torment" mentioned in verses 10 and 11. The light of self-observation causes self-knowledge to grow (2 Cor. 13:5) just as the light of the sun causes fruits to grow (Deut. 33:14), so "ripe" indicates that the associated self-knowledge is mature, or sufficiently developed.

16. And he that sat on the cloud thrust in his sickle on the earth; and the earth was reaped.

17. And another angel came out of the temple which is in heaven, he also having a sharp sickle.

18. And another angel came out from the altar, which had power over fire; and cried with a loud cry to him that had the sharp sickle, saying, Thrust in thy sharp sickle, and gather the clusters of the vine of the earth; for her grapes are fully ripe.

16. And so the aspirant, while remaining detached, uses his mind to uncover the beliefs that lie behind his suffering.[32]

17. The abstract reasoning of the causal body can discriminate among beliefs, but must wait and be receptive before beginning this work.[33]

18. Eventually, an intuition from the soul, which has power over abstract reasoning, comes to the causal body and instructs that reasoning, saying, "Categorize the observed beliefs as true or false, for all relevant beliefs have been uncovered."[34]

---

32. *ACIM*, vol. I, p. 64, states, "Watch your mind carefully for any beliefs that hinder its accomplishment."
33. The angel is receptive in verse 17, as shown by the message that is received in verse 18. Verse 17 is equivalent to the third step of receptive meditation given in Rev. 4:10.
34. Bailey, *Glamour*, pp. 36–37, describes the role of the soul: "In the process of dissipating glamour, the way of the greatest potency is to realise the necessity to act purely as a channel for the energy of the soul. If the disciple can make right alignment and consequent contact with his soul, the results show as *increased light*. This light pours down and irradiates not only the mind, but the brain consciousness as well." In verse 18, the "altar" is the causal body, "angel" is an intuition from the soul, and "fire" is abstract reasoning (see Rev. 8:3, 5:2, 1:15). The "grapes" are taken as beliefs.

19. And the angel thrust in his sickle into the earth, and gathered the vine of the earth, and cast *it* into the great winepress of the wrath of God.

19. And so the illumined reasoning of the causal body examines the beliefs that underlie the suffering of the personality, discerns those that are false,[35] and transmutes the false beliefs into new principles of wisdom.[36]

---

35. Verses 15 through 19 describe the application of three factors: the light of the knowledge, which is the intellectual perception of the mind; the light of wisdom, which is the abstract reasoning of the causal body; and the light of the intuition, which is the illumination of the soul. Bailey, *Glamour*, p. 192, discusses the same factors: "You have therefore the light of knowledge, the light of wisdom and the light of the intuition, and these are three definite stages or aspects of the One Light. . . . These stages and their corresponding techniques are apt to be misunderstood if the student fails to remember that between them lie no real lines of demarcation but only a constant overlapping, a cyclic development and a process of fusion which is most confusing to beginners."

36. The image of a winepress comes from Isa. 63:3: "I have trodden the winepress alone; and of the people *there was* none with me: for I will tread them in mine anger, and trample them in my fury; and their blood shall be sprinkled upon my garments." The winepress symbolizes the use of the causal body for transmutation. Just as a winepress can transmute grapes into wine, the illumined reasoning of the causal body can transmute false beliefs into new principles of wisdom (see Rev. 3:9, 6:9).

20. And the winepress was trodden without the city, and blood came out of the winepress, even unto the horse bridles, by the space of a thousand *and* six hundred furlongs.

20. This process enables the causal body to gain new principles of wisdom whenever suffering occurs.[37] The new principles act through the mind[38] to bring the personality into alignment with the causal body.[39]

---

37. J. Krishnamurti, *Talks in Saanen 1974* (Beckenham, Kent, England: Krishnamurti Foundation Trust, 1975), pp. 50–51, explains the relationship between wisdom and suffering: "Wisdom is not a thing that you learn from books or from another. Wisdom comes in the understanding of suffering and all its implications." Verse 20 appears to be based on 1 Enoch 100:3: "The horse shall walk through the blood of sinners up to his chest." This text comes from Charlesworth, *The Old Testament Pseudepigrapha*, vol. I. A city in Biblical times was thought of as a refuge from conflict and suffering (Num. 35:26–27). In verse 20, the horses are without, or outside, the city, so they represent activities that bring about suffering. The winepress represents the causal body, so the blood that comes from the winepress symbolizes wisdom (see verse 19).

38. The bridles symbolize the controlling thoughts in the mind, as in James 1:26: "If any man among you seem to be religious, and bridleth not his tongue, but deceiveth his own heart, this man's religion *is* vain."

39. The distance in verse 20 can be interpreted in two ways but with a similar result. First, 1,600 is the product of the square of four, which represents the personality (see Rev. 4:7), and the square of ten, which represents completion (see Rev. 2:10), and so 1,600 furlongs of blood could be interpreted as meaning that the personality has been brought into alignment with the wisdom of the causal body. Second, Charles, *The Revelation of St. John*, vol. II, p. 26, refers to "the *Itinerarium* of Antoninus, according to which Palestine was said to be 1664 stades from Tyre to El-Arish." The *Catholic Encyclopedia*, vol. 8 (New York: Encyclopedia Press, 1913), p. 254, says that Antoninus wrote his book about 570 A.D. Here, "stades" has the same meaning as "furlongs," and El-Arish is located on the borders of Egypt, and so the length of the land settled by the Israelites is approximately 1,600 furlongs, or about 184 miles. Because the Israelites symbolize the personality (see Rev. 2:14), 1,600 furlongs of blood could be taken as meaning that the full range of the personality's activities is aligned with wisdom.

CHAPTER 15

THE SEVEN CHOHANS

The seven chohans, the presiding officers of the spiritual kingdom,
transmit seven realizations that bring about seven trials on the
spiritual journey.

KING JAMES VERSION

1. And I saw another sign in heaven, great and marvellous, seven angels having the seven last plagues; for in them is filled up the wrath of God.

PSYCHOLOGICAL INTERPRETATION

1. The aspirant understands another characteristic of the spiritual kingdom:[1] It has seven presiding officers,[2] sometimes called "chohans,"[3] who bring about seven final trials. With these trials, all suffering from being unrighteous is ended.[4]

---

1. To see means to understand (see Rev. 1:17), and heaven refers to the spiritual kingdom (see Rev. 14:2). "Sign" is a translation of the Greek word (*semeion*) that sometimes means "distinguishing mark" (2 Thess. 3:17, NASB).
2. Chapter 15 is based on Ezek. 9 and 10. Ezek. 9:1–2 states: "Cause them that have charge over the city to draw near. . . . And, behold, six men came from the way of the higher gate, which lieth toward the north, and every man a slaughter weapon in his hand; and one man among them *was* clothed with linen, with a writer's inkhorn by his side." Other versions state more clearly that seven men came altogether (e.g., RSV). The phrase "them that have charge" could be translated as "officers" (Isa. 60:17). Ezek. 9 says that these seven officers were sent by God and administered God's punishment, so they could be called "angels of God" because the word "angel" means "messenger" (see Rev. 1:1). In verse 1,

2. And I saw as it were a sea of glass mingled with fire: and them that had gotten the victory over the beast, and over his image, and over his mark, *and* over the number of his name, stand on the sea of glass, having the harps of God.

2. The aspirant understands the goal of the spiritual journey, which is to overcome all emotional turmoil through the illumination of the mind. He also understands that members of the spiritual kingdom have preceded him on this journey and achieved their own victory over glamour, fantasy, maya, and illusion. Their emotional nature is now calm and reflects the harmony of God.[5]

"great" indicates a position of authority (see Rev. 1:10). Accordingly, the seven angels in verse 1 are similar to, and may be the same as, Ezekiel's seven officers.

3. In Theosophy, the spiritual kingdom, or Hierarchy, is said to have seven officers who preside over it; these officers are sometimes called "chohans," which is a Tibetan word that simply means "Lords." For example, Leadbeater, *The Masters and the Path*, p. 256, says, "The title Chohan is given to those Adepts . . . who hold very definite and exalted offices in the Hierarchy." A. A. Bailey, *The Externalisation of the Hierarchy* (1957; reprint; New York: Lucis Publishing Company, 1976), p. 527, says, "The seven major centres or Ashrams within the Hierarchy are each presided over by Masters of Chohan rank." The seven angels of verse 1 are identified with the seven chohans of Theosophy, because they share the same abilities and functions, as shown by the footnotes for Rev. 15:6, 16.1, 17.1, 21.10 and 21.15.

4. For verse 1, *A Commentary on the Book of the Revelation*, p. 167, interprets the plagues as "trials in which the soul may overcome its Karma." The wrath of God brings suffering for unrighteousness (see Rev. 11:18). The phrase "seven last plagues" in verse 1 is taken to mean that these seven trials induce righteousness and thereby end all suffering from being unrighteous.

5. Bailey, *Initiation, Human and Solar*, p. 24, says, "this Hierarchy is composed of those Who have triumphed over matter, and Who have achieved the goal by the very self-same steps that individuals tread today." In verse 2, the sea of glass, fire, beast, image of the beast, mark of the beast, number of the beast, and harps symbolize stilled emotions, thoughts, glamour, fantasy of wish fulfillment, maya, illusion, and harmony, respectively (see Rev. 4:6; 1:15; 13:1, 13:14, 13:16, 13:17, 5:8).

3. And they sing the song of Moses the servant of God, and the song of the Lamb, saying, Great and marvellous *are* thy works, Lord God Almighty; just and true *are* thy ways, thou King of saints.

3. Members of the spiritual kingdom sing a song of praise and victory, which is what Moses sang when God delivered the Israelites out of bondage to Egypt. It is the song of the soul, because they achieved their deliverance through the power of the soul.[6] They sing: "God is great, marvelous, and omnipotent; divine laws are just and consistent; and divine purpose rules everyone having wisdom.[7]

4. Who shall not fear thee, O Lord, and glorify thy name? for *thou* only *art* holy: for all nations shall come and worship before thee; for thy judgments are made manifest.

4. Who will not respect God and praise his nature? For God alone is holy. Eventually everyone will take the spiritual journey and acknowledge the presence and power of God, because that outcome has been decreed by God and so must occur."[8]

---

6. The Lamb is the soul (see Rev. 5:6). The deliverance of the Israelites out of bondage to Egypt symbolizes the deliverance of the personality out of bondage to illusion, with Moses being a symbol for the soul. Moses' song of praise is recorded in Exod. 15:1–18.
7. In verse 3, the saints represent accumulated wisdom (see Rev. 5:8). The sources for the song in verses 3 and 4 include: Psal. 86:9, 111:3; Deut. 32:4; and Jer. 10:7.
8. Verse 4 is similar in meaning to Isa. 45:23 (NIV): "By myself I have sworn, my mouth has uttered in all integrity a word that will not be revoked: Before me every knee will bow; by me every tongue will swear." Rom. 14:11 is also similar. Verse 4 promises universal enlightenment. Reincarnation appears to be necessary, because one life does not seem to be enough for most people to achieve enlightenment. Other verses that suggest reincarnation are Rev. 3:12 and 14:4.

5. And after that I looked, and, behold, the temple of the tabernacle of the testimony in heaven was opened:

5. After that song is sung, the aspirant understands it, which shows that his causal body has become receptive, or open, to abstract telepathic impressions.[9]

6. And the seven angels came out of the temple, having the seven plagues, clothed in pure and white linen, and having their breasts girded with golden girdles.

6. The seven chohans sequentially transmit their realizations of their divine nature through the aspirant's causal body,[10] bringing about seven trials[11] in which their purity, innocence, holiness, and righteousness are contrasted with the aspirant's lower nature.[12]

---

9. Ezek. 9:3 (ICB) mentions "the place in the Temple where the door opened." In verse 5, "the temple of the tabernacle of the testimony in heaven" is the causal body (see Rev. 11:19). A. A. Bailey, *A Treatise on Cosmic Fire*, p. 192, speaks of "telepathy or that wordless communication . . . in the causal body on the formless levels of the mental plane." In addition, M. Bailey, *A Learning Experience*, p. 19, says, "Great teachers . . . communicate on causal levels." Accordingly, the causal body, which is the organ of abstract thought (see Rev. 4:10), can be used to receive abstract telepathic impressions. In verse 5, "looked" is a translation of the Greek word (*eido*) that can also mean to get knowledge of, or to understand (see Rev. 1:17).

10. Bailey, *Discipleship in the New Age*, vol. I, pp. 91–92, describes the telepathic assistance that a Master, or member of the spiritual kingdom, provides: "Initiation might be defined at this point as the moment of crisis wherein the consciousness hovers on the very border-line of revelation. . . . It is at this process, the Master *presides*. He is able to do nothing because it is the disciple's own problem. He can only endeavor to enhance the desire of the soul by the power of His directed thought."

11. Bailey, *Discipleship in the New Age*, vol. I, p. 92, describes the kind of trial faced by the aspirant: "The demands of the soul and the suggestions of the Master might be regarded as in conflict with the demands of time and space, focussed in the personality or the lower man. You will have, therefore, in this situation a tremendous pull between the pairs of opposites; the field of tension or the focus of the effort is to be found in the disciple 'standing at the midway point.' Will he respond and react consciously to the higher pull and pass on to new and higher areas of spiritual experience? Or will he fall back into the glamour of time and space and into the thralldom of the personal life?"

12. One of the seven officers in Ezek. 9:2 is dressed in linen, whereas all seven angels in verse 6 wear the same outfit including linen. Clothing symbolizes the nature of the wearer (see Rev. 7:9). Linen represents holiness, because it was worn by priests (Exod. 28:39). The Greek word (*lampros*) that is translated as "white" in the KJV appears as "bright" or "shining" in most modern translations (e.g., ICB, NIV, RSV); that word is interpreted here as signifying innocence. Golden girdles signify righteousness (see Rev. 1:13).

7. And one of the four beasts gave unto the seven angels seven golden vials full of the wrath of God, who liveth forever and ever.

7. The aspirant's emotional body adds consecrated feelings that reflect the realizations transmitted by the seven chohans,[13] which in turn reflect the seven aspects or rays of the eternal divine will.[14]

8. And the temple was filled with smoke from the glory of God, and from his power; and no man was able to enter into the temple, till the seven plagues of the seven angels were fulfilled.

8. The aspirant's causal body gains additional principles of wisdom[15] from this transmission of the illumination and power of God.[16] Yet he cannot raise his consciousness into his causal body until he goes through all seven trials brought about by the seven chohans.[17]

---

13. Verse 7 is based on Ezek. 10:7 (ICB): "One living creature put out his hand to the fire that was among them. The living creature took some of the fire. And he put it in the hands of the man dressed in linen." In verse 7, "one of the four beasts" is the emotional body, which is one part of the four-fold personality (see Rev. 4:7). Golden means consecrated, and each vial is a feeling that reflects the corresponding realization transmitted through the causal body (see Rev. 5:8).

14. The "wrath of God" is taken as the will of God, which has seven aspects, or rays (see Rev. 4:3). The chohans' realizations cannot contain the actual divine will, because those realizations are temporal but verse 7 indicates that the divine will is eternal. Leadbeater, *The Masters and the Path*, p. 266, says that the seven chohans are a "reflection" of the seven archangels, who are sometimes called "Dhyan Chohans" (see the footnotes for Rev. 1:4). Similarly, the "seven golden vials full of the wrath of God" are taken to mean that the seven realizations of the chohans *reflect* the seven aspects of the eternal divine will.

15. Verse 8 is based on Ezek. 10:4 (ICB): "The Temple was filled with the cloud. And the courtyard was full of the brightness from the glory of the Lord." As in verses 5 and 6, the temple represents the causal body. Smoke is interpreted as additional principles of wisdom for two reasons. First, "the temple was filled with smoke," just as the causal body is the receptacle for principles of wisdom (see Rev. 4:4). Second, the wrath of God is a form of punishment that brings wisdom, as shown in Prov. 21:11: "When the scorner is punished, the simple is made wise."

16. Ezek 1:28 (NASB) describes the glory of God: "As the appearance of the rainbow in the clouds on a rainy day, so *was* the appearance of the surrounding radiance. Such *was* the appearance of the likeness of the glory of the Lord." The glory of God is taken as illumination, because it is similar to the appearance of radiant light.

17. In verse 8, "to enter into the temple" means to shift the polarization of consciousness from the personality to the causal body. Rev. 9:1 also refers to this shift in consciousness.

CHAPTER 16

THE SEVEN TRIALS

*The aspirant undergoes seven trials that purify his lower nature
and gains increased clarity regarding his physical behavior,
emotions, essential worthiness, self-images, subconscious feelings,
fearful reactions, and inner purpose.*

KING JAMES VERSION

1. And I heard a great voice out of the temple saying to the seven angels, Go your ways, and pour out the vials of the wrath of God upon the earth.

PSYCHOLOGICAL INTERPRETATION

1. The aspirant, via the abstract thinking of his causal body, invokes the assistance of the seven chohans,[1] saying, "Go your ways, and transmit your realizations of the seven aspects or rays of the divine will[2] to my personality.[3]

---

1. Bailey, *The Externalisation of the Hierarchy*, p. 414, predicts, "The science of invocation and evocation will take the place of what we now call prayer and worship." In verse 1, the "temple" is the causal body, the "voice" is abstract thinking, and the "seven angels" are the seven chohans (see Rev. 11:19, 4:10, 15:1). This verse describes the aspirant's invocation, or call, for help from the chohans; the rest of the chapter describes the subsequent evocation, or provision, of help.
2. Bailey says that "Chohans . . . are focal points of powerful Ashrams," "every Ashram radiates some one major quality according to the ray of the Master at the centre," and "the seven major Ashrams . . . are the custodians, transmitters and distributors of the seven ray energies" (*The Externalisation of the Hierarchy*, pp. 522, 527; *Discipleship in the New Age*, vol. I, p. 754). In verse 1, "the vials of the wrath of God" are the chohans' realizations that reflect the seven aspects, or rays, of the divine will (see Rev. 15:7).
3. The realization transmitted by each chohan in chapter 15 brings about one of the seven trials mentioned in chapter 16, is received during one of the seven stages described in chapters 2 and 3, and leads to one

2. And the first went, and poured out his vial upon the earth; and there fell a noisome and grievous sore upon the men which had the mark of the beast, and *upon* them which worshipped his image.

3. And the second angel poured out his vial upon the sea; and it became as the blood of a dead *man*: and every living soul died in the sea.

4. And the third angel poured out his vial upon the rivers and fountains of waters; and they became blood.

2. The first chohan transmits his realization to the aspirant, and it illuminates physical behavior, revealing the disgusting and onerous nature of compulsions and indulgent fantasies.[4]

3. The second chohan's realization illuminates lower emotions, revealing the emptiness and meaninglessness of selfish desires and ambitions, and causing those feelings to pass away.[5]

4. The third chohan's realization strengthens higher emotions like devotion and aspiration so that they become spiritual love.[6]

---

of the seven purificatory experiences discussed in chapters 6 and 8. Thus, chapters 2, 3, 6, 8, 15, and 16 depict the same seven stages of the spiritual journey but from multiple perspectives.

4. Verse 2 is based on Exod. 9:9–11, which describes a plague that causes sores and boils to break out upon people and beasts throughout the land of Egypt. In verse 2, the earth, mark of the beast, and image are the physical body, maya, and fantasy, respectively (see Rev. 3:10; 13:17, 14).

5. Verses 3 and 4 are based on Exod. 7:20–21, which describes a plague that turns the waters of Egypt into blood. Verses 3 and 4 distinguish between lower waters (sea) and higher waters (rivers and fountains). The lower waters are the lower emotions associated with the solar plexus chakra, and the higher waters are the higher emotions associated with the heart chakra (see Rev. 7:1, 17; 8:10).

6. Verses 3 and 4 distinguish between two kinds of blood. In verse 3, the sea is turned into "the blood of a dead man," which means that it is unable to support any life, signifying the emptiness of selfish desires. In verse 4, the higher waters are turned into simply "blood," signifying spiritual love (see Rev. 1:5).

5. And I heard the angel of the waters say, Thou art righteous, O Lord, which art, and wast, and shalt be, because thou hast judged thus.

6. For they have shed the blood of saints and prophets, and thou hast given them blood to drink; for they are worthy.

7. And I heard another out of the altar say, Even so, Lord God Almighty, true and righteous *are* thy judgments.

5. The aspirant reasons, via his causal body, "You, O God, must be impartial and eternal, because of the way you have judged me.[7]

6. For my past decisions have misused the energies of my causal body and personality, and yet you have given them spiritual love to ingest, which conveys the feeling of present worthiness."[8]

7. The aspirant concludes, via his causal body, "I must be worthy, because God is all-powerful and cannot be confused about anything."[9]

---

7. Angel means messenger (see Rev. 1:1), and waters refer to emotions (see Rev. 1:15). "The angel of the waters" in verse 5 is taken as the causal body for three reasons. First, the causal body is the messenger of spiritual love in that it is the channel through which spiritual love passes into the emotional body (see Rev. 22:1). Second, verses 5 and 6 indicate that this angel is capable of abstract reasoning, which is a primary function of the causal body (see Rev. 4:10). Third, the "altar" in verse 7 represents the causal body (see Rev. 6:9, 8:3) and so the word "another" in verse 7 indicates that the voice in verse 5 must also be from the causal body. In verse 5, "righteous" is a translation of the Greek word (*dikaios*) that Vine, *Vine's Complete Expository Dictionary*, p. 534, says "signifies 'just,' without prejudice or partiality."

8. Verse 6 provides the argument for the conclusions reached in verse 5. First, God must be impartial, because he makes spiritual love available to everyone without prejudice. Matt. 5:45 says, "he maketh his sun to rise on the evil and on the good, and sendeth rain on the just and on the unjust." Second, God must be eternal, because he does not condemn. *ACIM*, vol. I, p. 237, says, "You are not guiltless in time, but in eternity." In verse 6, the saints and prophets are the causal, emotional, and vital bodies (see Rev. 11:18).

9. The altar represents the causal body (see Rev. 6:9, 8:3).

8. And the fourth angel poured out his vial upon the sun; and power was given unto him to scorch men with fire.

9. And men were scorched with great heat, and blasphemed the name of God, which hath power over these plagues: and they repented not to give him glory.

10. And the fifth angel poured out his vial upon the seat of the beast; and his kingdom was full of darkness; and they gnawed their tongues for pain,

11. And blasphemed the God of heaven because of their pains and their sores, and repented not of their deeds.

8. The fourth chohan's realization transforms the mind into the searchlight of the soul, with the power to illuminate the thoughts in which self-images appear.[10]

9. Consequently, this searchlight highlights many self-images, their resentment toward the inner light that reveals their flaws, and their excuses and rationalizations.[11]

10. The fifth chohan's realization brings subconscious feelings, which underlie glamour, to the surface of consciousness. These feelings had been repressed because of their gnawing guilt.[12]

11. They embody the fear that God is wrathful and punishing, which is a slanderous aspersion on the true nature of God. These feelings attempt to justify themselves with more excuses and rationalizations.[13]

---

10. Bailey, *The Rays and the Initiations*, p. 460, says, "This lower concrete mind is . . . capable of pronounced soul illumination, proving eventually to be the searchlight of the soul." In verse 8, the sun is a metaphor for the soul, fire represents thoughts, and men are self-images (see Rev. 7:16, 1:15, 3:7).

11. 1 John 1:5: "God is light, and in him is no darkness at all." In verse 9, the name of God represents the nature of God (see Rev. 2:3), which is inner light.

12. 1 John 1:9 states: "If we confess our sins, he is faithful and just to forgive us *our* sins, and to cleanse us from all unrighteousness." Bailey, *Glamour*, pp. 267–268, describes the stage in which "all unresolved problems, all undeclared desires, all latent characteristics and qualities, all phases of thought and of self-will, all lower potencies and ancient habits . . . are brought to the surface of consciousness, there to be dealt with in such a way that their control is broken." In verse 10, the beast is glamour (see Rev. 13:1), and "they gnawed their tongues for pain" depicts gnawing guilt.

13. Perry, *A Course Glossary*, p. 23, explains the relationship between guilt and the fear of God: "The ego persuades us to condemn our brothers, so that we will feel guilty, so that we will punish ourselves with pain, sickness and death. Then, through projection, we see God as standing at the head of this system of 'justice.' We think that He is an angry god, Who believes in our guilt and seeks to punish us for our sins, and Who should thus be feared."

12. And the sixth angel poured out his vial upon the great river Euphrates; and the water thereof was dried up, that the way of the kings of the east might be prepared.

13. And I saw three unclean spirits like frogs *come* out of the mouth of the dragon, and out of the mouth of the beast, and out of the mouth of the false prophet.

12. The sixth chohan's realization illuminates fearful reactions so they can be observed without fear, so that the way of receiving new insights may be prepared.[14]

13. The aspirant sees that illusion, glamour, and maya are forms of fear[15] that operate through his negative, automatic thoughts.[16]

---

14. Prov. 3:25 says, "Be not afraid of sudden fear, neither of the desolation of the wicked, when it cometh." In verse 12, "the great river Euphrates" is the pervasive emotion of fear (see Rev. 9:14). "East" symbolizes the direction from which light comes from the soul (see Rev. 7:2), and so "the kings of the east" represent new insights from the soul.

15. *ACIM*, vol. I, p. 338, says, "Every illusion is one of fear, whatever form it takes." Krishnamurti, *Commentaries on Living, First Series*, p. 113, makes a similar point: "fear breeds illusion." Verse 13 lists the unholy triumvirate: the "dragon" is illusion (see Rev. 12:3); the "beast" refers to the beast out of the sea in Rev. 13:1 and is glamour; and the "false prophet" refers to the beast out of the earth in Rev. 13:11 and is maya.

16. James 3:8 speaks of the power of negative words and thoughts: "But the tongue can no man tame; *it is* an unruly evil, full of deadly poison." The unclean spirits in verse 13 are taken as negative, automatic thoughts, because they are likened to frogs, which are classified as unclean animals (Lev. 11:10) and are known for their endless croaking. Verses 13 through 16 are similar to the series of steps in cognitive therapy. According to A. T. Beck, *Cognitive Therapy of Depression* (New York: The Guilford Press, 1979), p. 4, cognitive therapy teaches each patient the following steps: "(1) to monitor his negative, automatic thoughts (cognitions); (2) to recognize the connections between cognition, affect, and behavior; (3) to examine the evidence for and against his distorted automatic thoughts; (4) to substitute more reality-oriented interpretations for these biased cognitions."

14. For they are the spirits of devils, working miracles, *which* go forth unto the kings of the earth and of the whole world, to gather them to the battle of that great day of God Almighty.

14. These automatic thoughts are deceitful, seeming to work miracles by giving meaning to the unmeaningful and importance to the unimportant. They corrupt all other thoughts and feelings, gathering them to an inner battle during this ongoing period of objective self-observation.[17]

15. Behold, I come as a thief. Blessed *is* he that watcheth, and keepeth his garments, lest he walk naked, and they see his shame.

15. The soul conveys the following insight:[18] "Happiness comes from observing inner battles from above with spiritual love.[19] Otherwise, fear will affect the observation, and the various forms of illusion will take advantage of this weakness."[20]

---

17. The kings of the earth are interpreted as thoughts, because thoughts rule the rest of the personality, molding desires and behavior. Prov. 23:7 makes a similar point: "For as he thinketh in his heart, so *is* he." The world is the emotional body (see Rev. 3:10), so the kings of the world are feelings. The "great day of God Almighty" is the period of objective self-observation that began in verse 12 (see Rev. 6:17).

18. The phrase "I come as a thief" in verse 15 is similar to "I will come on thee as a thief" in Rev. 3:3, which in turn symbolizes the coming of an insight from the soul.

19. *ACIM*, vol. I, p. 497, says, "When the temptation to attack rises to make your mind darkened and murderous, remember you *can* see the battle from above." In verse 15, to watch means to be self-observant (see Rev. 3:2–3), and the garments symbolize spiritual love (see Rev. 3:18).

20. Bailey, *Letters on Occult Meditation*, p. 137, describes the effects of fear: "Fear causes weakness; weakness causes a disintegration; the weak spot breaks and a gap appears, and through that gap evil force may enter. The factor of entrance is the fear of the man himself, who opens thus the door." In verse 15, nakedness symbolizes fear (see Rev. 3:17).

16. And he gathered them together into a place called in the Hebrew tongue Armageddon.	16. The negative, automatic thoughts[21] bring about an inner battle, but its senselessness is quite apparent from the quiet place above the battleground.[22]
17. And the seventh angel poured out his vial into the air; and there came a great voice out of the temple of heaven, from the throne, saying, It is done.	17. The seventh chohan's realization strengthens the intuitive nature,[23] enabling the abstract thoughts of the causal body to become unified in purpose with the heart of God and express the spiritual will.[24]

---

21. Although the KJV uses the word "he" as the second word in verse 16, most modern versions (e.g., RSV, NRS, and NIV) instead use the word "they," which refers back to the "three unclean spirits" of verse 13.
22. The Hebrew name Armageddon literally means "Mountain of Megiddo." The plain of Megiddo was one of the great battlegrounds that involved the people of Israel (Judg. 5:19; 2 Kings 9:27 and 23:29). The geographical fact that there is no Mountain of Megiddo has confused many commentators. For example, G. A. Krodel, *Revelation* (Minneapolis, MN: Augsburg Publishing House, 1989), p. 287, writes: "Yet there is no 'mount' of Megiddo, and the name has eluded all attempts to define it geographically." The people of Israel symbolize the personality (see Rev. 2:14), so the plain of Megiddo symbolizes the inner battleground. Armageddon is taken as the quiet higher place from which that battleground can be clearly seen, because a mountain's vantage point enables the surrounding plain to be clearly seen. *ACIM*, vol. I, p. 498, mentions this higher place: "The senselessness of conquest is quite apparent from the quiet sphere above the battleground."
23. Air symbolizes the intuitive nature (see Rev. 9:2).
24. The only place where the phrase "It is done" appears in the Old Testament is Ezek. 39:8, according to which God speaks this phrase, and so this phrase is a symbol of the spiritual will. The temple in heaven is the causal body (see verse 1), and the throne is the heart of God (see Rev. 1:4). The voice in verse 17 comes from both the temple and throne, indicating that they have been unified by the spiritual will (see Rev. 8:4).

18. And there were voices, and thunders, and lightnings; and there was a great earthquake, such as was not since men were upon the earth, so mighty an earthquake, *and* so great.

19. And the great city was divided into three parts, and the cities of the nations fell: and great Babylon came in remembrance before God, to give unto her the cup of the wine of the fierceness of his wrath.

18. Afterward, kundalini awakens and shifts the polarization of consciousness into the causal body. This shift brings about a greater change in the personality than any previous effort.[25]

19. Emerging thoughts are divided into three categories based upon their content: past, present, and future. Thoughts that look back to the past or forward to the future fall away, leaving only thoughts concerned with the present.[26] The ego, or personal self, is shown to be unreal by God's ideas, which are brought forth through alignment with his will.[27]

---

25. Bailey, *Letters on Occult Meditation*, p. 28, says, "It is by meditation, or the reaching from the concrete to the abstract, that the causal consciousness is entered, and man—during this final period—becomes the Higher Self and not the Personality." In verse 18, "voices, and thunders, and lightnings" symbolize the vital energies of the throat, crown, and heart chakras, whose union within the basic chakra awakens kundalini (see Rev. 7:1, 8:5). "A great earthquake" is a symbol of a great change in the personality due to divine discernment (see Rev. 6:12). For two reasons, this earthquake is taken as the achievement of causal consciousness. First, awakened kundalini is able to bring about causal consciousness (see Rev. 9:1). Second, the verse says that the earthquake is greater than any previous one, and causal consciousness would bring about a change in the personality greater than any previous effort.

26. Verse 19 describes how illusion, which is the dragon of verse 13, is overcome. The first part of this verse is related to Luke 9: 62: "And Jesus said unto him, No man, having put his hand to the plough, and looking back, is fit for the kingdom of God." In verse 19, "great city" refers to an internal center of authority (see Rev. 14:8); it is taken as the collection of thoughts, because thoughts control the personality and can be divided into three parts based upon time. "The cities of the nations fell" is taken as the falling away of thoughts that look back to the past or forward to the future.

27. Babylon is the ego, or personal self (see Rev. 14:8). A cup is a container. The cup in verse 19 is taken as the "little book" in Rev. 10:2, which in turn is the plane of divine ideas. The wrath of God is the will of God (see verse 1).

20. And every island fled away, and the mountains were not found.

21. And there fell upon men a great hail out of heaven, *every stone* about the weight of a talent: and men blasphemed God because of the plague of the hail; for the plague thereof was exceeding great.

20. Feelings of separateness disappear, and feelings of pride are gone.[28]

21. Motives based on spiritual love supersede compulsive patterns, with every motive affirming unity rather than separation. The compulsive patterns blame God's ideas for their loss of egotistical advantages, because they cannot overcome the new spiritual motives.[29]

---

28. Verse 20 describes how glamour, which is the beast of verse 13, is overcome. Islands are feelings of separateness and mountains are feelings of pride (see Rev. 6:14).

29. Verse 21 describes how maya, which is the false prophet of verse 13, is overcome. Yogananda, *Autobiography of a Yogi*, p. 170, says: "Man *is* a soul, and *has* a body. When he properly places his sense of identity, he leaves behind all compulsive patterns." In verse 21, the men are compulsive patterns, and the great hail is spiritual love expressed through physical behavior (see Rev. 11:19). The weight of one talent is taken as the affirmation of unity.

CHAPTER 17

THE EGO

The aspirant learns about the ego, or personal sense of identity,
and its relation to guilt, the chakras, and desires.

KING JAMES VERSION	PSYCHOLOGICAL INTERPRETATION
1. And there came one of the seven angels which had the seven vials, and talked with me, saying unto me, Come hither; I will shew unto thee the judgment of the great whore that sitteth upon many waters:	1. One of the seven chohans comes to the aspirant and says,[1] "Raise your consciousness and I will show you the truth about your ego, which is a controlling, corrupt, and deluded sense of identity supported by your many emotional reactions.[2]

---

1. Bailey, *A Learning Experience*, p. 20, states: "The moment a man has equipped his vehicles with matter of the higher subplanes, he becomes a subject of unremitting care to some ego more advanced than himself, later, as progress is made, to some lesser chela, then to some advanced disciple, next to an initiate, until he reaches his Master." Here, *chela* is a Sanskrit word that means "disciple." In verse 1, the seven angels are the seven chohans, who are the presiding officers of the spiritual kingdom (see Rev. 15:1). The aspirant has passed through the seven trials of chapter 16, and so he has earned the right to be taught directly by a chohan.
2. The word *ego* is Latin for "I" and has several meanings. Although theosophical writers sometimes use the word ego to denote the soul, or higher self, this commentary uses it to denote a false personal sense

2. With whom the kings of the earth have committed fornication, and the inhabitants of the earth have been made drunk with the wine of her fornication.

3. So he carried me away in the spirit into the wilderness: and I saw a woman sit upon a scarlet coloured beast, full of names of blasphemy, having seven heads and ten horns.

2. Your thoughts have become idolatrous through your ego. Your feelings and motives have been deluded by the idolatrous beliefs of your ego."[3]

3. The chohan helps the aspirant achieve a detached state of mind that is receptive to intuitive instruction.[4] Then the aspirant sees that his ego is maintained by his guilt,[5] which is full of judgments and rage, and which controls his seven chakras and all of his desires.[6]

---

of identity, which is consistent with the usage in *ACIM* and recent books on yoga and Buddhism; refer to later footnotes in this chapter for examples. Paul refers to the ego with the phrase "old self" in Eph. 4:22 (NRSV): "You were taught to put away your former way of life, your old self, corrupt and deluded by its lusts." In verse 1, "whore" is taken as symbolizing the ego, because a whore is corrupt and deluded by lusts; "great" indicates control or authority (see Rev. 1:10); and "waters" are emotional reactions (see Rev. 1:15).

3. *ACIM*, vol, II, p. 467, states: "The ego is idolatry." In verse 2, the inhabitants of the earth are taken as feelings and motives, because the earth refers to the personality (see Rev. 5:3). In addition, the kings of the earth, wine, and fornication are thoughts, beliefs, and idolatry, respectively (see Rev. 16:14, 14:8).

4. The wilderness symbolizes a condition of detachment (see Rev. 12:6).

5. The beast in verse 3 is an emotion, because verse 1 says that its rider "sitteth upon many waters" and waters represent emotions. This beast is a form of glamour, because it shares the characteristics of the beast described in Rev. 13:1. This beast can be taken as guilt, because its scarlet color can be a symbol of iniquity, as shown in Isa. 1:18: "though your sins be as scarlet, they shall be as white as snow." Moreover, verse 8 says that this beast ascends "out of the bottomless pit," which is where guilt feelings arise (see Rev. 9:1–11). Perry, *A Course Glossary*, p. 31, says, "Guilt maintains the ego's existence," which is consistent with taking the scarlet beast as guilt and its rider as the ego.

6. Name signifies nature (see Rev. 2:3). Blasphemy refers to slander and verbal abuse (see Rev. 2:9). The seven heads are the seven chakras, and the ten horns are the full range of desires (see Rev. 12:3).

4. And the woman was arrayed in purple and scarlet colour, and decked with gold and precious stones and pearls, having a golden cup in her hand full of abominations and filthiness of her fornication:

5. And upon her forehead *was* a name written, MYSTERY, BABYLON THE GREAT, THE MOTHER OF HARLOTS AND ABOMINATIONS OF THE EARTH.

4. The ego appears very attractive, because it offers self-glorification through prominence, prosperity, and valuable things. Its offering, however, is actually idolatrous and therefore corrupting.[7]

5. The ego's consciousness has a hidden purpose to enslave the personality through great confusion, many kinds of temptation, and idolatrous experiences.[8]

---

7. In verse 4, scarlet is used as a symbol of prosperity, as in 2 Sam. 1:24: "Ye daughters of Israel, weep over Saul, who clothed you in scarlet, with *other* delights, who put on ornaments of gold upon your apparel." Purple is a symbol of royalty or prominence, as in Judg. 8:26: "purple raiment that *was* on the kings of Midian." The Bible often uses the word "abomination" to denote practices that are derived from idolatry; see 2 Kings 23:13, Jer. 16:18, and Luke 16:15.

8. Yogananda, *Autobiography of a Yogi*, p. 160, says, "Though the ego in most barbaric ways conspires to enslave him, man is not a body confined to a point in space but is essentially the omnipresent soul." *ACIM*, vol. I, p. 317, states: "The ego wishes no one well. Yet its survival depends on your belief that you are exempt from its evil intentions." Both quotations speak of the ego as though it has its own consciousness with a hidden evil purpose. In verse 5, "mystery" is a translation of the Greek word (*musterion*) that sometimes means hidden purpose or will (2 Thess. 2:7). Forehead and Babylon signify consciousness and confusion, respectively (see Rev. 7:3, 14:8).

6. And I saw the woman drunken with the blood of the saints, and with the blood of the martyrs of Jesus: and when I saw her, I wondered with great admiration.

6. The aspirant sees that his ego takes pride[9] in his displays of wisdom and his expressions of spiritual love through following Jesus' example.[10] Upon having this insight, he is amazed at how his ego can subvert and corrupt even his spiritual practices.[11]

7. And the angel said unto me, Wherefore didst thou marvel? I will tell thee the mystery of the woman, and of the beast that carrieth her, which hath the seven heads and ten horns.

7. The chohan says to the aspirant, "Why are you amazed? I will tell you the deeper truths about the ego, including its relationship to guilt, chakras, and desires.

---

9. The drunkenness in verse 6 is interpreted as pride, since that is what is offered in verse 4. Sophocles (495–406 B.C.), a Greek tragic poet, also used drunkenness as a metaphor for pride: "The tyrant is a child of Pride who drinks from his great sickening cup recklessness and vanity, until from his high crest headlong he plummets to the dust of hope" (*Oedipus Rex*, line 872, translated by D. Fitts and R. Fitzgerald).

10. In verse 6, the "blood of the saints" is wisdom, because the saints symbolize the causal body (see Rev. 5:8, 14:20). "The blood of the martyrs of Jesus" is spiritual love expressed through following Jesus' example, because blood is a symbol of spiritual love (see Rev. 1:5) and martyr is a translation of the Greek word (*martus*) that means "witness."

11. C. Trungpa, *Cutting Through Spiritual Materialism* (Boston: Shambhala Publications, 1973), pp. 3, 7, describes how the ego can distort even spiritual practices: "Walking the spiritual path properly is a very subtle process. . . . We can deceive ourselves into thinking we are developing spiritually when instead we are strengthening our egocentricity through spiritual techniques. This fundamental distortion may be referred to as *spiritual materialism*. . . . Ego is able to convert everything to its own use, even spirituality."

8. The beast that thou sawest was, and is not; and shall ascend out of the bottomless pit, and go into perdition: and they that dwell on the earth shall wonder, whose names were not written in the book of life from the foundation of the world, when they behold the beast that was, and is not, and yet is.

8. The guilt you see in yourself was imagined by you and is not based on any true belief or idea.[12] When a guilt feeling rises from the subconscious nature into full awareness, it disappears.[13] Nevertheless, feelings that are identified with the physical body, whose underlying beliefs are inconsistent with divine ideas, are enthralled by this form of glamour that was imagined, is unreal, and yet is powerful.[14]

9. And here *is* the mind which hath wisdom. The seven heads are seven mountains, on which the woman sitteth.

9. Here is a clue for those who can understand it. The seven chakras in the vital body are the means through which the ego affects the physical body.[15]

12. B. Haskell, *Journey Beyond Words* (Marina del Rey, CA: DeVorss and Company, 1994), p. 251, refers to the unreal nature of guilt: "Guilt is simply that which you have imagined, And as such, should not, and cannot, exist."
13. The bottomless pit is the subconscious nature from which guilt feelings arise (see Rev. 9:1–3).
14. "They that dwell upon the earth" are feelings of identification with the physical body; the world is the emotional body (see Rev. 3:10). The name of a feeling is its underlying belief, the foundation of the world is the set of all such beliefs, and the book of life is the plane of divine ideas (see Rev. 13:8).
15. Regarding verse 9, Pryse, *The Apocalypse Unsealed*, p. 190, says that "the seven mountains are the seven *chakras*." The physical body is symbolized by the surrounding level ground, which is implicit in the concept of a mountain.

10. And there are seven kings: five are fallen, and one is, *and* the other is not yet come; and when he cometh, he must continue a short space.

10. Each chakra governs a portion of the physical body.[16] Five chakras can be dominated by the throat chakra, from which the ego works. The heart chakra, however, can overcome the ego. Working from the heart chakra requires only a short time before spiritual love replaces the feeling of separateness engendered by the ego.[17]

11. And the beast that was, and is not, even he is the eighth, and is of the seven, and goeth into perdition.

11. Guilt, which was imagined and is unreal, is even a governing center of energy, because it is the cause of all pain. Guilt arises from the misuse of the seven chakras, and so it will eventually go away.[18]

---

16. Most modern versions (e.g., NIV, NRSV, and RSV) use "they" instead of "there" in the first part of verse 10, which makes it clear that the seven heads mentioned in verse 9 are the seven kings mentioned in verse 10. Each chakra is like a king because it exercises dominion, as Bailey, *Esoteric Healing*, p. 194, explains: "Each of the seven major centres governs or conditions . . . the area of the physical body in which it is found."

17. Bailey, *A Treatise on Cosmic Fire*, pp. 986–987, describes the roles of the heart and throat chakras: "The Brother of Light . . . learns to work from the heart, and therefore to manipulate that energy which streams from the 'Heart of the Sun.'. . . The Brothers of the left hand path work . . . from the throat centre almost entirely." Here, brothers of light are people who work under the influence of the soul; the Heart of the Sun is the heart of God; and brothers of the left hand path are people who work under the influence of their egos and so exploit other human beings.

18. Perry, *A Course Glossary*, pp. 30–31, describes guilt's dominion: "Guilt is at the core of our experience here. It maintains linear time, for it rests on *past* mistakes and demands *future* punishment. . . . It is the essence of our perception of the world. It is the sole cause of all pain. . . . Since guilt is the only thing that keeps us from God, the journey home consists entirely of teaching and learning the unreality of guilt through forgiveness."

12. And the ten horns which thou sawest are ten kings, which have received no kingdom as yet; but receive power as kings one hour with the beast.

13. These have one mind, and shall give their power and strength unto the beast.

14. These shall make war with the Lamb, and the Lamb shall overcome them: for he is Lord of lords, and King of kings: and they that are with him *are* called, and chosen, and faithful.

12. The desires that you see in yourself, which govern your activities, do not have any real power. They have the illusion of power, however, as long as guilt seems to have power, because the attainment of desires brings a feeling of superiority that compensates for the feeling of inferiority that guilt imposes.[19]

13. Your desires promote the hidden purpose of your ego, because they reinforce the power and strength of your guilt.

14. Your desires are in conflict with the soul. The soul will eventually overcome them, because it is intrinsically more powerful.[20] When that victory finally comes, your physical, vital, emotional, and mental bodies will be receptive, consecrated, and obedient to the soul."

---

19. A. Adler, *Understanding Human Nature* (1927; reprint; New York: Fawcett Premier, 1954), p. 67, found "the awakening desire for recognition developing itself under the concomitant influence of the sense of inferiority, with its purpose the attainment of a goal in which the individual is seemingly superior to his environment." In other words, the striving for superiority is a compensation for the feeling of inferiority.
20. The phrase "Lord of lords, and King of kings" is similar to several passages in the Old Testament: Deut. 10:17; Psal. 136:2, 3; and Dan. 2:47. Because the Lamb is the soul (see Rev. 5:6), this phrase indicates that the soul is very powerful. Bailey, *A Treatise on White Magic*, p. 231, says, "the soul is omnipotent."

15. And he saith unto me, The waters which thou sawest, where the whore sitteth, are peoples, and multitudes, and nations, and tongues.

15. The chohan also says to the aspirant, "The emotions you see in yourself, which support your ego, are actually the collective emotions of people of every community, race, nation, and language throughout the world.[21]

16. And the ten horns which thou sawest upon the beast, these shall hate the whore, and shall make her desolate and naked, and shall eat her flesh, and burn her with fire.

16. Your desires, which try to compensate for your guilt, bring suffering to your ego, making it lonely and afraid. Frustrated desires cause your ego to ruminate upon itself and to attack itself with its own judgments.[22]

21. Bailey, *Glamour*, p. 72, writes, "It might almost be said that the astral body of a person comes into being as a part of the general world glamour." Here, astral is a synonym for emotional.

22. Yogananda, *Science of Religion*, p. 35, says that "desire is the root of all misery, which arises out of the sense of identification of the 'self' with mind and body." The notion that desire is the root of all suffering is the second of the "four noble truths" of Buddhism; see *The Shambhala Dictionary of Buddhism and Zen*, p. 71. The language of verse 16 comes from Ezek. 23:22–35, which describes the punishment of the adulterous Jerusalem. In verse 16, "naked" means fearful and "fire" refers to thoughts (see Rev. 3:17, 1:15).

17. For God hath put in their hearts to fulfil his will, and to agree, and give their kingdom unto the beast, until the words of God shall be fulfilled.

17. For God has given desires an important role in the evolution of consciousness. Desires reinforce each other and reinforce guilt, thereby providing the incentive to invoke intuitions from the soul. The resulting illumination, when complete, will eliminate all desires.[23]

18. And the woman which thou sawest is that great city, which reigneth over the kings of the earth.

18. Your ego, as you now understand, is an internal center of authority that reigns over your thoughts."[24]

---

23. Yogananda, *Science of Religion*, p. 35, says, "you will ultimately learn to *disown* your own petty desires." Bailey, *Esoteric Healing*, p. 499, says that one can "dissolve the last remaining vestiges of all desire by means of *illumination*." In verse 17, words of God are intuitions from the soul (see Rev. 6:9).

24. In verse 18, "sawest" is a translation of the Greek word (*eido*) that can also mean "understand" (see Rev. 1:17). "Great city" refers to an internal center of authority (see Rev. 14:8).

CHAPTER 18

ELIMINATION
OF THE EGO

The aspirant is illumined by the soul, realizes what must be done,
and takes action to eliminate his ego.

KING JAMES VERSION	PSYCHOLOGICAL INTERPRETATION
1. And after these things I saw another angel come down from heaven, having great power; and the earth was lightened with his glory.	1. After receiving the preceding instruction, the aspirant realizes that the soul is approaching him from the spiritual world. It has great power and illumines his personality.[1]

---

1. In verse 1, the angel, heaven, and earth symbolize the soul, spiritual world, and personality, respectively (see Rev. 8:3, 4:1, 5:3). This verse is similar to Rev. 10:1, because both depict the same stage in which the soul approaches the aspirant.

2. And he cried mightily with a strong voice, saying, Babylon the great is fallen, is fallen, and is become the habitation of devils, and the hold of every foul spirit, and a cage of every unclean and hateful bird.

3. For all nations have drunk of the wine of the wrath of her fornication, and the kings of the earth have committed fornication with her, and the merchants of the earth are waxed rich through the abundance of her delicacies.

2. The soul conveys a clear intuition, saying, "Your ego is a sense of identity without permanent or independent substance. It is the home of false concepts of God, habitat of all wickedness, and domain of every impure and hateful thought.[2]

3. For all parts of your personality have imbibed the idolatrous beliefs of your ego. Your thoughts have become idolatrous through your ego, and your feelings have swelled with pride and vanity through the many things that your ego has made attractive."[3]

---

2. *The Shambhala Dictionary of Buddhism and Zen*, p. 8, states: "In Buddhism the methods for the attainment of liberation concentrate on doing away with the belief in an ego." Such elimination is also the emphasis in this chapter. In verse 2, Babylon represents the ego, or personal self, and its fallen condition indicates that the ego lacks intrinsic substance (see Rev. 14:8). The last part of verse 2 is based on Isa. 13:19–22, which describes a series of strange animals that will live in Babylon after it is overthrown. Devils are false concepts of God (see Rev. 9:20).

3. *The Shambhala Dictionary of Buddhism and Zen*, p. 8, states: "Clinging to the concept of an ego is the primary cause of all passions." In verse 3, fornication symbolizes idolatry (see Rev. 14:8), and the kings of the earth represent thoughts (see Rev. 16:14). The merchants of the earth are taken as feelings, because both merchants and feelings are concerned with the value of things.

4. And I heard another voice from heaven, saying, Come out of her, my people, that ye be not partakers of her sins, and that ye receive not of her plagues.
5. For her sins have reached unto heaven, and God hath remembered her iniquities.

6. Reward her even as she rewarded you, and double unto her double according to her works: in the cup which she hath filled fill to her double.

4. Next, the aspirant uses his abstract thoughts to instruct his personality,[4] saying, "Disengage from the ego, so that you no longer participate in the ego's beliefs and receive its suffering.[5]
5. For the ego's beliefs have been brought up to the intuitive level, where they are shown to be false through comparison with God's ideas.[6]
6. Give back to the ego what the ego gave you, and then some. The ego brought suffering to you; now you must help to eliminate it.[7]

---

4. Bailey, *Esoteric Astrology*, p. 207, describes the role of the personality in the elimination of the ego: "Eventually, the light of the personal self fades out and wanes in the blaze of glory which emanates from the Angel. Then the greater glory obliterates the lesser. This is, however, only possible when the personality eagerly enters into this relation with the Angel, recognises itself as the Dweller and—as a disciple—begins the battle between the pairs of opposites." Here, Dweller and Angel are synonyms for ego and soul. In verse 4, the voice from heaven is the abstract thinking of the causal body, which has power over the personality (see Rev. 10:4, 9:13). In verses 4 through 20, this voice instructs the personality so that it will fulfill the role that is described in Bailey's quotation.
5. The last part of verse 4 echoes Jer. 51:45: "My people, go ye out of the midst of her." The meaning of this part is similar to Goldsmith, *The Infinite Way*, p. 171: "Withdraw from personal consciousness as rapidly as possible. Let 'I' die."
6. In Rev. 16:19, the ego is compared with divine ideas and is shown to be unreal.
7. Verse 6 echoes two passages from Jeremiah: "recompense her according to her work; according to all that she hath done, do unto her" (50:29); "and destroy them with double destruction" (17:18).

7. How much she hath glorified herself, and lived deliciously, so much torment and sorrow give her: for she saith in her heart, I sit a queen, and am no widow, and shall see no sorrow.

7. The ego lived pridefully and wantonly, so give it a like measure of torment and sorrow. The fundamental lie within the ego's thought system is that one can be prideful without being lonely and without feeling sorrow.[8]

8. Therefore shall her plagues come in one day, death, and mourning, and famine; and she shall be utterly burned with fire: for strong *is* the Lord God who judgeth her.

8. Therefore the ego will be purged in three successive stages in a brief time. Then it will be utterly vanquished by illumination, for ideas from God can reveal the illusoriness of the ego in each stage.[9]

9. And the kings of the earth, who have committed fornication and lived deliciously with her, shall bewail her, and lament for her, when they shall see the smoke of her burning,

9. In the first stage, your selfish thoughts, which became idolatrous and prideful through the ego, will miss it and lament its elimination.[10]

---

8. Verse 7 is based on Isa. 47:8: "Therefore hear now this, *thou that art* given to pleasures, that dwellest carelessly, that sayest in thine heart, I *am*, and none else beside me; I shall not sit *as* a widow, neither shall I know the loss of children." Verse 7 describes the ego's fundamental lie, which Perry, *Relationships as a Spiritual Journey*, p. 8, also discusses: "Specialness is the ego's solution to the hole we feel in our souls. . . . Who does not think that being really special would make us really happy? . . . Consider this for a moment: Feeling better than others does not deliver any real sense of worth at all. It only delivers loneliness and guilt."

9. Bailey, *Glamour*, p. 268, says that the personal self, or ego, is destroyed in three stages: "The personal self is now very highly developed; it is a useful instrument which the soul can use. . . . Can it and should it be sacrificed so that (esoterically speaking) its life is lost and in its place consecration and devotion are substituted? This is a hard problem for all disciples to solve, to understand and to make effectively practical. Only by crossing the burning ground three successive times are all impediments to the free use of the will destroyed." In verse 8, "death, and mourning, and famine" are taken as the three stages required to obliterate the ego. Fire is a symbol of thoughts (see Rev. 1:15), so the fire from God is taken as divine ideas.

10. Verses 9 through 19 describe how the kings, merchants, and mariners of the earth will lament over the destruction of the city of Babylon. These verses are modeled after Ezekiel's lamentation over the destruction of the city of Tyre, which mentions the same three groups of mourners (Ezek. 27). Verses 9 through 19 are interpreted as preparing the personality for the destruction of the personal self, or ego, that is about to occur. Cayce had a similar perspective, because he answered "It does" to the question: "Does Rev. 18 give some idea in symbols of the effect of the fall of self—selfishness?" (Van Auken, *Edgar Cayce on the Revelation*, p. 196).

10. Standing afar off for the fear of her torment, saying, Alas, alas, that great city Babylon, that mighty city! for in one hour is thy judgment come.

11. And the merchants of the earth shall weep and mourn over her; for no man buyeth their merchandise any more:

12. The merchandise of gold, and silver, and precious stones, and of pearls, and fine linen, and purple, and silk, and scarlet, and all thine wood, and all manner vessels of ivory, and all manner vessels of most precious wood, and of brass, and iron, and marble,

13. And cinnamon, and odours, and ointments, and frankincense, and wine, and oil, and fine flour, and wheat, and beasts, and sheep, and horses, and chariots, and slaves, and souls of men.

10. Murmuring from a distance in fear of sharing the ego's fate, they will regret that such a key notion, an overarching world-view, could so suddenly be rejected.

11. In the second stage, your selfish feelings will grieve for and mourn the loss of the ego, because no effort will be made to acquire special things like[11]

12. precious metals and gems, ostentatious clothing, exotic and extravagant building materials,[12]

13. spices, perfumes, ointments, wine, fine food, excessive wealth, servants, and affection of human beings.[13]

---

11. Perry, *A Course Glossary*, p. 74, defines "specialness": "The idea of being set apart from others *and* set above others. Having more or being more than others. Specialness is the great pay-off promised by the ego. . . . No price is too dear for us to pay for obtaining specialness. We seek it in our special relationships, where others give us special love and their special selves. . . . We seek it with our body, adorning our body in order to attract it. We also seek it by accumulating idols." Eccles. 12:8 makes a similar point: "Vanity of vanities, saith the preacher; all *is* vanity."

12. Most of the twenty-eight commodities listed in verses 12 and 13 are also mentioned in Ezek. 27:12–22. Verse 12 is the only place where thyine wood is mentioned in the Bible. Thyine wood grows in North Africa, is a member of the cypress family, and is sometimes called the arar tree. In the days of the Roman Empire, this wood was used for luxurious furniture and ornamental work.

13. The word soul is a translation of a Greek word (*psuche*) that is used in many different ways, one of which is to denote the seat of the sentient element that enables us to have feeling, desire, or affection. For examples, see Luke 2:35 and Acts 14:2. Accordingly, gaining the "souls of men" is interpreted as receiving their affection. The point is that we may feel special by receiving affection, such as expressions of warmth and tenderness, from people whom we regard as special due to their beauty, intelligence, wealth, power, or fame.

14. And the fruits that thy soul lusted after are departed from thee, and all things which were dainty and goodly are departed from thee, and thou shalt find them no more at all.

15. The merchants of these things, which were made rich by her, shall stand afar off for the fear of her torment, weeping and wailing,

16. And saying, Alas, alas, that great city, that was clothed in fine linen, and purple, and scarlet, and decked with gold, and precious stones, and pearls!

17. For in one hour so great riches is come to nought. And every shipmaster, and all the company in ships, and sailors, and as many as trade by sea, stood afar off,

18. And cried when they saw the smoke of her burning, saying, What *city is* like unto this great city!

14. The special things that you once desired, the things that seemed attractive and good, will be gone from you and you will no longer seek them.

15. The feelings associated with those things, which had been made prideful by the ego, will stand at a distance and look upon the loss of the ego with fear, sadness, disappointment,

16. and regret, because the feeling of being special will not accompany the possession of special things.

17. For in a short amount of time, this feeling will no longer be valued. In the third stage, your selfish motives, fantasies, and images, which had sought prideful feelings, will be isolated.[14]

18. They will be frustrated when observing the elimination of the ego, for the ego was the center of their existence.

---

14. Paul, in Phil. 2:3 (ICB), advises: "When you do things, do not let selfishness or pride be your guide." In verse 17, ships are motives (see Rev. 8:9), and the sea is the emotional body (see Rev. 4:6).

19. And they cast dust on their heads, and cried, weeping and wailing, saying, Alas, alas, that great city, wherein were made rich all that had ships in the sea by reason of her costliness! for in one hour is she made desolate.

20. Rejoice over her, *thou* heaven, and *ye* holy apostles and prophets; for God hath avenged you on her.

19. These vital impulses will feel a loss, because the ego, which justified seeking prideful feelings through obtaining special things, will be eliminated in a short amount of time.[15]

20. Rejoice over the ego, O illumined personality, along with your holy thoughts, feelings, and motives. For God's ideas have shown the ego to be unreal."[16]

---

15. Verse 19 is based on Ezek. 27:29–30: "And all that handle the oar, the mariners, *and* all the pilots of the sea, shall come down from their ships, they shall stand upon the land; And shall cause their voice to be heard against thee, and shall cry bitterly, and shall cast up dust upon their heads, they shall wallow themselves in the ashes." Casting dust on one's head is a sign of mourning (Josh. 7:6, Job 2:12).

16. In verse 1, the personality was illumined by the great power from "heaven," or the spiritual world. In verse 20, "heaven" is the recipient of the instruction; it is taken as the illumined personality, because the latter has been the recipient of the instruction in verses 4 through 19, and because it has the quality of light from the spiritual world. The apostles are taken as thoughts, because the latter are the leaders of the personality. In addition, the prophets are feelings and motives (see Rev. 11:18).

21. And a mighty angel took up a stone like a great millstone, and cast *it* into the sea, saying, Thus with violence shall that great city Babylon be thrown down, and shall be found no more at all.

21. Having become confident through illumination, the aspirant[17] brings forth spiritual love and casts it into his emotional body, while affirming, "This decisive action will throw out my ego so that it will no longer be found."[18]

---

17. Bailey, *Glamour*, pp. 270–271, clarifies the aspirant's role: "It is the disciple who, in full consciousness, *acts*. He initiates all the processes himself. It is not the Angel or the Dweller but the spiritual man himself who has to employ the will and take definite forward moving action. Once the disciple has taken the necessary steps and moved irrevocably forward, the response of the Angel is sure, automatic and all-enveloping. Complete obliteration of the personal self in three successive stages is the immediate and normal result." Here, Angel and Dweller are synonyms for soul and ego; the "three successive stages" are the ones prepared for in verses 9 through 19, which are also listed in Rev. 11:13. In verse 21, the "mighty angel" is the aspirant, who has become a messenger of the soul (see Rev. 1:1).

18. Verse 21 is based on Jer. 51:63–64 (NRSV): "When you finish reading this scroll, tie a stone to it, and throw it into the middle of the Euphrates, and say, 'Thus shall Babylon sink, to rise no more, because of the disasters that I am bringing on her.'" The "great millstone" in verse 21 is taken as the "great hail" in Rev. 11:19 or 16:21, which in turn is spiritual love expressed through behavior. Thus, the clue given in Rev. 17:10, which is to use spiritual love for overcoming the ego, is applied here. Yogananda, *Autobiography of a Yogi*, p. 252, describes the result: "the true yogic fire ceremony, in which all past and present desires are fuel consumed by love divine."

22. And the voice of harpers, and musicians, and of pipers, and trumpeters, shall be heard no more at all in thee; and no craftsman, of whatsoever craft *he be*, shall be found any more in thee; and the sound of a millstone shall be heard no more at all in thee;

23. And the light of a candle shall shine no more at all in thee; and the voice of the bridegroom and of the bride shall be heard no more at all in thee: for thy merchants were the great men of the earth; for by thy sorceries were all nations deceived.

22. Nevertheless, the aspirant will still enjoy music, songs, festivals, and theaters, but will do so without an ego.[19] He will still function as a craftsman in whatever craft he may have learned, but will do so without an ego. He will still perform the duties of life, but will do so without a personal self.[20]

23. The ego will no longer distort his intellect, and so it will neither corrupt his sexual nature nor use emotions to deceive his personality with false values.[21]

---

19. Verse 22 is partly based on Ezek. 26:13: "And I will cause the noise of thy songs to cease; and the sound of thy harps shall be no more heard." Charles, *The Revelation of St. John*, vol. II, pp. 109–110, argues that "singers" should be the translation used in verse 22 instead of "musicians." In addition, he reports that flute players, or pipers, played at Roman festivals and that trumpeters played at Roman theaters.

20. J. S. Goldsmith, *The Nineteen Hundred Fifty-Nine Infinite Way Letters* (London: L. N. Fowler, 1960), p. 86, appears to summarize all of chapter 18 and especially verse 22: "The personal sense of 'I' is always under the necessity of acquiring, achieving, or attaining. Once this is perceived, it quickly appears that this personal sense is not a part of God's universe, never was, and never can be. We begin to understand that there is a spiritual Presence and a spiritual Power, and, in that perception, the personal sense of 'I' is lost, and spiritual harmony begins to appear. To all appearances, we remain the same as we have always been, except often with improved health of body or improved condition of purse. Outwardly, we are the same person, but inwardly we are now living by Grace."

21. Verses 22 and 23 are partly based on Jer. 25:10: "Moreover I will take from them the voice of mirth, and the voice of gladness, the voice of the bridegroom, and the voice of the bride, the sound of the millstones, and the light of the candle." Yogananda, *Sayings of Yogananda*, p. 64, says, "Saints do not act unwisely, because they have forsaken the ego and have found their true identity in God." In verse 23, the light of the candle represents the intellect, because fire is the symbol of the intellect (see Rev. 1:15). Sorcery refers to bewitchment by false beliefs (see Rev. 9:21).

24. And in her was found the blood of prophets, and of saints, and of all that were slain upon the earth.

24. The personality, causal body, and accumulated wisdom, which once supported the ego, will be applied constructively.[22]

---

22. "Blood of prophets, and of saints" are energies of the personality and causal body (see Rev. 16:6). The "blood of all that were slain upon the earth" is taken as wisdom (see Rev. 14:20).

CHAPTER 19

UNION WITH THE SOUL

The aspirant achieves union with the soul, and the soul eliminates the remaining forms of glamour and maya.

KING JAMES VERSION

1. And after these things I heard a great voice of much people in heaven, saying, Alleluia; Salvation, and glory, and honour, and power, unto the Lord our God:

PSYCHOLOGICAL INTERPRETATION

1. After eliminating his ego, the aspirant telepathically hears the collective voice of the spiritual kingdom, which says, "Let us praise God, because salvation, illumination, honor, and power belong to God.[1]

---

1. Alleluia, often written hallelujah, is derived from Hebrew and means "praise the Lord." The *Revelation* is the only book in the Bible where this word appears.

2. For true and righteous *are* his judgments: for he hath judged the great whore, which did corrupt the earth with her fornication, and hath avenged the blood of his servants at her hand.

3. And again they said, Alleluia. And her smoke rose up for ever and ever.

4. And the four and twenty elders and the four beasts fell down and worshipped God that sat on the throne, saying, Amen; Alleluia.

2. For the ideas from God are true and righteous: they show the unreality of our egos, which corrupt our personalities with idolatry; and our application of those ideas ends our suffering by eliminating our idolatry."[2]

3. Members of the spiritual kingdom repeat their praise of God. They persistently apply divine ideas to themselves and so remain free of their egos.[3]

4. The aspirant's causal body and personality respond by acknowledging God's power, by affirming the value of persistent application of divine ideas, and by praising God.[4]

---

2. The last part of verse 2 is based on Deut. 32:43, which states that "he will avenge the blood of his servants." In verse 2, the great whore is the ego, earth is the personality, fornication is idolatry, and to avenge blood is to eliminate the cause of suffering (see Rev. 17:1, 5:3, 14:8, 6:10). The servants of God are those who apply divine ideas to themselves.

3. The last part of verse 3 is similar to Isa. 34:10, in which God's judgment upon Edom is such that "the smoke thereof shall go up for ever." In verse 3, the phrase "for ever and ever" indicates persistent application of divine ideas. Goldsmith, *The Contemplative Life,* pp. 148–149, emphasizes the value of repeated practice: "I say to you, with all my years of practice behind me, that I would not be prepared when calls come for help if I should fail on any single day of the week to re-establish myself in the consciousness of the Presence and then go further to the realization that whatever problems I meet this day are appearing to me only as mesmeric suggestions."

4. The elders and four beasts refer to the causal body and four-fold personality, respectively (see Rev. 4:4, 4:7). The throne of God is the heart of God (see Rev. 1:4), but it is taken here as a symbol of God's power.

5. And a voice came out of the throne, saying, Praise our God, all ye his servants, and ye that fear him, both small and great.

6. And I heard as it were the voice of a great multitude, and as the voice of many waters, and as the voice of mighty thunderings, saying, Alleluia: for the Lord God omnipotent reigneth.

5. One of the seven chohans, who are messengers from the heart of God, comes to the aspirant,[5] saying, "Practice the presence of God, in addition to your persistent efforts to apply divine ideas to yourself, and bring all of your activities—small and great—into alignment with God's nature."[6]

6. Next, the aspirant telepathically hears the collective voice of the spiritual kingdom, with their spiritual feelings and intention. This voice says, "Praise God for what God's power has accomplished.[7]

---

5. The voice that "came out of the throne" in verse 5 is not God's voice, because it refers to God as an object, and so it must be the voice of a messenger of God. The instructor in verse 5 is interpreted as one of the seven chohans, because Rev. 15:1 indicates that the seven chohans are messengers of God, and because the instructor in chapter 17 is also one of them.

6. The phrase "praise our God" is interpreted as telling the aspirant to practice the presence of God, in the sense of acknowledging God's presence and power in all circumstances. This practice is illustrated in Rev. 11:16–18 and in verses 1–3 of this chapter. Bailey, *Glamour*, p. 180, describes this practice as the "definite and sustained effort to sense the Presence throughout the Universe in all forms and in all presentations of truth." This practice is a deepening and extension of the instruction given in Rev. 2:13. The servants of God are those who apply divine ideas to themselves (see verse 2). Fearing God means to be aligned with God's nature (see Rev. 11:18).

7. The voice of many waters and the voice of mighty thunderings are taken as collective spiritual feelings and intention, respectively (see Rev. 14:2).

7. Let us be glad and rejoice, and give honour to him: for the marriage of the Lamb is come, and his wife hath made herself ready.

7. Let us be glad and rejoice, and give honor to God,[8] for the mystical marriage of the soul is about to occur, and the aspirant's personality is now ready for such union."[9]

8. And to her was granted that she should be arrayed in fine linen, clean and white: for the fine linen is the righteousness of saints.

8. The aspirant's personality has been given the necessary holiness; it is free of fear and guilt.[10] For this holiness is the elimination of the ego by the aspirant, who is still polarized in his causal body.[11]

---

8. The first part of verse 7 is related to Luke 15:10: "I say unto you, there is joy in the presence of the angels of God over one sinner that repenteth." *ACIM*, vol. II, p. 140, describes a similar celebration: "The world and Heaven join in thanking you, for not one Thought of God but must rejoice as you are saved, and all the world with you."

9. *A Commentary on the Book of the Revelation*, p. 175, interprets the marriage of the Lamb in verse 7 as the "union of the evolved self with the Overself." Goldsmith, *The Gift of Love*, p. 43, gives a similar definition for the "mystical marriage": "When an individual under the sense of separation from God becomes reunited in Spirit and finds in the relationship conscious union with God, this is termed the mystical marriage." Bailey, *Esoteric Psychology*, vol. I, p. 314, also uses the expression "mystical marriage": "the spiritually new-born . . . will be those who have brought together, consciously and within themselves, the two aspects of soul and body, and thus have consummated the 'mystical marriage.'" In verse 7, the "Lamb" is the soul (see Rev. 5:6), and "his wife" is the aspirant's personality.

10. Verses 7 and 8 may be based on Ezek. 16:8–10 (NRSV), which compares the Israelites with a betrothed woman: "I pledged myself to you and entered into a covenant with you, says the Lord GOD, and . . . I bound you in fine linen." In verse 8, linen represents holiness (see Rev. 15:6). The word "white" generally appears as "bright" or "shining" in most modern translations and represents innocence, or lack of guilt (see Rev. 15:6).

11. Bailey, *Glamour*, pp. 269–271, describes the situation when the ego is eliminated: "The personality remains; it still exists but is seen no more as of old. The light of the Angel envelops it; the burning ground has done its work and the personality is now nothing more or less than the purified shell or form through which the light, the radiance, the quality and the characteristics of the Angel can shine. . . . When this 'occult obliteration' has taken place, what then is the destiny of the disciple? It is complete control by the soul." In verse 8, "saints" denote the causal body (see Rev. 5:8), so "the righteousness of saints" refers to the right action of the causal body.

9. And he saith unto me, Write, Blessed *are* they which are called unto the marriage supper of the Lamb. And he saith unto me, These are the true sayings of God.

10. And I fell at his feet to worship him. And he said unto me, See *thou do it* not: I am thy fellow servant, and of thy brethren that have the testimony of Jesus: worship God: for the testimony of Jesus is the spirit of prophecy.

9. The chohan tells the aspirant, "Apply the following principle, Happy are they who are united consciously with the soul." He also says, "Such unions are God's great objectives in the evolutionary process."[12]

10. The aspirant tries to praise the chohan, thinking of him as either being Jesus or being like him. But the chohan says: "Do not praise me, for I am your fellow servant and a member of the community in which everyone has the mind of Jesus. Therefore, practice the presence of God, for you can have the mind of Jesus by uniting consciously with the soul."[13]

12. Bailey, *Esoteric Psychology*, vol. I, p. 289, considers the union between soul and personality to be "god's great objective in the evolutionary process." In verse 9, to write means to apply to oneself (see Rev. 1:11).

13. Paul, in Phil. 2:5, writes: "Let this mind be in you, which was also in Christ Jesus." J. S. Goldsmith, *A Parenthesis in Eternity* (New York: Harper and Row, 1963), p. 52, explains: "When we have broken through this human exterior of mind and, through meditation, have contacted the Source, we are then one with the spiritual mind of the universe, which is the mind of the Buddha, of Jesus, of Lao-tse, and the mind of every spiritual saint and seer. We have become one with it when we have become one with the Source of our own life."

11. And I saw heaven opened, and behold a white horse; and he that sat upon him *was* called Faithful and True, and in righteousness he doth judge and make war.

11. After following this instruction, the aspirant realizes that his consciousness has risen up into the soul through an opening in his causal body, which has become a pure vehicle of manifestation for use by the soul.[14] The soul is faithful to God and without fault; it is righteous when judging mental, emotional, and physical activities and making war with the parts that still need correction.[15]

12. His eyes *were* as a flame of fire, and on his head *were* many crowns; and he had a name written, that no man knew, but he himself.

12. The soul has penetrating insight, the capacity to govern the causal body and personality, and a nature that can be known only through an understanding that comes from the soul itself.[16]

---

14. Verse 11 has a meaning similar to Rev. 11:19, which describes the shift of consciousness into the soul. Bailey, *A Treatise on Cosmic Fire*, says, "in considering the causal body, we are dealing specifically with the vehicle of manifestation of a solar Angel" (p. 1110) and uses solar Angel as a synonym for soul (p. 48). In verse 11, heaven refers to the causal body (see Rev. 5:3), and the horse is also taken as the causal body, because the latter is the vehicle of the soul. White means pure (see Table 4).

15. According to verse 11, the soul engages in both righteous judgment and war. John 7:24 refers to righteous judgement: "Judge not according to the appearance, but judge righteous judgment." Collins, *Light on the Path*, pp. 9–10, refers to the soul as an inner warrior: "Stand aside in the coming battle, and though thou fightest be not the warrior. Look for the warrior and let him fight in thee. Take his orders for battle and obey them. Obey him not as though he were a general, but as though he were thyself, and his spoken words were the utterance of thy secret desires; for he is thyself, yet infinitely wiser and stronger than thyself."

16. Bailey, *Discipleship in the New Age*, vol. I, p. 140, speaks of "that aspect of the soul which expresses itself in understanding." In verse 12, eyes of flame symbolize penetrating insight (see Rev. 1:14), and the name of anything represents its nature (see Rev. 2:3).

13. And he *was* clothed with a vesture dipped in blood: and his name is called The Word of God.

14. And the armies *which were* in heaven followed him upon white horses, clothed in fine linen, white and clean.

15. And out of his mouth goeth a sharp sword, that with it he should smite the nations: and he shall rule them with a rod of iron: and he treadeth the winepress of the fierceness and wrath of Almighty God.

13. The soul is clothed with spiritual love[17] and its nature is the Will of God.[18]

14. The soul is aided by other spiritual forces like the spiritual kingdom, divine ideas, chohans, and archangels. These forces also operate through pure vehicles of manifestation and are holy by being free of guilt and fear.

15. Intuitions derive from the soul that can discriminate between truth and illusion. With these intuitions, the soul can discipline all aspects of the personality, rule them via awakened kundalini in the spinal column, and then use the causal body to transmute any imperfections into new principles of wisdom.[19]

---

17. Blood is spiritual love (see Rev. 1:5, 5:9).

18. J. S. Goldsmith, *The Nineteen Hundred Fifty-Four Infinite Way Letters* (1954; reprint; Austell, GA: Acropolis Books, 1996), p. 7, says, "This Selfhood is your Soul identity, and God's Will is forever functioning through It." Bailey, *Discipleship in the New Age*, vol. I, p. 391, makes a similar point: "the will of your soul . . . is the Will of God." Accordingly, the Word of God in verse 13 is interpreted as the Will of God. In Rev. 6:9, the word of God, without the capitalization, is an intuition from the soul.

19. Verse 15 fulfills the prediction made in Rev. 12:5, which is that the soul will rule via awakened kundalini in the spinal column. The "sharp sword" symbolizes the soul's intuitions (see Rev. 1:16). The "rod of iron" is the spinal column with awakened kundalini (see Rev. 2:27). The "winepress of the fierceness and wrath of Almighty God" represents the use of the causal body for transmuting imperfections into new wisdom (see Rev. 14:19).

16. And he hath on *his* vesture and on his thigh a name written, KING OF KINGS, AND LORD OF LORDS.

17. And I saw an angel standing in the sun; and he cried with a loud voice, saying to all the fowls that fly in the midst of heaven, Come and gather yourselves together unto the supper of the great God;

18. That ye may eat the flesh of kings, and the flesh of captains, and the flesh of mighty men, and the flesh of horses, and of them that sit on them, and the flesh of all *men, both* free and bond, both small and great.

16. For all these reasons, the soul is omnipotent, both outwardly and inwardly.[20]

17. The aspirant sees that the soul is acting through him as a channel for God.[21] The soul sends a clear intuition to the abstract thoughts of the causal body, saying, "Come and learn from the imperfections that are revealed by divine ideas,[22]

18. that you may extract wisdom from the pride of power, the pride of superiority, the pride of strength, the pride of both following and leading, the pride of both independence and association, and the pride of both humility and authority."[23]

---

20. Isa. 11:5 may provide the background for a name written on clothing and the thigh: "And righteousness shall be the girdle of his loins, and faithfulness the girdle of his reins." The clothing and thigh are taken as signifying outward and inward, respectively. The name "King of kings, and Lord of lords" signifies omnipotence (see Rev. 17:14).

21. Yogananda, *The Science of Religion*, pp. 54–55, writes: "The man of Self-realization knows that God is the Doer—all power to perform actions flows into us from Him. He that is centered in his Spiritual self feels himself to be the *dispassionate seer* of all actions, whether he is seeing, hearing, feeling, smelling, tasting, or undergoing various other experiences on earth." In verse 17, the angel is the soul (see Rev. 8:3). The sun is a symbol with several meanings; in addition to symbolizing external teachers and the soul (see Rev. 6:12, 7:16), the sun can also symbolize God. For example, Psal. 84:11 says, "For the LORD God *is* a sun and shield"; and Blavatsky, *The Secret Doctrine*, vol. I, p. 479, says, "The Sun is . . . the symbol of Divinity."

22. Verses 17 and 18 are based on Ezek. 39:17–20 (NRSV): "Speak to the birds of every kind and to all the wild animals: Assemble and come, gather from all around to the sacrificial feast that I am preparing for you. . . . You shall eat the flesh of the mighty, and drink the blood of the princes of the earth. . . . And you shall be filled at my table with horses and charioteers, with warriors and all kinds of soldiers." The fowls of heaven are taken as abstract thoughts, because the causal body, denoted by heaven, is the instrument of such thoughts (see Rev. 4:10, 5:3).

23. Some of these forms of pride are also listed in Rev. 6:15.

19. And I saw the beast, and the kings of the earth, and their armies, gathered together to make war against him that sat on the horse, and against his army.

20. And the beast was taken, and with him the false prophet that wrought miracles before him, with which he deceived them that had received the mark of the beast, and them that worshipped his image. These both were cast alive into a lake of fire burning with brimstone.

21. And the remnant were slain with the sword of him that sat upon the horse, which *sword* proceeded out of his mouth: and all the fowls were filled with their flesh.

19. The aspirant observes the resistance of factors that attempt to subvert the soul and its forces—glamour, associated thoughts, and their other allies still present within his personality.[24]

20. Glamour is overcome and also maya, which had fulfilled desires fostered by glamour and brought about compulsive behavior and fantasy.[25] Both glamour and maya are cast into the triple light of the intuition, which blends the lights of God, soul, and personality.[26]

21. The remaining imperfections are eliminated with intuitions that operate through the causal body and come from the soul; and the abstract thoughts of the causal body are filled with new wisdom extracted from those imperfections.

---

24. Goldsmith, *A Parenthesis in Eternity*, p. 220, describes the stage depicted in verses 19 to 21: "When this experience of living in God first comes to us, it is disturbing because . . . now we are 'dying' all over again. This is not only an annihilation of our undesirable humanhood, but it is also an annihilation even of our good humanhood, and at first it is frightening and disconcerting as veil after veil drops away, and we come face to face with naked truth." In verse 19, the beast and kings of the earth refer to glamour and thoughts, respectively (see Rev. 13:1, 16:14).

25. The false prophet, mark, and image are maya, compulsive behavior, and fantasy, respectively (see Rev. 16:13; 13:16, 14).

26. The *Revelation* is the only book in the Bible that has the notion of a "lake of fire," but extra-Biblical Jewish writings have similar concepts: 1 Enoch 54:1 refers to the place of judgment as "a valley, deep and burning with fire"; and 2 Enoch 10:2 describes a place of terror including "a river of fire." These texts come from Charlesworth, *The Old Testament Pseudepigrapha*, vol. I. Bailey, *Glamour*, p. 181, says that "the triple light of the intuition . . . is formed by the blending of the light of the personal self, focussed in the mind, the light of the soul, focussed in the Angel, and the universal light which the Presence emits." In verse 20, fire is taken as the thoughts of God (see Rev. 18:8), lake as the soul (since verse 17 indicates that the soul is a channel for God), and burning brimstone as the light of the personality, and so the "lake of fire burning with brimstone" is taken as the triple light of the intuition.

CHAPTER 20

DEATH AND RESURRECTION

Following a period of reigning with the soul, the aspirant senses a subconscious feeling that rises to the level of consciousness and judges it according to whether its underlying beliefs are consistent with God's ideas.

KING JAMES VERSION

1. And I saw an angel come down from heaven, having the key of the bottomless pit and a great chain in his hand.

PSYCHOLOGICAL INTERPRETATION

1. The aspirant sees an intuition come down from the soul. It exercises authority over his subconscious nature and has power to restrict the influence of what is there.[1]

---

1. Verses 1 and 2 may be based on 2 Pet. 2:4: "God spared not the angels that sinned, but cast *them* down to hell, and delivered *them* into chains of darkness, to be reserved unto judgment." Verse 1 is similar to Rev. 9:1, because in both verses the aspirant sees something coming down from heaven with the key of the bottomless pit. The aspirant is in a more advanced position in verse 1 than in Rev. 9:1, because he sees an "angel" rather than a "star." As interpreted here, an angel is an intuition (see Rev. 5:2), whereas a star is the light of self-observation. The bottomless pit is the subconscious nature (see Rev. 9:1), and the key is a symbol of authority, as in Isa. 22:22 and Matt. 16:19.

2. And he laid hold on the dragon, that old serpent, which is the Devil, and Satan, and bound him a thousand years,

2. This intuition ensures that illusion—which is a tempter, a liar, and an adversary[2]—cannot interfere with the fulfillment of the external, mental, and subconscious conditions needed for each subconscious feeling to emerge.[3]

---

2. Verse 2 brings together four of the symbols by which illusion is represented in the *Revelation*: dragon, serpent, Devil, and Satan. Table 6 lists the verses with those symbols.

3. The duration of "a thousand years" is significant, because it occurs six times in verses 2 through 7. Many commentaries have interpreted this duration in a literal way, which brought about the various millenarian movements in Christianity. A symbolic interpretation, however, is given here. Ten means completeness (see Rev. 2:10) and a thousand is ten cubed, so a thousand represents completeness with respect to three processes simultaneously (see Rev. 7:4, 11:13). A subconscious feeling rises to consciousness when an event in the external world triggers a thought in the mind, which then draws out an associated memory from the subconscious nature. For this combination to occur, favorable conditions must be present simultaneously in all three domains: external, mental, and subconscious. Accordingly, "a thousand years" is taken as the fulfillment of those conditions.

3. And cast him into the bottomless pit, and shut him up, and set a seal upon him, that he should deceive the nations no more, till the thousand years should be fulfilled: and after that he must be loosed a little season.

3. The soul's intuition confines illusion to the subconscious nature and closes the channel through which its deceptive power operates. The influence of illusion is sealed while it is confined, so that it can no longer deceive the aspirant into suppressing or denying any subconscious feeling.[4] Consequently, each subconscious feeling emerges when its needed conditions are fulfilled. This emergence brings illusion into the conscious level for a brief time.[5]

---

4. Verse 3 is related to Matt. 27:66 (NIV): "So they went and made the tomb secure by putting a seal on the stone and posting the guard." In Rev. 16:13, the mouth of the dragon symbolizes the channel through which the deceptive power of the dragon operates. "Shut him up" in verse 3 is interpreted as closing that channel.

5. Bailey, *Esoteric Astrology*, pp. 207–208, describes the stage depicted in verse 3: "The disciple puts himself into the positive or conditioning environment wherein the trials and the discipline are unavoidable and inevitable. When the mind has reached a relatively high stage of development, the memory aspect is evoked in *a new and conscious manner* and then every latent pre-disposition, every racial and national instinct, every unconquered situation and every controlling fault rises to the surface of consciousness and then—the fight is on." This quotation mentions favorable conditions that are present simultaneously in the external, mental, and subconscious domains, and so it supports the symbolic meaning of 1000 given earlier.

4. And I saw thrones, and they sat upon them, and judgment was given unto them: and *I saw* the souls of them that were beheaded for the witness of Jesus, and for the word of God, and which had not worshipped the beast, neither his image, neither had received *his* mark upon their foreheads, or in their hands; and they lived and reigned with Christ a thousand years.

4. The aspirant sees a hierarchical order formed by the soul, and the causal, mental, emotional, vital, and physical bodies, with each element governing its immediate successor. He also sees their new lives.[6] The causal and mental bodies have lost their leadership positions, because decisions are now made the way Jesus makes them— with intuitions from the soul.[7] The emotional body is no longer ruled by glamour; the vital body is no longer impelled by fantasies of wish-fulfillment; the physical body no longer has its consciousness and strength controlled by maya. This period of reigning with the soul only lasts, however, until the emergence of a subconscious feeling.[8]

---

6. The word soul is a translation of the Greek word (*psuche*) that is sometimes used to denote the seat of the new life, such as in Luke 21:19, 1 Pet. 2:11, and 3 John 2. Accordingly, "souls" in verse 4 are interpreted as new lives.

7. *ACIM*, vol. III, p. 89, states: "Jesus is the manifestation of the *Holy Spirit*." Here, Holy Spirit has the same meaning as soul (see Rev. 2:7).

8. Goldsmith, *The Contemplative Life*, p. 200, writes: "There is within every one of us this Infinite Invisible which, in Christian mysticism, is called the Christ or Spirit of God in man. . . . No change takes place in our outer life except in proportion to our awareness of the inner Presence and Power, but as we awaken to this Spirit within us, It becomes the very substance, life, law, and activity of our experience in the without." In verse 4, word of God, beast, image, mark, and Christ refer to intuition from the soul, glamour, fantasy, maya, and soul, respectively (see Rev. 6:9, 13:1, 13:14, 13:17, 11:15).

5. But the rest of the dead lived not again until the thousand years were finished. This *is* the first resurrection.

6. Blessed and holy *is* he that hath part in the first resurrection: on such the second death hath no power, but they shall be priests of God and of Christ, and shall reign with him a thousand years.

5. Subconscious feelings do not have any influence during a period of reigning with the soul. This period is the first resurrection considered in this chapter.[9]

6. The aspirant is happy and abides in spiritual love while he participates in the first resurrection. He therefore has no need for the second death, which is the progressive ending of selfishness. Instead, he shows forth the blessings of God and the soul, but only until a subconscious feeling emerges.[10]

---

9. The first resurrection is emergence into the world of the soul. Paul, in Eph. 2:4–6, writes about this type of resurrection: "But God, who is rich in mercy, for his great love wherewith he loved us, Even when we were dead in sins, hath quickened us together with Christ, And hath raised *us* up together, and made *us* sit together in heavenly *places*."

10. 1 Pet. 2:9 states: "But ye *are* a chosen generation, a royal priesthood, an holy nation, a peculiar people; that ye should shew forth the praises of him who hath called you out of darkness into his marvellous light." In verse 6, blessed and holy refer to happiness and spiritual love, respectively (see Rev. 1:3, 3:7). The second death was first mentioned in Rev. 2:11.

7. And when the thousand years are expired, Satan shall be loosed out of his prison,

8. And shall go out to deceive the nations which are in the four quarters of the earth, Gog and Magog, to gather them together to battle: the number of whom *is* as the sand of the sea.

7. When a period of reigning with the soul is over, a subconscious feeling rises to the level of consciousness,[11]

8. deceives the four principal parts of the personality, and musters them for battle.[12] They thus become forces of illusion and guilt,[13] consisting of many thoughts, feelings, and motives.[14]

---

11. Goldsmith, *A Parenthesis in Eternity*, p. 221, describes the stage depicted in verses 7 to 9: "This is a difficult period because we have glimpses of what spiritual living can be, and yet at the same time we have the frustrating experience of not being able to live in the Spirit continuously. While our old unillumined self does not dominate the scene, its shadow still lingers, and we are often tempted to indulge in the old habits and modes of life." The emergence of a subconscious feeling in verse 7 is the second resurrection considered in this chapter.

12. The NEB provides a clearer translation of verse 8: "and he will come out to seduce the nations in the four quarters of the earth and to muster them for battle, yes, the hosts of Gog and Magog, countless as the sands of the sea." The four quarters of the earth are taken as the mental, emotional, vital, and physical bodies, because the earth is the personality (see Rev. 4:7, 5:3).

13. According to Ezek. 38–39, Magog is a country or tribe that assails the people of Israel, and Gog is their chief prince; the people of Magog have a calvary and are armed with bows and arrows. The people of Israel represents the personality (see Rev. 2:14). Magog is taken as guilt, which is the role played by the locusts in Rev. 9:3–11, because Magog and the locusts share two characteristics: a calvary, signifying preparedness for battle; and arrows (or stingers), signifying self-condemnation. Gog, being the chief prince, is taken as the illusory belief that governs guilt, which is the role of Abaddon in Rev. 9:11.

14. Many commentators have not understood why an additional battle is necessary in chapter 20, even after the kings of the earth and their armies were killed in Rev. 19:19–21. For example, Mounce, *The Book of Revelation*, p. 363, writes, "It is futile to speculate just why there needs to be yet another conflict." Bailey, *The Rays and the Initiations*, p. 452, explains: "The unalterable tendency of the subconscious nature to penetrate to the surface of consciousness [is] a reflex activity in the establishing of continuity of consciousness. This reflex activity of the lower nature corresponds to the development of continuity between the superconscious and the consciousness which develops upon the Path of Discipleship." Chapter 19 describes the development of continuity between the superconscious (or soul) and the consciousness (or personality). Chapter 20 describes the reflex action of the subconscious nature, which brings about the additional battle.

9. And they went up on the breadth of the earth, and compassed the camp of the saints about, and the beloved city: and fire came down from God out of heaven, and devoured them.

9. During such a period, illusion and guilt affect the entire personality, limit the wisdom of the causal body, and disrupt the harmony of the preceding period of reigning with the soul.[15] They are, however, destroyed by illuminating ideas coming down from God.[16]

10. And the devil that deceived them was cast into the lake of fire and brimstone, where the beast and the false prophet *are*, and shall be tormented day and night for ever and ever.

10. In particular, any false belief associated with a subconscious feeling is cast into the triple light of the intuition, which is how glamour and maya were handled in the preceding chapter. The first step in this process is to have an attitude of perpetual vigilance, which means continually examining every thought, feeling, and motive in the personality.[17]

---

15. The camp of the saints is the causal body, because the saints constitute wisdom (see Rev 5:8). The beloved city is the New Jerusalem, which is the spiritually transformed personality (see Rev. 3:12). Rev. 13:7 also contains the notion that illusion can subvert both the causal body and personality.
16. The last part of verse 9 is based upon Ezek. 39:6: "And I will send a fire on Magog, and among them that dwell carelessly in the isles: and they shall know that I *am* the LORD." See also Ezek. 38:22. Fire from God represents divine ideas (see Rev. 18:8).
17. 1 Pet. 5:8 states: "Be sober, be vigilant; because your adversary the devil, as a roaring lion, walketh about, seeking whom he may devour." *ACIM*, vol. I, p. 111, makes a similar point: "Vigilance is not necessary for truth, but it is necessary against illusions." In verse 10, the torment that the devil receives "day and night for ever and ever" is the result of perpetual vigilance. The "lake of fire and brimstone" is the triple light of the intuition (see Rev. 19:20).

11. And I saw a great white throne, and him that sat on it, from whose face the earth and the heaven fled away; and there was found no place for them.

12. And I saw the dead, small and great, stand before God; and the books were opened: and another book was opened, which is *the book* of life: and the dead were judged out of those things which were written in the books, according to their works.

11. After observing any emergent feeling, the aspirant reestablishes his awareness of the presence of God—immanent and transcendent[18]—in which all dualities are absorbed, and all distinctions and differences lose their meaning.[19]

12. Afterward, the aspirant is ready to compare the emergent feelings—small and great—with divine standards. The beliefs underlying those feelings are identified, the plane of divine ideas is accessed,[20] and the emergent feelings are judged according to whether their underlying beliefs are consistent with divine ideas.[21]

---

18. "A great white throne" is the heart of God, which is God immanent; "him that sat on it" is God transcendent; and "whose face" is the presence of God (see Rev. 1:4, 4:2, 6:16). Paul, in 2 Cor. 12:3–5, seems to describe the experience of contacting this presence: "And I knew such a man, (whether in the body, or out of the body, I cannot tell: God knoweth); How that he was caught up into paradise, and heard unspeakable words, which it is not lawful for a man to utter. Of such an one will I glory: yet of myself I will not glory, but in mine infirmities."

19. Verse 11 is similar to Isa. 51:6: "the heavens shall vanish away like smoke, and the earth shall wax old like a garment." Bailey, *Discipleship in the New Age*, vol I, p. 390, describes how the presence of God dissolves all dualistic thinking: "But, behind them all looms—immanent, stupendous, and glorious—that of which these dualities are but the aspects: the Presence, immanent yet transcendent, of Deity. In the nature of this *One*, all dualities are absorbed and all distinctions and differences lose their meaning." In verse 11, earth and heaven are taken simply as symbolizing duality.

20. Verse 12 may be based on Dan. 7:10: "the judgment was set, and the books were opened." In verse 12, "the dead" are emergent feelings, and "the books" are the underlying beliefs. The "book of life" is the "little book" encountered in Rev. 10:2, which is the plane of divine ideas (see Rev. 13:8). John 8:32 states: "And ye shall know the truth, and the truth shall make you free." If "the truth" is a divine idea, then this quotation is similar to verse 12.

21. Verse 12 is closely related to Platonic philosophy, which associates divinity with the highest objects of knowledge and rational aspiration; in English translations, these objects are generally denoted as "Ideas" or "Forms." In the *Phaedo*, Plato states that the Ideas are changeless (p. 78d), are revealed to us by thought rather than sensation (p. 79a), are different from both body and soul (p. 79b-c), and serve as absolute standards of comparison (p. 75c-d). For example, these standards include absolute beauty, goodness, uprightness, and holiness.

13. And the sea gave up the dead which were in it; and death and hell delivered up the dead which were in them: and they were judged every man according to their works.

14. And death and hell were cast into the lake of fire. This is the second death.

15. And whosoever was not found written in the book of life was cast into the lake of fire.

13. Eventually, the emotional body gives up all of its repressed contents, including all buried feelings of limitation and guilt. These feelings are judged according to their consistency with the divine standards.[22]

14. Consequently, limitation and guilt are dispelled by the triple light of the intuition.[23] This elimination is the second death.

15. And anything found to be inconsistent with God's ideas is also dispelled by the triple light of the intuition.

---

22. Although many commentators have attempted to give a literal meaning to the symbols in this chapter, it is difficult to do so in a coherent way. As Krodel, *Revelation*, p. 338, observes: "No answers are given to silly timetables or questions such as: How can there still be a sea to give up the dead (20:13), when the earth has already vanished (20:11)?" The psychological meaning of verse 13 is similar to Eccl. 12:14: "For God shall bring every work into judgment, with every secret thing, whether *it be* good, or whether *it be* evil." In verse 13, the sea, dead, death, and hell represent the emotional body, repressed feelings, limitation, and guilt, respectively (see Rev. 4:6, 9:6, 1:18).

23. Paul, in 1 Cor. 15:26, says, "The last enemy *that* shall be destroyed *is* death." The destruction of death and hell, representing limitation and guilt, in verse 14 fulfills the promise made in Rev. 1:18.

CHAPTER 21

SPIRITUAL TRANSFORMATION

*The aspirant completes the spiritual journey; John returns to his
normal consciousness and receives further instruction.*

KING JAMES VERSION

1. And I saw a new heaven and a new earth: for the first heaven and the first earth were passed away; and there was no more sea.

PSYCHOLOGICAL INTERPRETATION

1. The aspirant realizes that the spiritual and physical worlds are united, for his earlier perceptions of separate worlds have passed away.[1] He realizes that the emotional world does not exist.[2]

---

1. The first part of verse 1 echoes Isa. 65:17: "For, behold, I create new heavens and a new earth: and the former shall not be remembered, nor come into mind." In verse 1, "saw" means understand, and "heaven" and "earth" are the spiritual and physical worlds, respectively (see Rev. 1:17, 10:6). The Gospel of Thomas, logion 113, states: "the Father's kingdom is spread out upon the earth, and people don't see it." This text is taken from R. J. Miller, ed., *The Complete Gospels: Annotated Scholars Version* (Santa Rosa, CA: Polebridge Press, 1994). This quotation suggests that heaven and earth are united but generally misperceived.
2. In verse 1, the "sea" is the emotional world (see Rev. 10:6), which is sometimes called the "astral plane." Bailey, *A Treatise on White Magic*, p. 615, writes, "The secret of the Master is the discovery that there is no astral plane; he finds that the astral plane is a figment of the imagination and has been created through the uncontrolled use of the creative imagination." In Bailey's quotation, the Master is any member of the spiritual kingdom, implying that the insight in the last part of verse 1, which is the realization that the emotional world does not exist, is a distinguishing insight of that kingdom. Thus, verse 1 suggests that the aspirant has become a member of the spiritual kingdom.

2. And I John saw the holy city, new Jerusalem, coming down from God out of heaven, prepared as a bride adorned for her husband.

2. The aspirant also realizes that his personality is transformed, embodying ideas coming down from God out of the spiritual world. It is thus prepared as an instrument through which the soul can manifest.[3]

3. And I heard a great voice out of heaven saying, Behold, the tabernacle of God *is* with men, and he will dwell with them, and they shall be his people, and God himself shall be with them, *and be* their God.

3. The aspirant hears the soul say,[4] "As you can see, your personality has become a sanctuary in which divine ideas dwell. Your thoughts, feelings, and activities will demonstrate the power of God to the external world, for they will embody and express ideas from God.[5]

4. And God shall wipe away all tears from their eyes; and there shall be no more death, neither sorrow, nor crying, neither shall there be any more pain: for the former things are passed away.

4. God's ideas will eliminate all emotional reactions that prevent clear perception. There will be no more feelings of limitation, sorrow, self-pity, or pain, for they are gone."[6]

---

3. The KJV includes the name John in verse 2; most modern translations (e.g., ASV, NIV, and RSV), however, are based on a different Greek text that does not include this name in the verse. Both the New Jerusalem and adorned bride denote the spiritually transformed personality (see Rev. 3:12, 19:7), so the corresponding husband must be the soul.

4. A "voice out of heaven" can denote either the soul (see Rev. 18:1–2) or causal body (see Rev. 10:4). The word "great" suggests that the voice in verse 3 is the soul.

5. Verse 3 is based upon Lev. 26:11–12: "And I will set my tabernacle among you: and my soul shall not abhor you. And I will walk among you, and will be your God, and ye shall be my people." The meaning of verse 3 is similar to Bailey, *Esoteric Psychology*, vol. II, p. 267: "the personality, when fully developed, is the 'appearance of God on earth.'" In verse 3, the "men" are taken as the thoughts, feelings, and activities of a fully-developed personality.

6. Collins, *Light on the Path*, p. 29, states, "Before the eyes can see they must be incapable of tears." In verse 4, a tear is taken as an emotional reaction, because water is a symbol of emotions (see Rev. 1:15). Death symbolizes limitation (see Rev. 1:18).

5. And he that sat upon the throne said, Behold, I make all things new. And he said unto me, Write: for these words are true and faithful.

5. The soul, which now occupies its rightful place of rulership, also says, "As you can see, my intuitions enable you to meet everything anew."[7] The soul then says, "Note this effect in yourself, because it is your present experience."[8]

6. And he said unto me, It is done. I am Alpha and Omega, the beginning and the end. I will give unto him that is athirst of the fountain of the water of life freely.

6. The soul also says to the aspirant, "Your spiritual journey is complete. It began and ended with me, and was guided throughout by me.[9] I will freely provide unto you spiritual love, joy, and peace.[10]

---

7. Verse 5 is related to Isa. 43:19: "Behold, I will do a new thing." J. Krishnamurti, *The First and Last Freedom* (1954; reprint; London: Victor Gollencz, 1972), p. 248, describes how we can perceive all things in a new way: "There can be a meeting of the new only when the mind is fresh; and the mind is not fresh so long as there is the residue of memory. . . . So long as experience is not completely understood, there is residue, which is the old, which is of yesterday, the thing that is past; the past is always absorbing the new and therefore destroying the new. It is only when the mind is free from the old that it meets everything anew, and in that there is joy."

8. Bailey, *The Rays and the Initiations*, pp. 468–469, says, "*Knowledge-wisdom* must be superseded by intuitive understanding; this is, in reality, inclusive participation in the creative activity of divinity." In verse 5, the aspirant perceives things differently, because he no longer relies on the knowledge of his personality and the wisdom of his causal body. Those guides are based on the past, so following them had made everything seem old and familiar. To write means to apply to oneself (see Rev. 1:11).

9. Blavatsky, *The Voice of the Silence*, p. 62, says, "Thy way to final freedom is within thy SELF. That way begins and ends outside of Self." Here, SELF and Self are soul and personality.

10. James 3:17 states: "But the wisdom that is from above is first pure, then peaceable, gentle, *and* easy to be intreated, full of mercy and good fruits, without partiality, and without hypocrisy." In verse 6, the fountain of the water of life consists of spiritual love and other higher emotions (see Rev. 7:17).

7. He that overcometh shall inherit all things; and I will be his God, and he shall be my son.

7. By overcoming the trials on your journey, you have gained your inheritance, which is membership in the spiritual kingdom. You now consistently follow my guidance and are consciously united with me.[11]

8. But the fearful, and unbelieving, and the abominable, and murderers, and whoremongers, and sorcerers, and idolaters, and all liars, shall have their part in the lake which burneth with fire and brimstone: which is the second death.

8. Nevertheless, you must remain vigilant and place all observed fear, doubt, wickedness, hatred, lust, confusion, idolatry, and false belief into the triple light of the intuition. Dispelling these imperfections is the second death."[12]

9. And there came unto me one of the seven angels which had the seven vials full of the seven last plagues, and talked with me, saying, Come hither, I will shew thee the bride, the Lamb's wife.

9. The long vision that began in chapter 12 has finally ended, so John returns to his normal consciousness. One of the seven chohans comes and says, "Raise your consciousness, and I will show you how your personality appears when it is united with the soul."[13]

---

11. According to Rev. 14:4, consistently following the soul's guidance is a sufficient condition for being a member of the spiritual kingdom. The last part of verse 7 indicates that the aspirant is now satisfying that condition. Matt. 25:34 characterizes such membership as inheritance: "Then shall the King say unto them on his right hand, Come, ye blessed of my Father, inherit the kingdom prepared for you from the foundation of the world."

12. Both verse 8 and Rev. 19:3 indicate the need for continual vigilance by members of the spiritual kingdom. Murderer, whoremonger, and sorcerer symbolize hatred, lust, and confusion, respectively (see Rev. 9:21, 2:14). The lake of fire is the triple light of the intuition (see Rev. 19:20). The second death is mentioned in Rev. 2:11, 20:6, and 20:14.

13. The seven angels are the seven chohans (see Rev. 15:1). The Lamb is the soul and the bride is the personality (see Rev. 5:6, 19:7), so "the Lamb's wife" is the personality when united with the soul. The aspirant in John's past vision attained conscious union with the soul and observed the personality from that perspective (see Rev. 19:11). The listener in verse 9, however, does not know how the personality would appear when united with the soul, so that listener must be John in his normal consciousness, who has not yet attained union with the soul.

10. And he carried me away in the spirit to a great and high mountain, and shewed me that great city, the holy Jerusalem, descending out of heaven from God,

10. The chohan helps John attain temporary union with the soul, enabling him to observe his personality as it is being transformed by ideas descending out of the spiritual world from God.[14]

11. Having the glory of God: and her light *was* like unto a stone most precious, even like a jasper stone, clear as crystal;

11. With the illumination of God, John's personality has become like a translucent stone transmitting the light of the sun.[15]

12. And had a wall great and high, *and* had twelve gates, and at the gates twelve angels, and names written thereon, which are *the names* of the twelve tribes of the children of Israel:

12. It is protected from illusion;[16] it is open to all possible types of intuitions and receives these types continually;[17] it has an obedient nature similar to that of the twelve sons of Jacob.[18]

---

14. Verse 10 is based on Ezek. 40:2 (NIV): "In visions of God he took me to the land of Israel and set me on a very high mountain, on whose south side were some buildings that looked like a city." A mountain provides a lofty vantage point, which could symbolize the highest point of mental consciousness, the causal body, or the soul. In verse 10, the mountain is said to be "great and high," so it is taken as the soul. Bailey indicates that union with the soul may only be temporary (*Glamour*, p. 180) and that an aspirant's consciousness can be raised through the dynamic influence of a Master's aura, or radiatory activity (*Discipleship in the New Age*, vol. I, pp. 754–756).
15. The glory of God is illumination (see Rev. 15:8).
16. Both Isa. 26:1 and Zech. 2:5 use a wall as a metaphor of security. Regarding verse 12, Avanhov, *The Book of Revelations*, p. 178, writes: "A wall is a protection; the wall surrounding the Heavenly City is the symbol of a powerful aura that surrounds and protects man, for he who possesses a powerful aura is protected by the radiance of his own light."
17. Regarding verse 12, Avanhov, *The Book of Revelations*, p. 178, says, "it is through these gates that the currents and forces and invisible entities at work in the universe enter and influence man." The angels are intuitions (see Rev. 5:2), and each gate is taken as the capacity to receive a type of intuition. The number twelve represents the divine pattern (see Rev. 7:4), which in this case is the range of possible types of intuition.
18. Ezek. 48:30–34 also describes a city with twelve gates that are named after the twelve tribes of Israel. In the *Revelation*, the name of something represents its underlying nature (see Rev. 2:3). The twelve tribes were descended from and named after the twelve sons of Jacob. Gen. 49 describes the obedient nature of these sons: when summoned by their father, they gathered themselves around him to hear his prophecies concerning them.

13. On the east three gates; on the north three gates; on the south three gates; and on the west three gates.

13. In particular, John's mental body can receive the lights of wisdom, the soul, and God. Similarly, his emotional, vital, and physical bodies can each receive the same three kinds of intuitions.[19]

14. And the wall of the city had twelve foundations, and in them the names of the twelve apostles of the Lamb.

14. John's personality is integrated with and supported by his causal body, which has an illumined nature similar to that of the twelve apostles on the day of Pentecost.[20]

15. And he that talked with me had a golden reed to measure the city, and the gates thereof, and the wall thereof.

15. The chohan has the ability to assess the degree of perfection attained by human beings, including their receptivity to intuitions and their defenses against illusion.[21]

---

19. The four directions represent the four parts of the personality, which are the mental, emotional, vital, and physical bodies (see Rev. 4:7, 20:8).

20. Verse 14 is related to Eph. 2:19–20: "Now therefore ye are . . . of the household of God; And are built upon the foundation of the apostles and prophets." Verse 14 is also related to Acts 2:4, according to which the twelve apostles (including Matthias as the replacement for Judas) on the day of Pentecost "were all filled with the Holy Ghost, and began to speak with other tongues, as the Spirit gave them utterance." In verse 14, the Lamb is the soul, which is a synonym for the Holy Ghost, or Spirit (see Rev. 2:7). The twelve foundations are taken as the causal body, because the latter can both support the personality and be illumined.

21. Verse 15 is based on Ezek. 40:3–6, which describes a man with a measuring reed who has the "appearance of brass" and who takes careful measurements of the walls, gates, and rooms of the "house of Israel." This man's appearance shows that he is not ordinary but has special abilities. The house of Israel might refer to the personality, as Israel can symbolize the soul (see Rev. 2:14). Bailey, *A Treatise on White Magic*, pp. 138–139, tells how the "Great Ones" assess the degree of perfection achieved in a human being: "They look to see whether the inner flame—the result of effort wisely to work and think and do—burns with increased brilliance. . . . They look to see who can struggle and contend for principle with personalities, and yet keep the link of love intact. . . . The Great Ones look to see the faculty of pliability and adaptability working out. . . . Above all, They look for an enlarged channel from the soul to the physical brain, via the mind."

16. And the city lieth foursquare, and the length is as large as the breadth: and he measured the city with the reed, twelve thousand furlongs. The length and the breadth and the height of it are equal.

17. And he measured the wall thereof, an hundred *and* forty *and* four cubits, *according to* the measure of a man, that is, of the angel.

18. And the building of the wall of it was *of* jasper: and the city *was* pure gold, like unto clear glass.

16. John's personality has become a sanctuary in which divine ideas dwell,[22] and the chohan's assessment is that each part is fulfilling its divine pattern.[23]

17. The chohan also sees that John's personality is protected against illusion through the integration of the physical and spiritual worlds, so that human concerns are resolved with divine ideas.[24]

18. Each part of his personality is a clear transparency, permitting the full shining forth of the inner divine radiance.[25]

---

22. Verse 16 states that the city lies foursquare, referring to a cube whose length, breadth, and height are all equal. 1 Kings 6:19–20 describes how King Solomon prepared an inner sanctuary within the temple to receive the "ark of the covenant of the LORD." This sanctuary had the shape of a perfect cube, with each dimension being twenty cubits. Accordingly, a cube symbolizes a sanctuary.

23. Verse 16 states that the height of the city is 12,000 furlongs, which is approximately 1,400 miles; verse 17 states that the height of the walls is 144 cubits, which is approximately 220 feet. Krodel, *Revelation*, p. 359, says, "The discrepancy between the height of the city and the measurement of the wall . . . is so tremendous as to be ludicrous." The point is that these numbers must be interpreted symbolically. The number 12,000 symbolizes the fulfillment of the divine pattern, because the number 12 represents the divine pattern and the number 1,000 represents fulfillment with respect to multiple criteria (see Rev 7:4).

24. The number 144, which is 12 times 12, is taken as representing two divine patterns working together simultaneously, namely, those of the physical and spiritual worlds.

25. Bailey, *The Rays and the Initiations*, p. 6, says, "one by one those bodies which veil the Self are brought to a point where they are simply transparencies, permitting the full shining forth of the divine nature." The personality in verse 18 has become a transparency, because it is symbolized by walls of jasper, which in turn is "clear as crystal" (see verse 11).

19. And the foundations of the wall of the city *were* garnished with all manner of precious stones. The first foundation *was* jasper; the second, sapphire; the third, a chalcedony; the fourth, an emerald;

20. The fifth, sardonyx; the sixth, sardius; the seventh, chrysolite; the eighth, beryl; the ninth, a topaz; the tenth, a chrysoprasus; the eleventh, a jacinth; the twelfth, an amethyst.

19. John's causal body is enriched with all kinds of principles of wisdom, which are rare and valuable like precious stones.[26]

20. The spiritual will emanates from his causal body with seven aspects or rays[27]—like a rainbow with seven colors[28]—just as the divine will emanates from the heart of God like a rainbow with seven colors.[29]

---

26. The Bible sometimes speaks of wisdom as though it were a type of precious stone, such as in Job 28:18–19 (ICB): "The price of wisdom is much greater than rubies. The topaz from Cush cannot compare to wisdom." See also Prov. 8:11. In verse 19, the "foundations" and "precious stones" represent the causal body and principles of wisdom, respectively, so "garnished with" depicts the causal body's function of storing principles of wisdom (see verse 14, Rev. 3:1, and 4:4).

27. Table 7 gives the modern equivalents of the stones listed in verses 19 and 20, but these equivalents are not known with certainty. For example, even though the Greek name of the first stone, *iaspis*, is translated as jasper in the KJV, this stone cannot be identical with the jasper known in our day, because ancient jasper is transparent (see verse 11) but modern jasper is opaque. Consequently, Table 7 shows that there is disagreement among Bible versions on how the Greek names of the stones should be translated. Nevertheless, Pryse, *The Apocalypse Unsealed*, p. 214, makes the following observation: "Placed in a circle, as if incorporated in the aura, these colored stones form approximately the prismatic scale, and are thus identical with the rainbow (iv. 3) which encircles the throne of the God." The rainbow represents the divine will in Rev. 4:3; it represents the spiritual will in both Rev. 10:1 and verses 19 and 20.

28. Bailey, *A Treatise on Cosmic Fire*, pp. 538, 763, 802, characterizes the causal body in a way that is quite similar to verses 19 and 20. In particular, the causal body is pictured as the "Twelve-Petalled Egoic Lotus" with its petals arranged in a circle; the unfoldment of a petal symbolizes the acquisition of wisdom. After spiritual transformation occurs, this lotus is "palpitating with every colour in the rainbow, and is of a wide radius; the streams of electrical energy circulating in it are so powerful that they are escaping beyond the periphery of the circle, resembling the rays of the sun." Here, "electrical energy" is a synonym for "will-impulse."

29. Gen. 1:27 says, "So God created man in his *own* image, in the image of God created he him." In particular, the seven chakras, causal body, spiritual will, and soul within the human being, or microcosm, resemble the seven archangels, heart of God, divine will, and God, respectively, within the divine whole, or macrocosm. See Bailey, *A Treatise on Cosmic Fire*, pp. 357, 632; *Esoteric Astrology*, p. 47; *A Treatise on White Magic*, pp. 39, 555–556.

21. And the twelve gates *were* twelve pearls; every several gate was of one pearl: and the street of the city *was* pure gold, as it were transparent glass.

21. The types of intuitions received by John's personality are the effects of the principles of wisdom he has learned. Each type of intuition is the effect of a single principle.[30] Internal channels of communication transmit his intuitions throughout his personality without distortion.[31]

22. And I saw no temple therein: for the Lord God Almighty and the Lamb are the temple of it.

22. John realizes that no part of his personality acts as an authority, because God and the soul are the only authorities that are accepted.[32]

23. And the city had no need of the sun, neither of the moon, to shine in it: for the glory of God did lighten it, and the Lamb *is* the light thereof.

23. John's personality is not dependent on any external teachers or teachings, because it receives the illumination of God via the soul.[33]

---

30. Gems are often placed into two categories: minerals and organic materials. All of the gems mentioned in verses 19 and 20 are minerals. Pearls, which are mentioned in verse 21, are organic materials, because they are produced by certain molluscs, such as pearl oysters, as a response to the entrance of foreign matter into their shells. The mineral gems symbolize the principles of wisdom stored within the causal body; the pearls symbolize the response of the personality, in the form of openness or receptivity, to the stored principles.
31. The street of the city consists of the internal communication channels within the personality (see Rev. 11:8).
32. Regarding verse 22, M. Grosso, *The Millennium Myth* (Wheaton, IL: Theosophical Publishing House, 1995), p. 22, says, "The temple is the supreme symbol of external authority."
33. Verse 23 is based on Isa. 60:19: "The sun shall be no more thy light by day; neither for brightness shall the moon give light unto thee: but the LORD shall be unto thee an everlasting light, and thy God thy glory." The sun is an external teacher, and the moon is an external teaching such as found in books (see Rev. 6:12).

24. And the nations of them which are saved shall walk in the light of it: and the kings of the earth do bring their glory and honour into it.

24. All parts of his personality are guided by the illumination and spiritual will that are received through his mind.[34]

25. And the gates of it shall not be shut at all by day: for there shall be no night there.

25. Each type of receptivity is always active, because John's consciousness is continuous day and night, even while his physical body is asleep.[35]

26. And they shall bring the glory and honour of the nations into it.

26. And so these receptive channels continually bring illumination and spiritual will into his personality.

27. And there shall in no wise enter into it any thing that defileth, neither *whatsoever* worketh abomination, or *maketh* a lie: but they which are written in the Lamb's book of life.

27. Nothing can enter John's personality that is based on selfishness, idolatry, or false beliefs, for the only thoughts that can enter are those consistent with the divine ideas conveyed by the soul.[36]

---

34. Verse 24 is similar to Isa. 2:5: "let us walk in the light of the LORD." In verse 24, the "kings of the earth" are thoughts (see Rev. 16:14). "Honour" is a translation of the Greek word (*time*) that sometimes means "honorable use" or "noble purpose" (Rom. 9:21, NASB and NIV); it is taken as a reference to the spiritual will.

35. Verse 25 may be based Isa. 60:11, which makes this prediction for the restored Jerusalem: "Therefore thy gates shall be open continually; they shall not be shut day or night." Verse 25 is taken as a reference to sleep, the nature of which is described by Powell, *The Astral Body*, pp. 83, 87: "In sleep, then, a man is simply using his astral body instead of his physical: it is only the physical body that is asleep, not necessarily the man himself. . . . When a man has also bridged over the chasm between astral and physical consciousness, day and night no longer exist for him, since he leads a life unbroken in its continuity."

36. Verse 27 is similar to Isa. 52:1: "put on thy beautiful garments, O Jerusalem, the holy city: for henceforth there shall no more come into thee the uncircumcised and the unclean." In verse 27, the "book of life" is the plane of divine ideas (see Rev. 13:8, 20:12).

CHAPTER 22

POWER OF DECISION

Human beings have the power of decision and can choose to accept spiritual love with its redemption and illumination.

KING JAMES VERSION

1. And he shewed me a pure river of water of life, clear as crystal, proceeding out of the throne of God and of the Lamb.

PSYCHOLOGICAL INTERPRETATION

1. The chohan summarizes a few key points for John:[1] "Spiritual love is a pure river free of all self-centeredness.[2] It proceeds from the heart of God and then passes through the soul and causal body of a human being.[3]

---

1. Chapter 22 is a continuation of chapter 21, so the instructor in verse 1 is likely to be the same as the instructor in Rev. 21:9, who was identified as one of the chohans from chapters 15 and 16.
2. Verses 1 and 2 are based on the description of the sacred river in Ezek. 47:1–12. This river originates from under the threshold of the temple, flows past the altar, and eventually reaches the Dead Sea, where it heals the water of its saltiness so that fish can live; along the banks are trees bearing fresh fruit each month and having leaves that can be used for healing. Regarding verse 1, St. John of the Cross, *Collected Works*, vol. II, p. 328, says, "The waters of this river, since they are the inmost love of God, flow into the inmost soul and give her to drink this torrent of love."
3. Yogananda, *Autobiography of a Yogi*, p. 423, writes, "Man as an individualized soul is essentially causal-bodied." In verse 1, the throne of God is the heart of God, and the Lamb is the soul (see Rev. 1:4, 5:6). The footnotes for Rev. 19:11 and 21:20 indicate that the causal body is the vehicle of the soul and corresponds to the heart, or throne, of God. Accordingly, the throne of the soul is taken as the causal body.

2. In the midst of the street of it, and on either side of the river, *was there* the tree of life, which bare twelve *manner of* fruits, *and* yielded her fruit every month: and the leaves of the tree *were* for the healing of the nations.

3. And there shall be no more curse: but the throne of God and of the Lamb shall be in it; and his servants shall serve him:

4. And they shall see his face; and his name *shall be* in their foreheads.

2. Spiritual love gives access to the plane of divine ideas. These ideas provide progressive revelations regarding the organization of the divine whole, and they can redeem human beings.[4]

3. With this love, human beings will no longer be cursed by a belief of separation from God: instead they will feel connected to God and the soul, and will serve God.[5]

4. And they will intuitively perceive the presence of God and be conscious of their own divine nature.[6]

---

4. The "tree of life" represents the plane of divine ideas (see Rev. 2:7), and so it is equivalent to the "little book" in Rev. 10:2 and the "book of life" in Rev. 13:8. The "twelve manner of fruits" mentioned in verse 2 are interpreted as ideas that bring progressive revelation of the divine organization, because the number 12 represents the divine pattern or organization (see Rev. 7:4).

5. J. S. Goldsmith, *The Mystical I* (New York: Harper and Row, 1971), p. 31, writes: "All discord, all inharmony, and all error are experienced because of a sense of separation from God. But this sense of separation from God is not your fault personally. It is the universal belief that has come down to us from the allegorical experience of Adam and Eve being cast out of the Garden of Eden." The first part of verse 3 is based on Zech. 14:11 (RSV): "there shall be no more curse; Jerusalem shall dwell in security." The "curse" in verse 3 is taken as a belief of separation from God. The last part is similar to 1 John 4:16: "he that dwelleth in love dwelleth in God, and God in him."

6. The face of God, name of God, and forehead represent the presence of God, nature of God, and consciousness, respectively (see Rev. 6:16, 14:1, 7:3). Matt. 5:8 gives a requirement similar to that of verse 4 for seeing God: "Blessed *are* the pure in heart: for they shall see God." These requirements are similar, because the heart chakra becomes pure when it receives spiritual love from the heart of God.

5. And there shall be no night there; and they need no candle, neither light of the sun; for the Lord God giveth them light: and they shall reign for ever and ever.

6. And he said unto me, These sayings *are* faithful and true: and the Lord God of the holy prophets sent his angel to shew unto his servants the things which must shortly be done.

7. Behold, I come quickly: blessed *is* he that keepeth the sayings of the prophecy of this book.

5. In addition, they will be free of ignorance and will not rely on their own intellects or any external teacher. Instead, they will be illumined by ideas from God, which will enable them to rule over their personalities forever."[7]

6. The chohan also says to John, "These teachings are faithful and true, because God has sent me as a messenger to show his servants their next immediate steps on the spiritual journey.[8]

7. As you can observe, I come quickly to you by conveying inspiration: happiness is found by applying the inspired teachings of this book."[9]

---

7. In verse 5, night, candle, and sun symbolize ignorance, intellect, and an external teacher, respectively (see Rev. 8:12, 18:23, 6:12).

8. An angel is a messenger (see Rev. 1:1). Rev. 15:1 indicates that the seven chohans are messengers of God, because they are referred to as "angels" who bring "the wrath of God" to human beings. Accordingly, when the chohan in verse 6 speaks about the angel sent by God, he is speaking about himself. This verse indicates that the chohan instructing John has the same mission that Rev. 1:1 attributes to Jesus, namely, to show the experiences that must shortly occur to God's servants. Thus, verse 6 seems to suggest that this chohan is Jesus.

9. Vine, *Vine's Complete Expository Dictionary*, p. 492, gives this definition: "Prophecy . . . is the declaration of that which cannot be known by natural means." Inspiration is prophecy that is transmitted from the spiritual kingdom to the human kingdom. Bailey, *The Rays and the Initiations*, p. 230, says, "the main technique of the Hierarchy is that of conveying inspiration." Here, Hierarchy is a synonym for spiritual kingdom. Rev. 1:2 indicates that inspiration could come through intuitions, clairaudience, or clairvoyance. In verse 7 and the rest of this chapter, "prophecy" is taken to mean inspiration.

8. And I John saw these things, and heard *them*. And when I had heard and seen, I fell down to worship before the feet of the angel which shewed me these things.

9. Then saith he unto me, See *thou do it* not: for I am thy fellowservant, and of thy brethren the prophets, and of them which keep the sayings of this book: worship God.

10. And he saith unto me, Seal not the sayings of the prophecy of this book: for the time is at hand.

8. John testifies that he saw and heard these things. And when he had heard and seen them, he tried to praise the chohan who showed these things to him.[10]

9. Then the chohan says to John, "Do not praise me, for I am a fellow servant with you, with other people I have inspired, and with all who apply the teachings of this book. Therefore, praise only God."[11]

10. The chohan also says to John, "Do not ignore the inspired teachings of this book, for now is the time to apply them.[12]

---

10. Many modern commentators find verse 8 to be confusing. For example, Krodel, *Revelation*, p. 374, says, "It is odd that in spite of the rebuke by the angel (19:10), John for the second time falls down to worship at the feet of the angel (22:8–9)." This confusion vanishes if a distinction is made between John and the role that John plays in his visions. John's visions dramatize the various stages of the spiritual journey, including stages that John has not yet attained in his ordinary consciousness. In verse 8, John reaches the stage in his own spiritual evolution that is depicted in Rev. 19:10.

11. Matt. 19:16–17 describes an encounter with Jesus: "And, behold, one came and said unto him, Good Master, what good thing shall I do, that I may have eternal life? And he said unto him, Why callest thou me good? *there is* none good but one, *that is*, God: but if thou wilt enter into life, keep the commandments." Just as Jesus stopped someone from calling him good, saying that only God is good, the chohan in verse 9 stopped John from worshiping him, saying that only God should be worshiped. This similarity between the words of the chohan and those of Jesus is further evidence that the chohan may be Jesus.

12. The instruction that John receives in verse 10 is the opposite to what Daniel receives in Dan. 12:4 (RSV): "But you, Daniel, shut up the words, and seal the book, until the time of the end." Both verse 10 and Rev. 1:3 announce that "the time is at hand." Mounce, *The Book of Revelation*, p. 406, observes: "In view of the fact that nearly two millennia have passed since the announcement that the time was at hand, some have concluded that John was simply wrong in his eschatological expectation." John appears to be wrong only if his visions are interpreted as describing events out in the external world. There is no discrepancy if his visions describe psychological events because, as Krishnamurti, *The First and Last Freedom*, p. 135, has noted, "regeneration is only possible in the present, not in the future."

11. He that is unjust, let him be unjust still: and he which is filthy, let him be filthy still: and he that is righteous, let him be righteous still: and he that is holy, let him be holy still.

12. And, behold, I come quickly; and my reward *is* with me, to give every man according as his work shall be.

13. I am Alpha and Omega, the beginning and the end, the first and the last.

14. Blessed *are* they that do his commandments, that they may have right to the tree of life, and may enter in through the gates into the city.

11. If anyone decides to be unjust or impure, let us respect that decision by not opposing it. But if anyone decides to be righteous or holy, let us respect that decision by supporting it.[13]

12. Moreover, as can be observed, I come quickly to any call for help, and give help to everyone according to his or her need.[14]

13. I am eternal, everlasting, and always available to provide assistance.[15]

14. Happy are they who apply intuitions from God, that they may contact the plane of divine ideas and then bring this illumination, via their receptivity and alignment, into their lower nature.[16]

---

13. *ACIM* is composed as if it were written by Jesus and states (vol. I, p. 145): "Your will is as free as mine, and God Himself would not go against it. . . . I cannot oppose your decision without competing with it and thereby violating God's will for you. . . . If you want to be like me I will help you, knowing that we are alike. If you want to be different, I will wait until you change your mind."

14. *ACIM*, vol. I, pp. 254, 294, states: "Love always answers, being unable to deny a call for help. . . . A call for help is given help." This process of invocation and evocation is illustrated in chapter 16, according to which the chohans transmit their realizations only after the aspirant has invoked their assistance in Rev. 16:1.

15. The characterization "Alpha and Omega" indicates divinity, because it was previously applied to God in Rev. 1:8 and to the soul in Rev. 1:11 and 21:6. According to Rev. 14:1, all members of the spiritual kingdom are consciously aware of their divine nature.

16. The commandments of God are intuitions (see Rev. 12:17). The gates of the city are portals within the personality through which intuitions may pass (see Rev. 21:12). Receptivity and alignment are required for these portals to be open (see Rev. 14:1 and 14:14).

15. For without *are* dogs, and sorcerers, and whoremongers, and murderers, and idolaters, and whosoever loveth and maketh a lie.

16. I Jesus have sent mine angel to testify unto you these things in the churches. I am the root and the offspring of David, *and* the bright and morning star.

15. For the outside world has many negative influences that must be overcome, including ignorance, confusion, lust, hatred, greed, and lies.[17]

16. I, Jesus,[18] have been teaching you through inspiration about the chakras.[19] Although I was born in the human kingdom as a descendent of King David, I now have insight and illumination.[20]

---

17. In the Bible, the term dog is often used as an epithet of contempt, indicating that the recipient is ignorant, dumb, or inattentive; see 1 Sam. 17:43, 2 Sam. 16:9, and Isa. 56:10–11. Sorcerers, murderers, and idolaters represent confusion, hatred, and greed, respectively (see Rev. 9:21, 2:14).

18. Jesus is designated as one of the seven chohans by several theosophical writers: Leadbeater, *The Masters and the Path*, p. 268; Powell, *The Causal Body and the Ego*, p. 323; Bailey, *A Treatise on Cosmic Fire*, p. 439; and R. Ellwood, *Theosophy* (Wheaton, IL: Theosophical Publishing House, 1994), p. 142. Verse 16 identifies Jesus as the chohan who has been instructing John, which is consistent with the clues given in verses 6 and 9.

19. Jesus' angel is inspiration, and the churches are the chakras (see Rev. 1:1, 1:11).

20. Paul, in Rom. 1:3 (NASB), speaks of Jesus as "born of a descendant of David according to the flesh." The bright star symbolizes insight, as in Dan. 12:3 (NASB): "And those who have insight will shine brightly like the brightness of the expanse of heaven." In addition, the morning star represents illumination (see Rev. 2:28).

17. And the Spirit and the bride say, Come. And let him that heareth say, Come. And let him that is athirst come. And whosoever will, let him take the water of life freely.

17. The guidance of the soul and the best interest of everyone's personality is to make progress on the spiritual journey.[21] Let everyone who understands the words of this book follow them.[22] Let everyone with a sense of need or emptiness change their lives. For if they so choose, they can freely access spiritual love with its redemption and illumination.[23]

18. For I testify unto every man that heareth the words of the prophecy of this book, If any man shall add unto these things, God shall add unto him the plagues that are written in this book:

18. I warn everyone who understands the inspired words of this book: If you apply practices that are inconsistent with your own understanding, the God-given power of that decision will bring about the inner conflicts described in this book;[24]

---

21. Spirit is short for Holy Spirit, which is a synonym for the soul (see Rev. 2:7). The bride is the personality (see Rev. 19:7).
22. In verse 17, "heareth" means hear with the ear of the mind, or understand (see Rev. 3:3).
23. The last part of verse 17 is similar to Jesus' invitation in John 7:37, which in turn echoes Isa. 55:1: "every one that thirsteth, come ye to the waters." The water of life is spiritual love (see verse 1).
24. Verses 18 and 19 are similar to Deut. 4:2: "Ye shall not add unto the word which I command you, neither shall ye diminish *ought* from it." Verses 18 and 19 could be interpreted as a warning to future scribes and translators who might be tempted to alter the text. A different interpretation is offered here: the warning is taken as applying to aspirants who hear the words of the *Revelation* in the sense of understanding them (see verse 17). To make progress on the spiritual journey, they must consistently apply to themselves what they understand (see Rev. 1:11, 19). These verses contain a notion that is stated explicitly in *ACIM*, vol. I, p. 145: "God gave your will its power."

19. And if any man shall take away from the words of the book of this prophecy, God shall take away his part out of the book of life, and out of the holy city, and *from* the things which are written in this book.

20. He which testifieth these things saith, Surely I come quickly. Amen. Even so, come, Lord Jesus.

21. The grace of our Lord Jesus Christ *be* with you all. Amen.

19. and if you neglect to apply what you understand, the God-given power of that decision will deny you access to the plane of divine ideas, a transformed personality, and the other rewards described in this book."[25]

20. Jesus, who gave these teachings, says, "Surely I come quickly." So it is. Accordingly, please come, Lord Jesus.[26]

21. Let the grace of our Lord Jesus Christ be with everyone. It is so.[27]

25. James 4:17 (NRSV) states: "Anyone, then, who knows the right thing to do and fails to do it, commits sin."
26. The last part of verse 20 echos 1 Cor. 16:22 (RSV): "Our Lord, come!"
27. Epistles often close with a benediction, as in 1 Cor. 16:23 and Eph. 6:24. The *Revelation* began as an epistle (Rev. 1:4), so it is appropriate that its last verse be a benediction.

Appendix A

Reference Tables

Table 1. The Seven Chakras

Greek Church Name	English Chakra Name	Sanskrit Chakra Name	Approximate Chakra Location
1. Ephesus	Sacral	Svadhisthana	Base of sexual organ
2. Smyrna	Solar Plexus	Manipura	Region of the navel
3. Pergamos	Heart	Anahata	Region of the heart
4. Thyatira	Throat	Vishuddha	Lower end of the throat
5. Sardis	Brow	Ajna	Area between eyebrows
6. Philadelphia	Crown	Sahasrara or Sahasradala	Top of head
7. Laodicea	Basic	Muladhara	Base of spine

TABLE 2. THE SEVEN CHURCHES AND THEIR ASSOCIATED CHAKRAS

Greek Church Name	Fillmore Meaning	Hitchcock Meaning	Potts Meaning	English Chakra Name	Chakra Function
1. Ephesus	Desirable; appealing	Desirable	Amiable; desirable; the end; patience	Sacral	Governs motives or strong desires
2. Smyrna	Myrrh; flowing; distilling; sweet; fragrant; aromatic; spirituous; gall; sorrow; lamentation; bitterness; rebellion	Myrrh	Cold habitation; myrrh; tribulation	Solar plexus	Transmits emotions
3. Pergamos	Strongly united; closely knit; tough texture; elevated; height; citadel	Height; elevation	Elevated; height; fortified; faith	Heart	Receives spiritual love from soul
4. Thyatira	Burning incense; rushing headlong; inspired; frantic; aromatic wood; perfume	A perfume; sacrifice of labor	Sacrifice of love or labor; perfume; burning incense	Throat	Formulates thoughts
5. Sardis	Precious stone; carnelian; sardonyx; sard; prince of joy	Prince of joy	The remainder; prince of joy; the sun; watchfulness	Brow	Receives wisdom from causal body
6. Philadelphia	Brotherly love; loving as brethren; love of brothers (or sisters); fraternal love	Love of a brother	Love of a brother; brotherly love; affection	Crown	Receives insights from soul
7. Laodicea	Justice of the people; judgment of the people	Just people	A just people; justice	Basic	Receives spiritual will from soul, via crown chakra

Sources: C. Fillmore, *The Metaphysical Bible Dictionary* (1931; reprint; Unity Village, MO: Unity School of Christianity, 1995); R. D. Hitchcock, "An Interpreting Dictionary of Scripture Proper Names" in *Hitchcock's Complete Analysis of the Holy Bible* (New York: A. J. Johnson, 1874); C. A. Potts, *Dictionary of Bible Proper Names* (New York: The Abingdom Press, 1922).

Table 3. Symbolic Meanings of Numbers

Number	Symbolic Meaning	Verses	Biblical Example
3 or 1/3	Activity of the spiritual will	Rev. 8:8, 10, 11, 12; 9:15, 18	"Thou shalt burn with fire a third part in the midst of the city, when the days of the siege are fulfilled: and thou shalt take a third part, *and* smite about it with a knife: and a third part thou shalt scatter in the wind" (Ezek. 5:2)
3.5, 42, or 1260	Period in which evil can operate	Rev. 11:2, 3, 9, 11; 12:6, 14; 13:5	"they shall be given into his hand until a time and times and the dividing of time" (Dan. 7:25)
4	Four-fold personality	Rev. 4:6, 7; 7:1; 9:14; 14:20; 20:8; 21:13	"Also out of the midst thereof *came* the likeness of four living creatures. And this *was* their appearance; they had the likeness of a man." (Ezek. 1:5)
5	Punishment	Rev. 9:5, 10	"He shall restore five oxen for an ox" (Exod. 22:1)
6	Illusion or imperfection	Rev. 13:18	"These six *things* doth the LORD hate" (Prov. 6:16)
7	Perfection	Rev. 5:6, 11:13	"God blessed the seventh day, and sanctified it" (Gen. 2:3)
10 or 1/10	Completion of a series	Rev. 2:10; 7:4; 11:13; 12:3; 13:1; 17:3	"And he wrote upon the tables the words of the covenant, the ten commandments" (Exod. 34:28)
12	Divine pattern or organization	Rev. 7:4; 12:1; 14:1; 21:16, 17; 22:2	"All these *are* the twelve tribes of Israel" (Gen. 49:28)
24	Passage of time	Rev. 4:4; 12:3	"Are there not twelve hours in the day?" (John 11:9); "at the third hour of the night" (Acts 23:23)
200,000,000	Indefinitely large number	Rev. 9:16	"The chariots of God are twenty thousand, even thousands upon thousands" (Psal. 68:17, ASV)

TABLE 4. SYMBOLIC MEANINGS OF COLORS

Color	Symbolic Meaning	Verses	Biblical Example
Black	Death	Rev. 6:5	"He hath made me to dwell in darkness, as those that have been long dead" (Psal. 143:3)
Green	Vitality and growth	Rev. 8:7; 9:4	"He *is* green before the sun, and his branch shooteth forth in his garden" (Job 8:16)
Purple	Royalty and prominence	Rev. 17:4; 18:12, 16	"Purple raiment that *was* on the kings of Midian" (Judg. 8:26)
Red	Struggle and conflict	Rev. 6:4; 12:3	"The shield of his mighty men is made red" (Nah. 2:3)
Scarlet	Guilt or iniquity	Rev. 17:3	"Though your sins be as scarlet, they shall be as white as snow" (Isa. 1:18)
Scarlet	Prosperity	Rev. 17:4; 18:12, 16	"Ye daughters of Israel, weep over Saul, who clothed you in scarlet, with *other* delights, who put on ornaments of gold upon your apparel" (2 Sam. 1:24)
White	Purity	Rev. 2:17; 3:4, 5, 18; 4:4; 6:2; etc.	"Many shall be purified, and made white" (Dan. 12:10)

Tribe of Israel	Fillmore Meaning	Hitchcock Meaning	Potts Meaning	Old Testament Example	Associated Physical Organ
1. Juda	Praise Jehovah; celebration of Jehovah	The praise of the Lord; confession	Praise of God; celebrated	"The sceptre shall not depart from Judah, nor a lawgiver from between his feet, until Shiloh come; and unto him *shall* the gathering of the people *be*." (Gen. 49:10)	Brain
2. Reuben	Behold a son; vision of the son	Who sees the son; the vision of the son	A son seen	"And Leah conceived, and bare a son, and she called his name Reuben: for she said, Surely the LORD hath looked upon my affliction." (Gen. 29:32)	Eyes
3. Gad	Abundance; dispenser of fortune; troop	A band; a troop	A troop or band	"Blessed *be* he that enlargeth Gad: he dwelleth as a lion, and teareth the arm with the crown of the head. And he provided the first part for himself, because there, *in* a portion of the lawgiver, *was he* seated; and he came with the heads of the people, he executed the justice of the LORD." (Deut. 33:20–21)	Pineal, pituitary, and carotid glands
4. Aser	Straight; prosperous; happiness; blessedness	Happiness	Proceeding right	"And Zilpah Leah's maid bare Jacob a second son. And Leah said, Happy am I, for the daughters will call me blessed: and she called his name Asher." (Gen. 30:12–13)	Heart

continued

207

Tribe of Israel	Fillmore Meaning	Hitchcock Meaning	Potts Meaning	Old Testament Example	Associated Physical Organ
5. Nephtalim	My wrestling; wrestling of Jehovah	That struggles or fights	My wrestling	"Naphtali *is* a hind let loose." (Gen. 49:21)	Lungs
6. Manasses	Causing forgetfulness; out of the forgotten	Forgetfulness; he that is forgotten	He made to forget; forgetting	"And Joseph called the name of the firstborn Manasseh: For God, *said he*, hath made me forget all my toil, and all my father's house." (Gen. 41:51)	Throat
7. Simeon	Hearing; harkening	That hears or obeys; that is heard	Gracious hearing	"Simeon and Levi *are* brethren; instruments of cruelty *are in* their habitations. O my soul, come not thou into their secret; unto their assembly, mine honour, be not thou united: for in their anger they slew a man, and in their selfwill they digged down a wall." (Gen. 49:5–6)	Sex organs
8. Levi	Joining; entwining; infolding; uniting	Associated with him	My joining; associated	"And she conceived again, and bare a son; and said, Now this time will my husband be joined unto me, because I have born him three sons: therefore was his name called Levi." (Gen. 29:34)	Stomach

continued

Tribe of Israel	Fillmore Meaning	Hitchcock Meaning	Potts Meaning	Old Testament Example	Associated Physical Organ
9. Issachar	He will bring reward; who brings hire	Reward; recompense	He brings a reward	"Issachar *is* a strong ass couching down between two burdens: And he saw that rest *was* good, and the land that *it was* pleasant; and bowed his shoulder to bear, and became a servant unto tribute." (Gen. 49:14–15)	Spleen
10. Zabulon	Dwelling; surrounded; habitation	Dwelling; habitation	Dwelling wished for	"Zabulun shall dwell at the haven of the sea; and he *shall be* for an haven of ships." (Gen. 49:13)	Skin and bony structure
11. Joseph	Whom Jehovah will add to; Jehovah shall increase	Increase; addition	He increases	"Joseph *is* a fruitful bough, *even* a fruitful bough by a well; *whose* branches run over the wall." (Gen. 49:22)	Three-fold nervous system
12. Benjamin	Son of good fortune; son of prosperity	Son of the right hand	The son of my right hand	"Benjamin shall ravin *as* a wolf; in the morning he shall devour the prey, and at night he shall divide the spoil." (Gen. 49:27)	Vascular or blood system

Sources: C. Fillmore, *The Metaphysical Bible Dictionary* (1931; reprint; Unity Village, MO: Unity School of Christianity, 1995); R. D. Hitchcock, "An Interpreting Dictionary of Scripture Proper Names" in *Hitchcock's Complete Analysis of the Holy Bible* (New York: A. J. Johnson, 1874); C. A. Potts, *Dictionary of Bible Proper Names* (New York: The Abingdom Press, 1922). The list of physical organs comes from A. A. Bailey, *A Treatise on White Magic* (New York: Lucis Publishing Company, 1974), p. 43, although Bailey did not associate the organs with the tribes of Israel.

TABLE 6. ASPECTS OF ILLUSION

Problem	Definition	Affected Body	Symbol
Illusion	False beliefs	Mental	Devil: Rev. 2:10, 12:9, 20:2; dragon: Rev. 12:3, 13:2,16:13, 20:2; number of the beast's name: Rev. 13:17, 15:2; Satan: Rev. 2:9, 3:9, 12:9, 20:2; serpent: Rev. 12:9, 20:2; six: Rev. 13:18
Glamour	Emotional reactions, which are false beliefs intensified by desire	Emotional	Beast: Rev. 14:9, 15:2, 16:10, 19:19, 20:4; beast from the sea: Rev. 13:1; name of the beast: Rev. 13:17; sixty: Rev. 13:18
Maya	Compulsions, which are false beliefs intensified by both desire and vital energy	Vital	Beast from the earth: Rev. 13:11; false prophet: Rev. 16:13, 19:20, 20:10; mark of the beast: Rev. 13:17, 14:9, 15:2, 16:2, 19:20, 20:4; mark of the beast's name: Rev. 14:11; six hundred: Rev. 13:18

TABLE 7. GREEK AND ENGLISH NAMES OF PRECIOUS STONES

Greek Name	Possible English Translations
1. Iaspis	Jasper (GNB, KJV, NEB, NIV, TNT); diamond (JB)
2. Sappheiros	Sapphire (GNB, KJV, NIV, TNT); lapis lazuli (NEB, JB)
3. Chalkendon	Agate (GNB, RSV); chalcedony (KJV, NIV, TNT); turquoise (JB)
4. Smaragdos	Emerald (GNB, KJV, NEB, NIV, TNT); crystal (JB)
5. Sardonux	Onyx (GNB, RSV); sardonyx (KJV, NEB, NIV, TNT); agate (JB)
6. Sardios	Carnelian (GNB, NIV, RSV); cornelian (NEB); ruby (JB); sardius (KJV, TNT)
7. Chrusolithos	Chrysolite (KJV, NEB, NIV, RSV, TNT); gold quartz (JB); yellow quartz (GNB)
8. Berullos	Beryl (GNB, KJV, NEB, NIV, RSV, TNT); malachite (JB)
9. Topazion	Topaz (GNB, JB, KJV, NEB, NIV, RSV, TNT)
10. Chrusoprasos	Chryoprase (KJV, NEB, NIV, TNT); emerald (JB); chalcedony (GNB)
11. Huakinthos	Jacinth (KJV, NIV, RSV, TNT); turquoise (NEB, GNB); sapphire (JB)
12. Amethustos	Amethyst (GNB, JB, KJV, NEB, NIV, RSV, TNT)

Sources: Good News Bible (GNB), Jerusalem Bible (JB), King James Version (KJV), New English Bible (NEB), New International Version (NIV), Revised Standard Version (RSV), and Translator's New Testament (TNT)

Appendix B

Related Perspectives

The Introduction described several ways to interpret the *Revelation of St. John*. Although the psychological interpretation described here differs from the external-temporal approaches used by the vast majority of commentators, it is related to the ideas of several earlier writers.

John Ruusbroec (1293–1381), a Flemish writer, is considered one of the greatest mystics of the Roman Catholic Church. He gave psychological explanations for a few verses in the *Revelation*, for instance, Rev. 2:17: "To him that overcometh will I give to eat of the hidden manna." According to Ruusbroec, the overcomer is anyone who transcends the personal self, and the hidden manna is "an interior, hidden savor and heavenly joy."[1] Ruusbroec explained Rev. 14:13 ("Blessed are the dead which die in the Lord from henceforth") thus:

> But when we rise above ourselves and in our ascent to God become
> so unified that bare love can envelop us at that high level where love
> itself acts, . . . we will then come to nought, dying in God to our-
> selves and to all that is our own. In this death we become hidden sons
> of God and discover in ourselves a new life, which is eternal.[2]

---

1. Ruusbroec, *The Spiritual Espousals*, p. 160.
2. Ruusbroec, *The Spiritual Espousals*, p. 170.

St. John of the Cross (1542–1591) was a Spanish mystic, poet, and Doctor of the Roman Catholic Church. He wrote masterly treatises on mystical theology that included psychological explanations for several symbols in the *Revelation*. In Rev. 13:1, for example, the seven heads of the beast represent the inner forces that aspirants must overcome as they leave "the sensual things of the world," climb "the seven steps of love," and enter into "purity of spirit."[3] In Rev. 22:1, the pure river of life's water that proceeds out of the throne of God is "the inmost love of God."[4]

Helena P. Blavatsky (1831–1891) was born in Russia and, in 1875, founded the Theosophical Society, which became a worldwide organization. Her influential books proclaimed that all great world religions come from the same root. Blavatsky wrote very little about the *Revelation*, although she did discuss the meaning of a few of its symbols. Nevertheless, she made the following point: "The fact is . . . the whole *Revelation*, is simply an allegorical narrative of the Mysteries and initiation therein of a candidate, who is John himself."[5] The theosophical notion of initiation is tantamount to the awakening of higher consciousness.

Swami Sri Yukteswar (1855–1936) was the guru, or head, of a school that taught yoga—a method for awakening higher consciousness. Although Yukteswar remained in India throughout his life, he became well known in the West through the writings of his most famous student, Paramahansa Yogananda. Yukteswar believed that there is an essential unity in all religions. His book, *The Holy Science* (1894), established the fundamental harmony between the Sankhya philosophy of India and the *Revelation of St. John*. In it, Yukteswar commented on only a few of the verses in the *Revelation*, but gave an intriguing interpretation for the seven churches that play a prominent role in the first three chapters. Most commentators believe that these churches refer to historical churches founded in Asia by early Christians. Yukteswar states, however, that the seven churches refer to the seven chakras, which Indian philosophy regards as subtle centers of energy.[6]

---

3. St. John of the Cross, *The Complete Works*, vol. I, pp. 107–108.
4. St. John of the Cross, *The Complete Works*, vol. II, p. 328.
5. H. P. Blavatsky, *Isis Unveiled*, vol. II (1877; reprint; Pasadena, CA: Theosophical University Press, 1976), p. 351.
6. Yukteswar, *The Holy Science*, pp. 71–72.

Paramahansa Yogananda (1893–1952) was born in India but moved to United States, where he lived for more than thirty years. He founded the Self-Realization Fellowship in 1920, with its headquarters in Los Angeles. Although Yogananda published relatively little about the *Revelation,* he did consider it to be a veiled treatise on yoga:

> Certainly in the Revelation of St. John we are led by means of metaphor into the profound insights of the yoga science in which Jesus initiated his advanced disciple John, and others, whose consciousness thereby ascended to the exalted Self-realized state of the kingdom of God within.[7]

Yogananda believed that Jesus varied the depth of his teachings depending on the receptivity of his students. According to this view, Jesus conveyed simple parables to instruct the general public, but taught the deeper mysteries, described symbolically in the *Revelation,* to those close disciples who were ready to receive them.[8]

Edgar Cayce (1877–1945) was a well-known medium who gave over 14,000 supposedly psychic messages (telepathic-clairvoyant readings) to more than 6,000 people over a period of forty-three years. The transcripts of these messages are preserved at the Association for Research and Enlightenment (ARE) in Virginia Beach, Virginia. Cayce gave these messages while in a trance state. He seemed not to have any conscious recollection of what he had said when he awoke. In 1930, he gave a message for a young girl who was suffering from a severe case of nervous instability. This message described the girl's physical condition and recommended that the girl's doctor read and understand the *Revelation,* because the forces operating in the girl's body were spoken of there.

Motivated by this message, a group of Cayce's colleagues began to study the *Revelation* and prepared a series of questions that they presented to Cayce while he was in a trance state. Cayce responded with a discourse on the *Revelation* that included the following:

---

7. Yogananda, *The Second Coming of the Christ,* pp. xxv–xxvi.
8. Yogananda, *The Second Coming of the Christ,* p. 87.

Why, then, ye ask now, was this written (this vision) in such a manner that is hard to be interpreted, save in the experience of every soul
who seeks to know, to walk in, a closer communion with Him? For
the visions, the experiences, the names, the churches, the places, the
dragons, the cities, all are but emblems of those forces that may war
within the individual in its journey through the material, or from the
entering into the material manifestation to the entering into the glory,
or the awakening in the spirit, in the inter-between, in the border-
land, in the shadow.[9]

This quotation agrees with two principles of the psychological interpretation given in the Introduction—namely, that the visions in the *Revelation*
describe the inner experiences that aspirants have on the spiritual journey and
that the symbols within each vision represent aspects of the aspirants' own consciousness. Although Cayce provided many clues as to how to interpret the
Revelation, much of what he said is obscure and incomplete, and he never
attempted to provide a verse-by-verse analysis.

Carl Gustav Jung (1875–1961), an eminent Swiss psychiatrist and the
founder of analytical psychology, also interpreted the *Revelation* in a psychological way, believing that John's visions were a product of repressed negative feelings:

We can take it as certain that the author of the Epistles of John made
every effort to practice what he preached to his fellow Christians. For
this purpose he had to shut out all negative feelings, and, thanks to a
helpful lack of self-reflection, he was able to forget them. But though
they disappeared from the conscious level they continued to rankle
beneath the surface, and in the course of time spun an elaborate web
of resentments and vengeful thoughts which then burst upon consciousness in the form of a revelation.[10]

Jung agreed with another principle given in the Introduction, namely, that
John's visions are similar to dreams. He compared those visions with the com-

---

9. Van Auken, *Edgar Cayce on the Revelation*, pp. 158–159.
10. C. G. Jung, *Answer to Job* (1954; reprint; Cleveland, OH: World Publishing Company, 1965), p. 147.

pensating dreams that people have when they deceive themselves about their own virtues. Although Jung considered John's visions to be the product of repression, the earlier commentary in this book is faithful to John's explanation that he was inspired by his teacher, Jesus.

Frederick (Fritz) Perls (1893–1970), founder of Gestalt psychotherapy, did not comment on the *Revelation*. Nevertheless, among the methods of dream interpretation devised by various psychologists, Perls' is perhaps the best approach for understanding the symbols in the *Revelation*. According to Perls:

> All the different parts of the dream are fragments of our personalities. Since our aim is to make every one of us a wholesome person, which means a unified person, without conflicts, what we have to do is put the different fragments of the dream together. We have to *re-own* these projected, fragmented parts of our personality, and *re-own* the hidden potential that appears in the dream.[11]

To understand a dream, Perls encourages you to write it down and make a list of all of its details—every person, every thing, and every mood. Perls considers each detail as a fragment of your self, and believes that you need to understand how and why it is such a fragment. The interactions and relations of details in dreams represent how the corresponding fragments interact or relate in your self. When you see that the details of your dreams are actually fragments of your self, you assimilate the dreams and achieve greater understanding and integration in your life.

According to the psychological interpretation of the *Revelation*, each episode represents a particular stage on the spiritual journey, and each symbol represents a key fragment of aspirants at the corresponding stage. In this sense, the *Revelation* is a roadmap for the spiritual journey. If you are at an intermediate stage in that journey, you can use the roadmap to understand the progress you have already made, the lessons you must learn to make further progress, and the issues you will confront in the future. For the *Revelation* to be a useful roadmap, however, you must use it in a manner similar to Perls' use of dreams. In particular, you must actually see, as part of your own first-hand knowledge,

---

11. Perls, *Gestalt Therapy Verbatim*, pp. 71–72.

how the symbols in each episode represent different fragments of your self. When you achieve this insight, you will have assimilated that portion of the *Revelation* and gained greater understanding and integration in your life.

APPENDIX C

WHO WROTE THE
Revelation of St. John?

The author of the *Revelation* identifies himself as John in four places in the text. According to Rev. 1:1, Jesus' message was given to his "servant John," indicating that the author was one of his followers. Rev. 1:4 identifies the initial audience as "John to the seven churches that are in Asia." Rev. 1:9 indicates where the book was written: "I John, who also am your brother, . . . was in the isle that is called Patmos." And Rev. 22:8 describes the author as a faithful witness: "I John saw these things, and heard them." The text, however, does not explicitly state who John is.

The text does show, nonetheless, that its author was well-educated and intimately acquainted with the sacred scriptures of his era. Gerhard Krodel, a modern commentator, reports that the 404 verses of the *Revelation* allude 518 times to earlier sacred texts.[1] These earlier scriptures include books from the Old Testament, the New Testament, and the Pseudepigrapha.[2] Moreover,

---

1. Krodel, *Revelation*, p. 47.
2. The Pseudepigrapha consists of books that are not considered canonical but are Biblical in character. For example, the Pseudepigrapha includes: 1 Enoch, 2 Enoch, 4 Ezra, and the Testaments of the Twelve Patriarchs. The texts for these books are given by Charlesworth, *The Old Testament Pseudepigrapha*, vol. I.

there is textual evidence that the author was proficient in both Greek and Hebrew.[3]

Leaders of the second-century church were unanimous in their opinion that the *Revelation* was written by John the Apostle, son of Zebedee, the beloved disciple of Jesus. Justin Martyr wrote, in Ephesus during the first part of the second century (about A.D. 135), that John the Apostle was the author. Ephesus was one of the seven churches in Asia believed to be the initial audience for the text. Melito, Bishop of Sardis, acknowledged the *Revelation* as a genuine work by John the Apostle, and wrote a commentary on it (about A.D. 175). Sardis is another of the seven churches mentioned in the text. Irenaeus, Bishop of Lyons in southern Gaul, also supported the text's apostolic authorship. This is important, because Irenaeus had known people who had known John the Apostle. Other supporters included church leaders in many diverse regions: Tertuillian in Carthage, Clement and Origen in Egypt, Bishop Hippolytus in Italy, and Bishop Papias in Hierapolis, which was near Ephesus.[4]

Gnostic materials discovered in 1945 at Chenoboskion in Upper Egypt provide additional external evidence for apostolic authorship. One of the documents unearthed is the *Apocryphon of John,* which claims to have been written by "John, the brother of James, these who are the sons of Zebedee." It contains a passage similar to Rev. 1:13–18, and it cites Rev. 1:19. Andrew Helmbold, a contemporary scholar, believes that the *Apocryphon* was not written much later than 150 A.D. and cites authorities who believe it was written as early as the end of the first century. He concludes that "either date establishes the *Apocryphon* as an early witness, alongside the secondary testimony of Papias and Justin Martyr in Eusebius, for the Apostolic authorship of the Apocalypse."[5]

In spite of strong external evidence that the *Revelation* was written by John the Apostle, many modern scholars disagree based on internal evidence. At least three arguments have been given for this position:

---

3. The *Revelation* was written in the Greek language. According to Charles, *The Revelation of St. John*, vol. I, pp. x, lxvi, its author "thought in Hebrew, and he frequently reproduces Hebrew idioms literally in Greek. . . . An examination of the passages based on the O.T. makes it clear that our author draws his materials directly from the Hebrew (or Aramaic) text."

4. *Catholic Encyclopedia*, vol. I, pp. 594–595.

5. A. Helmbold, "A Note on the Authorship of the Apocalypse," *New Testament Studies*, vol. 8, 1961–2, pp. 77–79.

- The author calls himself a "servant" (Rev. 1:1), a "brother" (Rev. 1:9), and a "prophet" (Rev. 22:9), but does not call himself an apostle. The text, however, is written in the form of an epistle, or letter. Is it reasonable to assume that an apostle would necessarily identify himself as such in a letter to contemporaries? None of the *Epistles of John*, for instance, which are often attributed to the same author, contain the word "apostle."

- The text does not indicate that its author knew the historical Jesus. In contrast, the *Gospel of John* indicates that its author was present at many of the events that involved the historical Jesus. Again, should we assume that an apostle would necessarily include personal reminiscences in his letters? This may not be valid, because it fails to consider that the content of a writing depends upon its purpose, and that the purpose of the *Revelation* differed from that of the gospels.

- There are substantial linguistic differences between the *Gospel of John* and the *Revelation*—differences in grammar and diction, words used to express the same idea, and the meanings of common words.[6] This convinces many modern scholars that different writers composed the two books.[7] Establishing that different authors wrote these books does not necessarily disprove the apostolic authorship of the *Revelation*, since it is possible that John the Apostle provided the ideas for both books,[8] but had his students

---

6. Charles, *The Revelation of St. John*, vol. I, pp. xxix–xxxii, lists the many linguistic differences that would indicate different authors for the *Gospel of John* and the *Revelation*. This evidence is widely acknowledged and has been frequently discussed in academic literature.

7. Mounce, *The Book of Revelation*, p. 15, summarizes the current view among scholars: "Who, then, was the John who wrote the Revelation? Internal evidence has convinced the majority of writers that whoever he was, there is little possibility that he was also the author of the Fourth Gospel."

8. Charles, *The Revelation of St. John*, vol. I, pp. xxxii–xxxiii, asserts, "The Authors of the Apocalypse and the Fourth Gospel were in some way related to each other." He justifies this position by noting the common use of certain words, phrases, and ideas. Charles concludes, "The Evangelist was apparently at one time a disciple of the Seer, or they were members of the same religious circle in Ephesus."

or secretaries write the actual words in one or both of them.[9] Moreover, many modern scholars believe that the *Gospel of John* is the work of someone other than John the Apostle.[10]

Modern scholarship has failed to come to a definitive conclusion regarding the authorship of the *Revelation* by examining external and internal evidence. Several modern writers, however, claim to have opinions about the authorship of the book that were inspired by the spiritual dimension of life. Let's consider what they have to say.

Helena P. Blavatsky, mentioned briefly in Appendix A, believed that her work was inspired,[11] and referred to the author of the *Revelation* as "the apostle-kabalist John."[12] Edgar Cayce, also mentioned briefly in Appendix A, believed that he received messages from the spiritual world. One of those messages referred to the writer of the *Revelation* as "the apostle, the beloved, the last of those chosen."[13]

Alice A. Bailey (1880–1949) was born in England and moved to California, where she became a member of Blavatsky's Theosophical Society. She left the Society to found her own school for spiritual development in New York, the Arcane School, in 1923. Bailey published a series of books purportedly based on information received from the spiritual world.[14] One of these states that the *Revelation* was written by John, the beloved disciple of Jesus:

> In the *New Testament*, John, the beloved disciple, was privileged to
> gain a cosmic picture and a true prophetic vision which he embodied

---

9. The apostle Peter acknowledged that his first letter was written "by Silvanus" (1 Pet. 5:12), meaning that Silvanus acted as Peter's secretary. The apostle John may have also used one or more secretaries to convey his ideas, in which case his writings would appear as if they were composed by different people.

10. McKenzie, *Dictionary of the Bible*, p. 449, discusses the authorship of the *Gospel of John*: "Many modern critics believe that the tradition of the name and the composition at Ephesus around 100 are best preserved by attributing the Gospel not to the apostle but to John the Elder, mentioned by Papias."

11. H. P. Blavatsky, *The Key to Theosophy* (1889; reprint; Pasadena, CA: Theosophical University Press, 1972), pp. 290, 300.

12. Blavatsky, *Isis Unveiled*, vol. II, p. 229.

13. Van Auken, *Edgar Cayce on the Revelation*, p. 158.

14. Bailey, *The Rays and the Initiations*, pp. 250–251.

in the Apocalypse, but he is the only one who so achieved and he achieved because he loved so deeply, so wisely and so inclusively. His intuition was evoked through the depth and intensity of his love—as it was in his Master, the Christ.[15]

Blavatsky, Cayce, and Bailey may be the only modern writers who expressed an opinion about the authorship of the *Revelation* and also made the explicit claim of having received their information through inspiration. Moreover, they all agreed with the leaders of the second-century church on this point: the *Revelation* was written by John the Apostle.

---

15. Bailey, *Glamour*, p. 137.

BIBLIOGRAPHY

Adler, A. *Understanding Human Nature*. 1927. Reprint. New York: Fawcett Premier, 1954.

Aivanhov, O. M. *The Book of Revelations: A Commentary*. Second Edition. Los Angeles: Prosveta, 1997.

———. *Cosmic Moral Law*. Third Edition. Los Angeles: Prosveta, 1989.

Aurobindo, Sri. *The Integral Yoga*. Pondicherry, India: Sri Aurobindo Ashram, 1993.

———. *The Life Divine*. 1949. Reprint. Pondicherry, India: Sri Aurobindo Ashram, 1990.

———. *The Synthesis of Yoga*. Pondicherry, India: Sri Aurobindo Ashram, 1957.

Bailey, A. A. *Discipleship in the New Age*, vol. I. 1944. Reprint. New York: Lucis Publishing Company, 1976.

———. *Discipleship in the New Age*, vol. II. 1955. Reprint. New York: Lucis Publishing Company, 1972.

———. *Esoteric Astrology*. 1951. Reprint. New York: Lucis Publishing Company, 1979.

———. *Esoteric Healing*. 1953. Reprint. New York: Lucis Publishing Company, 1978.

————. *Esoteric Psychology*, vol. I. 1936. Reprint. New York: Lucis Publishing Company, 1979.

————. *Esoteric Psychology*, vol. II. 1942. Reprint. New York: Lucis Publishing Company, 1981.

————. *The Externalisation of the Hierarchy*. 1957. Reprint. New York: Lucis Publishing Company, 1976.

————. *Glamour: A World Problem*. 1950. Reprint. New York: Lucis Publishing Company, 1971.

————. *Initiation, Human and Solar*. 1922. Reprint. New York: Lucis Publishing Company, 1974.

————. *Letters on Occult Meditation*. 1922. Reprint. New York: Lucis Publishing Company, 1974.

————. *The Light of The Soul*. 1927. Reprint. New York: Lucis Publishing Company,   1978.

————. *The Rays and the Initiations*. 1960. Reprint. New York: Lucis Publishing Company, 1976.

————. *Telepathy and the Etheric Vehicle*. 1950. Reprint. New York: Lucis Publishing Company, 1975.

————. *A Treatise on Cosmic Fire*. 1925. Reprint. New York: Lucis Publishing Company, 1973.

————. *A Treatise on White Magic*. 1934. Reprint. New York: Lucis Publishing Company, 1979.

Bailey, M. *A Learning Experience*. New York: Lucis Publishing Company, 1990.

Beck, A. T., A. J. Rush, B. F. Shaw, and G. Emery. *Cognitive Therapy of Depression*. New York: The Guilford Press, 1979.

Bell-Ranske, J. *The Revelation of Man*. New York: William S. Rhode Company, 1924.

Blavatsky, H. P. *Collected Writings*. 15 vols. Wheaton, IL: Theosophical Society of America, 2002.

————. *Isis Unveiled*. 1877. 2 vols. Reprint. Pasadena, CA: Theosophical University Press, 1976.

————. *The Key to Theosophy*. 1889. Reprint. Pasadena, CA: Theosophical University Press, 1972.

————. *The Secret Doctrine.* 2 vols. 1888. Reprint. Pasadena, CA: Theosophical University Press, 1977.

————. *The Voice of the Silence.* 1889. Reprint. Wheaton, IL: Theosophical Publishing House, 1968.

Catholic Encyclopedia. 15 vols. New York: Encyclopedia Press, Inc. 1913.

Charles, R. H. *The Revelation of St. John.* 2 vols. 1920. Reprint. Edinburgh: T. and T. Clark, 1985.

Charlesworth, J. H. *The Old Testament Pseudepigrapha*, vol. I. New York: Doubleday, 1983.

Collins, M. *Light on the Path.* 1888. Reprint. Pasadena, CA: Theosophical University Press, 1976.

A Commentary on the Book of the Revelation Based on a Study of Twenty-Four Psychic Discourses of Edgar Cayce. 1945. Reprint. Virginia Beach, VA: A. R. E. Press, 1969.

Condron, B. *Kundalini Rising.* Windyville, MO: SOM Publishing, 1992.

A Course in Miracles. 3 vols. Second Edition. Glen Ellen, CA: Foundation for Inner Peace, 1992.

Eckhart, M. *Meister Eckhart: A Modern Translation.* Trans. R. B. Blakney. New York: Harper and Row, 1941.

Ellwood, R. *Theosophy.* Wheaton, IL: Theosophical Publishing House, 1994.

Fideler, D. *Jesus Christ, Sun of God.* Wheaton, IL: Theosophical Publishing House, 1993.

Fillmore, C. *Jesus Christ Heals.* Unity Village, MO: Unity School of Christianity, 1996.

————. *The Metaphysical Bible Dictionary.* 1931. Reprint. Unity Village, MO: Unity School of Christianity, 1995.

————. *The Twelve Powers of Man.* Unity Village, MO: Unity School of Christianity, 1995.

Freud, Sigmund. *Introductory Lectures on Psychoanalysis.* 1917. Reprint. New York: W. W. Norton, 1977.

Goldsmith, J. S. *Collected Essays of Joel S. Goldsmith.* Marina del Rey, CA: Devorss and Company, 1986.

————. *The Contemplative Life.* New Hyde Park, NY: University Books, 1963.

———. *The Gift of Love*. New York: Harper and Row, 1975.

———. *The Infinite Way*. 1947. Reprint. San Gabriel, CA: Willing Publishing Company, 1971.

———. *The Mystical I*. New York: Harper and Row, 1971.

———. *The Nineteen Hundred Fifty-Four Infinite Way Letters*. 1954. Reprint. Austell, GA: Acropolis Books, 1996.

———. *The Nineteen Hundred Fifty-Nine Infinite Way Letters*. London: L. N. Fowler, 1960.

———. *A Parenthesis in Eternity*. New York: Harper and Row, 1963.

———. *Practicing the Presence*. New York: Harper and Row, 1958.

———. *The Thunder of Silence*. New York: Harper and Row, 1961.

Grosso, M. *The Millennium Myth*. Wheaton, IL: Theosophical Publishing House, 1995.

Hall, M. P. *The Apocalypse Attributed to St. John*. Los Angeles: The Philosophical Research Society, 1981.

Hall, M. P. *The Secret Teachings of All Ages*. 1928. Reprint. Los Angeles: The Philosophical Research Society, 1975.

Haskell, B. *Journey Beyond Words*. Marina del Rey, CA: DeVorss and Company, 1994.

Helmbold, A. "A Note on the Authorship of the Apocalyse," *New Testament Studies*, vol. 8, 1961–2, pp. 77–79.

Hitchcock, R. D. "An Interpreting Dictionary of Scripture Proper Names," *Hitchcock's Complete Analysis of the Holy Bible*. New York: A. J. Johnson, 1874.

Hotema, H. *Awaken the World Within*. Pomeroy, WA: Health Research, 1962.

The Impersonal Life. 1941. Reprint. San Gabriel, CA: C. A. Willing, 1971.

John of the Cross, St. *Complete Works*. Translated and edited by E. A. Peers, 3 vols. London: Burns Oates and Washbourne, 1934.

Johnston, C. *The Yoga Sutras of Patanjali*. 1949. Reprint. London: Stuart and Watkins, 1968.

Judge, W. Q. *The Ocean of Theosophy*. 1893. Reprint. Los Angeles: The Theosophy Company, 1987.

Jung, C. G. *Analytic Psychology: Its Theory and Practice*. New York: Random House, 1970.

———. *Answer to Job*. Trans. by R. F. C. Hull. 1954. Reprint. Cleveland, OH: World Publishing Company, 1965.

Jurriaanse, A. *Bridges*. Cape, South Africa: Sun Centre, 1980.

Kiddle, M. *The Revelation of St. John*. London: Hodder and Stoughton, 1940.

Krishnamurti, J. *Commentaries on Living, First Series*. 1956. Reprint. Wheaton, IL: Theosophical Publishing House, 1970.

———. *Commentaries on Living, Third Series*. 1960. Reprint. Wheaton, IL: Theosophical Publishing House, 1970.

———. *The First and Last Freedom*. 1954. Reprint. London: Victor Gollancz, 1972.

———. *Freedom from the Known*. New York: Harper and Row, 1969.

———. *Krishnamurti on Education*. New Delhi: Orient Longman, 1974.

———. *Krishnamurti's Journal*. San Francisco: Harper and Row, 1982.

———. *Krishnamurti's Notebook*. New York: Harper and Row, 1976.

———. *Last Talks at Saanen 1985*. San Francisco: Harper and Row, 1986.

———. *Talks in Saanen 1974*. Beckenham, Kent, England: Krishnamurti Foundation Trust, 1975.

Krodel, G. A. *Revelation*. Minneapolis, MN: Augsburg Publishing House, 1989.

Lawrence, Brother. *The Practice of the Presence of God*. 1692. Reprint. Grand Rapids, MI: Fleming H. Revell Company, 1989.

Lawrence, D. H. *Apocalypse*. 1931. Reprint. New York: Penguin Books, 1995.

Leadbeater, C. W. *The Chakras*. 1927. Reprint. Wheaton, IL: Theosophical Publishing House, 1977.

———. *The Masters and the Path*. 1925. Reprint. Madras, India: Theosophical Publishing House, 1965.

Mackay, W. M. "Another look at the Nicolaitans," *The Evangelical Quarterly*, vol. 45, 1973, pp. 111–115.

McKenzie, J. L. *Dictionary of the Bible*. 1965. Reprint. New York: Simon and Schuster, 1995.

Miller, R. J. *The Complete Gospels: Annotated Scholars Version*. Santa Rosa, CA: Polebridge Press, 1994.

Ming-Dao, D. *Chronicles of Tao*. New York: Harper Collins, 1993.

Motoyama, H. *Theories of the Chakras*. Wheaton, IL: Theosophical Publishing House, 1984.

Mounce, R. H. *The Book of Revelation*. Revised. Grand Rapids, MI: William B. Eerdmans Publishing Company, 1998.

New Bible Dictionary. Third Edition. Downers Grove, IL: Intervarsity Press, 1996.

Nikhilananda, Swami. *The Gospel of Sri Ramakrishna*. Abridged Edition. New York: Ramakrishna-Vivekananda Center, 1958.

Pandit, M. P. *Sri Aurobindo on the Tantra*. 1967. Reprint. Pondicherry, India: Dipti Publications, 1999.

Perls, F. S. *Gestalt Therapy Verbatim*. 1969. Reprint. New York: Bantam Books, 1976.

Perry, R. *A Course Glossary*. West Sedona, AZ: The Circle of Atonement, 1996.

———. *Relationships as a Spiritual Journey*. West Sedona, AZ: The Circle of Atonement, 1997.

Plato, *The Collected Dialogues of Plato*. Ed. E. Hamilton and H. Cairns. Princeton, NJ: Princeton University Press, 1989.

Potts, C. A. *Dictionary of Bible Proper Names*. New York: The Abingdon Press, 1922.

Powell, A. E. *The Astral Body*. 1927. Reprint. Wheaton, IL: Theosophical Publishing House, 1978.

———. *The Causal Body and The Ego*. 1928. Reprint. Wheaton, IL: Theosophical Publishing House, 1978.

———. *The Etheric Double*. 1925. Reprint. Wheaton, IL: Theosophical Publishing House, 1979.

———. *The Mental Body*. 1927. Reprint. Wheaton, IL: Theosophical Publishing House, 1975.

Pryse, J. M. *The Apocalypse Unsealed*. 1910. Reprint. Kila, MT: Kessinger Publishing, 1997.

Rama, Swami. "The Awakening of Kundalini," in J. White (ed.), *Kundalini, Evolution and Enlightenment*. St. Paul, MN: Paragon House, 1990.

Ramacharaka, Yogi. *The Science of Psychic Healing*. 1909. Reprint. Chicago: Yogi Publication Society, 1937.

Ruusbroec, J. *The Spiritual Espousals and Other Works*. Introduction and translated by J. A. Wiseman. New York: Paulist Press, 1985.

Schleiermacher, F. *The Christian Faith*. 1821–22. Reprint. Edinburgh: T&T Clark, 1999.

The Shambhalla Dictionary of Buddhism and Zen. Boston: Shambhala Publications, 1991.

Smith, W. *A Dictionary of the Bible*. Hartford, CT: J. B. Burr and Hyde, 1873.

Steiner, R. *The Book of Revelation and the Work of the Priest*. London: Rudolf Steiner Press, 1998.

Taimni, I. K. *Self-Culture*. 1945. Reprint. Adyar, Madras, India: Theosophical Publishing House, 1976.

Thera, N. *The Heart of Buddhist Meditation*. York Beach, ME: Samuel Weiser, 1962.

Trungpa, C. *Cutting Through Spiritual Materialism*. Boston: Shambhala Publications, 1973.

Tyberg, J. M. *The Language of the Gods: Sanskrit Keys to India's Wisdom*. Los Angeles: East-West Cultural Center, 1970.

Van Auken, J. *Edgar Cayce on the Revelation*. Virginia Bearch, VA: A.R.E. Press, 2000.

Vine, W. E., M. F. Unger, and W. White. *Vine's Complete Expository Dictionary of Old and New Testament Words*. Nashville, TN: Thomas Nelson, 1985.

Vivekananda, Swami. *The Yogas and Other Works*. Second Edition. New York: Ramakrishna-Vivekananda Center, 1953.

Wainwright, A. W. *Mysterious Apocalypse: Interpreting the Book of Revelation*. Nashville, TN: Abingdon Press, 1993.

Walsch, N. D. *Communion with God*. New York: Penguin Putnam, 2000.

Watson, A. A. *Through Fear to Love*. West Sedona, AZ: The Circle of Atonement, 1994.

White, J. *Kundalini, Evolution and Enlightenment*. 1979. Reprint. St. Paul, MN: Paragon House, 1990.

Wilbur, K. "Are the Chakras Real?" in J. White (ed.), *Kundalini, Evolution and Enlightenment*. St. Paul, MN: Paragon House, 1990.

Wittgenstein, L. *Notebooks, 1914–1916*. Eds. G. H. von Wright and G. E. M. Anscombe. Trans. G. E. M. Anscombe. Oxford: Blackwell, 1961.

Yogananda, Paramahansa. *Autobiography of a Yogi*. 1946. Reprint. Los Angeles: Self-Realization Fellowship, 1969.

———. *Sayings of Yogananda*. 1952. Reprint. Los Angeles: Self-Realization Fellowship, 1968.

———. *Science of Religion*. 1953. Reprint. Los Angeles: Self-Realization Fellowship, 1969.

———. *The Second Coming of the Christ: The Resurrection of the Christ Within You*. Los Angeles: Self-Realization Fellowship, 2004.

Yukteswar, Swami. *The Holy Science*. 1894. Reprint. Los Angeles: Self-Realization Fellowship, 1977.

ABOUT THE AUTHOR

Zachary Lansdowne is a past president of the Theosophical Society in Boston. He has a Ph.D. in Engineering from Stanford University, an M.A. in Psychology from Antioch University, an M.A. in Philosophy and Religion from the California Institute of Integral Studies, and an M.S. in Engineering from the Massachusetts Institute of Technology. He has published dozens of articles in scholarly journals and four earlier books on philosophy and religion.

To Our Readers

Weiser Books, an imprint of Red Wheel/Weiser, publishes books across the entire spectrum of occult and esoteric subjects. Our mission is to publish quality books that will make a difference in people's lives without advocating any one particular path or field of study. We value the integrity, originality, and depth of knowledge of our authors.

Our readers are our most important resource, and we appreciate your input, suggestions, and ideas about what you would like to see published. Please feel free to contact us, to request our latest book catalog, or to be added to our mailing list.

Red Wheel/Weiser, LLC
P.O. Box 612
York Beach, ME 03910-0612
www.redwheelweiser.com